# TAKING SIDES

ALSO BY MICHAEL HARRINGTON

*The Other America*

*The Retail Clerks*

*The Accidental Century*

*Toward a Democratic Left*

*Socialism*

*Fragments of the Century*

*Twilight of Capitalism*

*The Vast Majority*

*Decade of Decision*

*The Next America*

*The Politics at God's Funeral: The Spiritual Crisis of Western Civilization*

*The New American Poverty*

# TAKING SIDES

## The Education of a Militant Mind

**Michael Harrington**

HOLT, RINEHART AND WINSTON · New York

Published by Holt, Rinehart and Winston,
383 Madison Avenue, New York, New York 10017.
Published simultaneously in Canada by Holt, Rinehart and Winston of Canada, Limited.

Library of Congress Cataloging in Publication Data
Harrington, Michael, 1928–
Taking sides.
Includes index.
1. Harrington, Michael, 1928– 2. Social scientists—United States—Biography. 3. Right and left (Political Science) I. Title.
H59.H36A37 1985 300'.92'4 [B] 85–7607
ISBN 0–03–004429–4

First Edition

Designed by Lucy Albanese
Printed in the United States of America
10 9 8 7 6 5 4 3 2 1



The following chapters originally appeared: In *Dissent*: "The Committee for Cultural Freedom," 1955; "Granville Hicks' Small Town," 1957; "The American Campus," 1962; "Straight Lesser-Evilism," 1968 (originally untitled); "The Misfortune of 'Great Memories': Historical Remarks on the Paris Commune," 1971; "What Socialists Would Do in America—If They Could," 1978. In *The New International*: "Is There a Political Novel? The Artistic Limits of the Political Novel Today," 1958. Reprinted by permission. In *New Republic*: "The Mystical Militants," 1966. Reprinted by permission. In *Commonweal*: "The Other America: Beyond the Neon Signs and the Coke Bottles, Another America Still Lives—As of Now," 1960; "Paradise or Disintegration: James Merrill's Unique Search for New Myths," 1983. Both reprinted by permission. In *The Village Voice*: "Does the Peace Movement Need the Communists?" 1965; "Harrington Replies," 1965; "Answering McReynolds: A Question of Philosophy, a Question of Tactics," 1967. All reprinted by permission. In *Commentary*: "Voting the Lesser Evil," 1968. Reprinted by permission. In *The Nation*: "Say What You Mean—Socialism," 1974. Reprinted by permission. In *Harper's*: "To the Disney Station," 1979. Reprinted by permission.

ISBN 0-03-004429-4

FOR IRVING HOWE
the original editor of six of these essays, but much
more than that, a man of enduring "steady work,"
a comrade, a friend

# Contents

# TAKING SIDES

# Introduction

Truths about society can be discovered only if one takes sides.

I have known this as a theory for a long time. More to the point of this collection of essays, I am living proof of that dry, epistemological proposition. But I will explore the theory first so as to avoid giving the impression that my autobiography is the stuff of some grand conceptual breakthrough. My experiences are an illustration of a basic idea discovered long before I was born.

You must stand somewhere in order to see social reality, and where you stand will determine much of what you see and how you see it. The data of society are, for all practical purposes, infinite. You need criteria that will provisionally permit you to bring some order into that chaos of data and to distinguish between relevant and irrelevant factors or, for that matter, to establish that there are facts in the first place. These criteria cannot be based upon the data for they are the precondition of the data. They represent—and the connotations of the phrase should be savored—a "point of view." That involves intuitive choices, a value-laden sense of what is meaningful and what is not.

The activist analysis of thinking was, of course, first systematized by one of the least activist, and greatest, of philosophers, Immanuel Kant. I have socialized his insight (here again, I follow in the footsteps of giants, like Marx and Durkheim, rather than blaze a new path).

The poor, I suggest, see a different social world from the rich—and so do those who think, whether consciously or not, from the vantage point of the poor or the rich. I was born into and have lived my life in the middle class. But I have tried to write from the point of view of the poor and excluded, those in the United States and elsewhere. I am therefore a deeply biased man, a taker of sides; but that is not really distinctive at all. Everyone else is as biased as I am, including the most "objective" social scientist. The difference between us is that I am frank about my values while many other analysts fool both themselves and their audiences with the illusion that they have found an intellectual perch that is free of Earth's social field of gravity.

Let me be specific. In the mid-1970s, the Congressional Budget Office published a careful, statistically documented study that suggested that the nation had been overestimating the poverty problem because it had not counted the cash value of the in-kind income of the poor (food stamps, Medicaid) in computing their real income. That seemingly impartial and scientific analysis was clearly a response to a conservative critique that had been building for some years. It was written—and I am not being the least facetious here—in a sincere desire to define the truth. For at least some who developed this thesis there was even a liberal and compassionate purpose: to show that the antipoverty efforts of the sixties had actually done much more than the official statistics recognized.

But there was also a shift of mood, of "point of view," in that study. Now one worked hard and honestly to show that there were fewer poor people, that the nation's conscience could rest easy; a decade before, one strove to show that there were more poor people and that the conscience must awaken. There is, Ludwik Fleck pointed out in his marvelously titled book, *Genesis and Development of a Scientific Fact*, a "thought style" that dominates every period and it is usually suffused with unstated, and unscientific, assumptions. So it was that the CBO tried, as objectively as possible, to estimate the overcount of the poor and ignored—did not even mention—the data suggesting an undercount of the poor. Such ignorance, Gunnar Myrdal once said, is never random. It is always related to values and when it is an unconscious ignorance the values are almost always those of established power.

I was never tempted by the myth of social objectivity. I began as a militant who wanted to change society, not as a scholar. That meant understanding society, of course, and being as ruthless with the unstated assumptions of the Left as with those of the Right. But the goal, the point of view, was always to change society. So it is that I interpret my intellectual life as a living demonstration of the analytic thesis I have just sketched. There was a paradigmatic moment in February 1973 that illuminates all this. I was appointed Professor of Political Science at Queens College of the City University of New York. Not too long after I was also made a member of the graduate faculty of the University.

In the winter of 1973 I taught the first political science course I ever attended. My highest earned degree was a masters in English literature from the University of Chicago, and I had taken only one course in economics, at Yale Law School, and one in sociology, at Holy Cross College. But how did a man who wrote his bachelor's thesis on Shakespeare's Prince Hal/King Henry V come to lecture on Power in America?

Joseph S. Murphy, then the president of Queens, now the chancellor of the entire University system, was part of the answer. An irreverent and maverick academic who had done a spell running the Peace Corps in Ethiopia, Murphy believed that a free public college—tuition did not come to the CUNY system until the New York City crisis of 1975—could, and should, be as intellectually serious as an Ivy League university. He was on the lookout for stimulating teachers, thought that I might be one, and simply ignored the fact that I lacked all of the formal credentials for the post to which he appointed me.

But the decision was not Murphy's alone. My department concurred and so did the Social Science Division of Queens and the

Board of Higher Education of the City of New York. The ideas that I had developed in the course of political involvement outside of the academy, they effectively said, were somehow the equivalent of a Ph.D.

That little history is more than an amusing autobiographical anecdote. It focuses, in hindsight, a central and unifying theme of these essays. My graduate school was the fight against McCarthyism; it was the trade unions and the civil rights movement. My professors were workers, some of them high school dropouts; and they were black activists, students, antiwar demonstrators, feminists, and, above all, democratic socialists. So it is that these essays do not simply record the education of a militant mind but also refract much of America's political and cultural history during the past three decades.

Also, I immodestly think that my analyses have some intrinsic value. Indeed in assembling these writings I was surprised by how much I still agreed with my past selves. I had even forgotten that, ten years before I published *The Other America*, I had written a little article in the *Catholic Worker* on "Poverty USA" that anticipated many of the themes of the book. And I think that my comments on liberal capitulation to McCarthyism in the 1950s, or the critique of some of the leftist oversimplifications in the sixties, say things that need to be remembered in the eighties. They are part of a history that is relevant to our future.

But perhaps they related to a vanishing past, too. I was and am an intellectual, which is to say a man of passionate, rather than merely academic, involvement with ideas and ideals. I learned about the Russian revolutionaries by trying to figure out what I would have done had I been in their place and whether they had anything to teach me about America. I acquired my Ph.D. equivalent as an itinerant thinker, a Bohemian, a hitchhiker. And I wonder if that social type might not be disappearing in a society in which roles are more and more defined by formal rules and qualifications. In any case, most of these essays were written before I entered the groves of academe in 1973; and even those that come after that date are, like me, somewhat extracurricular in spirit.

Indeed I have omitted my more traditional scholarly work. I

am proud of my lengthy discussions of Marxism and democracy and Marxism and ethics, but they do not illuminate a cultural history. There are three seeming exceptions to this approach: a commentary on the political novel, a historical note on the reactions of Marx and Engels to the Paris Commune, a probing of the difficulties of the transition to socialism. But, as we will see when I place those essays in hindsight, their abstractions resonate to social movements, they are a fusion of theory and practice.

Finally, this introduction should at least note how a middle-class, Jesuit-educated, Irish Catholic youth from St. Louis found his way into that university without walls located in the radical lofts and Bohemian bars of New York City. Those first learning experiences after college prepared my transition and turned a would-be poet into a practicing militant.

I knew I was going to be a writer when I was about ten years old—but I didn't discover what that meant until I was in my twenties. I was the sports editor of both my high school and college newspapers, a copyboy at the *St. Louis Post-Dispatch* working in the City Room on D Day in 1944, and by 1947 my short stories had been rejected by some of the best magazines in the country. That was when I realized that I really wanted to be a poet. For the next seven or eight years, I worked on my poems every single day.

A paradox now emerges. In the main I wrote unmilitant poetry that had more to do with private epiphanies than with the suffering of the people. Yet at the very same time I was immersing myself in Marx and walking picket lines against Spanish fascism and the Korean War. The point is, the relationship between culture—and individual writers—and society is always complex. Kant, Heinrich Heine once said, was more radical than Robespierre, yet he lived a sheltered and seemingly humdrum life; Marx's favorite novelist was Balzac, a reactionary.

Indeed, to turn now to a much more modest illustration of this insight, my own mentor was T. S. Eliot, a self-proclaimed monarchist and classicist, and even though I was a mere acolyte I was delighted that the great man and I both came from St. Louis. I encountered one of the trends of the Age of Eliot at the University of Chicago where the "Chicago Aristotelians" thrived in the late 1940s. The Chicago group constituted an independent subdivision of the dominant mode of interpreting literature, the New Criticism, and stressed a rigorous, even microscopic, reading of the text itself with little reference to any Freudian or Marxist analysis of the author's experience or intentions.

That theory related to a poetic praxis typical of the times: poems that were polished and controlled, often concerned with a minor revelation rather than a great cosmic truth. Eliot's rehabilitation of John Donne and the Metaphysical poets had put a considerable emphasis on elegance, wit, and virtuosity, often in the elaboration of religious themes.

Thus one of my poems of the early 1950s, written when I was living in voluntary poverty at the Catholic Worker in New York, was a defense of the aesthetic against the claims of society. That it was composed in a stuffy little room that I shared with a succession of homeless alcoholics and occasional rats only sharpens the paradox that it emerged in a period of growing social commitment on my part. The poem evoked a brief, but decisive, time of my life when I was a social worker for the St. Louis Board of Education at the Madison School and the poem assumed that the general reader knew that Plato wanted to banish poets from the good society.

*"Seldom is a Gothic head more beautiful than when broken."*

*—André Malraux*

*And in Saint Louis*
*Missouri, the slums*
*Near the river: red*
*Brick and an arching*
*Areaway, the windows*
*Are slim, and French*
*Predominates a court*
*Laid in the back of*
*The lovely building,*

*Where a dirty child*
*From Arkansas plays*
*Among the refuse. I*
*Must yet agree with*
*Malraux and a round*
*Arch, and with those*
*Platonists who may*
*Someday come to drive*
*Me out of their city.*

Even that poem is untypical in its social (or antisocial) stress. For the most part I explored private emotions in the laid-back style that was then in vogue.

*HEISENBERG'S INDETERMINACY PRINCIPLE*

*For any two cannonically conjugate magnitudes, only one can be measured to any desired degree of accuracy.*

*Somewhere bells,*
*And I where I was*
*In the afternoon.*
*I would tell you*
*Each detail, but*
*There were none.*
*If I should say,*
*Here, where I was*
*In the afternoon,*
*Then bells would*
*Not be ringing as*
*They were, and if*
*I should tell you*
*Their lingering you*
*Would not see me*
*Listening to them.*
*Somewhere, bells,*
*And I where I was,*

*Immense certitude*
*In the afternoon,*
*The secret whole.*

At times there was a vague social reference, as in my poem, "Daylight Saving Time":

*As usual, it*
*Had begun as*
*A triumph of*
*Our ingenuity:*
*The sun was*
*Stopped, and*
*The twilight*
*Staged more*
*Effectively.*

*This afternoon*
*It ended, and*
*One hour was*
*Unexpectedly*
*A season, and*
*In a rush of*
*This evening*
*The pent up*
*Shadows of*
*Our ingenuity*
*Fell as usual.*

After all of those years my published work amounted to five poems in *Poetry* (Chicago). One of them reflected my deeply religious engagement in those days:

*A prayer must*
*Be possible as*
*High buildings,*
*More quickly*

*The direction*
*Of the flesh*
*Than girls are,*
*As an edge is.*
*Look: Already*
*You have leapt.*

And there was my favorite, a bookish meditation on one of my literary heroes, James Joyce:

*That last second*
*Of his exile,*
*Were the knives*
*Laid out like*
*Bright pandybats?*
*Did his mind*
*Wander like Jews*
*And finally find*
*Some pun from*
*The Scandinavian*
*That told exactly*
*How ether smelled?*
*Or as the mask*
*Covered his face,*
*Did he sink back*
*Like Molly Bloom*
*And say, yes,*
*Oh yes yes*

At the same time that I was writing those poems, the focus of my imagination imperceptibly shifted from the bells lingering in the afternoon to the unjust city in which they rang. On the one hand, I had come to understand that, at best, I had the promise of an exceedingly minor poet. On the other, my deepening political involvement—the campaign for clemency for the Rosenbergs, opposition to the Korean War—set me to studying society, not in order to master political science, but to change the world. Thus it was that a talk on Martin Buber's analysis of utopian socialism led to both Marx and the Bureau of Labor Statistics' Urban Workers Budget. And on and on.

So part of that change was a painful recognition of my own limitations. But had I then abandoned the poet I once wanted to be? I think not.

There is a marvelous, almost untranslatable, Hegelian word, *Aufheben*. It describes how an epoch dies and is yet taken up in the new age, how, as Marx developed the notion, socialism is the realization of the possibility created within capitalism. But that concept applies to the intimate self as well as to the centuries. We never discard the past, no matter how radically we break from it. It is always part of our present and, when we die, it is a moment of our whole. That can be seen straightforwardly in the essays of this book, which shuttle back and forth between culture and society. Less prosaically, a few lines from Goethe's *Faust* might help one understand how the poet of my youth still lives in the socialist author of analytic books and even in the professor of political science.

At the end of his life, Faust loses his wager with Mephistopheles when he admits that contentment is indeed possible:

*If I could see a throng stand*
*Free among a free people*
*Then I would dare to say to the moment:*
*Stay, you are so fair.*

That is the poetry of my socialism, the vision not simply of an economic or political program but of the potential for beauty concealed in the ordinary lives of suffering humanity. It was in that spirit that I went to classes in the social structure of America and the world under the tutelage of Bowery outcasts and trade unionists and black activists. What follows are some of the truths I discovered by taking sides.

# PART 1

# 1
# Liberalism and the Left

American liberalism can be an infuriating movement to understand. It is amorphous and often anti-ideological; committed to reform, but within the system. Its right wing emphasizes the need to maintain the system and shades off into conservativism; its left wing stresses reform and sometimes reaches almost to radicalism.

In the twentieth century, the mass movements for social change in America—the unions, minorities, women, environmentalists, peace activists, and so on—have been predominantly liberal. The socialist and radical Left had to learn to understand, and relate to, that huge fact. When it failed to do so—when my friend Norman Thomas and the Socialist Party of the 1930s not only rightly pointed out how moderate and limited the New Deal was but wrongly failed to see that, for all those flaws, it was the focus of a genuine mass movement that included the entire American working class—it condemned itself to failure and irrelevance.

I encountered the liberals in the 1950s when many, but by no means all of them, were going through one of their worst periods. I was both right, and a little self-righteous, in my condemnation of those who capitulated to Senator Joe McCarthy's demagogic and reactionary anticommunism.

"McCarthyism" has entered American English as a proper noun, yet I suspect that the majority of Americans who know of it from books rather than experience do not realize how ugly those times were. McCarthy burst upon the public consciousness when he made a speech in West Virginia in February 1950, charging that Communist conspirators in the State Department, aided by liberal dupes, were the secret of Soviet success in the Cold War. That kind of accusation was hardly new; but this time it had an extraordinary impact, in part because North Korea invaded South Korea in June 1950, and American troops became involved in a shooting war with Communists. The issue was no longer a matter of ideology; it was now defined in blood.

But McCarthy, we anti-Stalinist radicals always pointed out, did not invent the witch-hunt even though he pushed it to a destructive extreme. The Attorney General's List of Subversive Organizations had been drawn up—without hearings or any other legal process—by Harry Truman's Attorney General, Tom Clark. And the Smith Act, which had first been invoked by the Roosevelt administration against Trotskyists in 1940—the Communists applauded this antilibertarian attack on their hated enemies—was used against the Communist Party in 1949 by the Truman administration.

Those liberal moves were part of a larger pattern. In 1935 the Communist International had ordered all of its member parties to seek a "united front" with non-Communist democrats who were opposed to fascism. In the United States that meant that the Communists, who had denounced Roosevelt prior to Moscow's switch in line, became supporters of the New Deal and worked closely with liberals in the process. That strategy led to the greatest success any American leftist organization had known since the heyday of Eugene Victor Debs in the first two decades of the century. Communists, often concealing their political identity, played a significant role in the mass-production unions, in civil rights struggles, Democratic Party politics, and cultural life.

Most of what the Communists did during those years was

positive and progressive; they were usually the most militant activists in practically every humane cause. At the same time, the crimes of Stalin were not widely known and the Soviet dictator was seen by many liberals as a respected leader of the antifascist movement and thus, despite his absolute power, a friend of freedom. That illusion was shattered in 1939 when Stalin signed a pact with the Nazis and even sent some German antifascists back to their homeland, where they were put into concentration camps. But only a year and a half later, Hitler invaded the Soviet Union. In the ensuing struggle, that country sacrificed millions of lives and, after Pearl Harbor, found itself allied with the United States.

So liberal illusions about Communism were once again possible. But then, it was not just liberals who made this shift. Captain Eddie Rickenbacker, a World War I hero and a vocal reactionary, went to the Soviet Union and praised the "iron discipline" that prevented workers from going on strike there. Monsignor Fulton Sheen, perhaps the most prominent Catholic preacher of those years, vaunted the family legislation in the Soviet Union as superior to the laws in the United States.

Still, when the Cold War began in 1946–47 and witch-hunting tendencies emerged within the Truman administration, many liberals felt that they in particular had to atone for past sins of naïveté toward the Soviet Union and cooperation with the American Communists in various united-front activities. The American Committee for Cultural Freedom appealed to that sentiment among intellectuals and formalized the capitulation of some liberals to a vicious, antidemocratic anti-Communism. This was one of the first issues on which I took sides.

"To the liberal," I wrote in the student antiwar magazine *Anvil* in 1955, "McCarthy has too often served the function of a ritual scapegoat. . . . In the passage of the Humphrey anti-Communist law"—one of the most antilibertarian statutes ever put on the books—"this view of the problem as a personal one reached its apogee; it was all right for a liberal to introduce a McCarthyite law, for after all, he was . . . a Vice President of Americans for Democratic Action and not Senator McCarthy."

I concluded: ". . . far from being able to 'fight' McCarthy, the liberal was actually an unwitting collaborator in his rise to prominence." In another article on the American Committee for Cultural Freedom, which follows, I even attacked a man who was to become a friend and mentor, Norman Thomas, for his involvement in the ACCF. In the worst days of the Cold War, Thomas was convinced by his friend Sidney Hook that Communism was a conspiratorial movement and that Communists therefore did not qualify for the liberties that one would accord to self-declared and open heretics. Fortunately, Norman Thomas moved sharply away from that attitude in the mid-fifties and once again became a towering figure of principled civil libertarianism.

Thomas's shift heartened me. And I knew, even as I wrote the article, that there were liberals who had refused to take the neo-McCarthyite path of the ACCF. Some of them are named in the article. I cite this complexity for an ironic reason: the young leftist historians of the sixties sometimes charged that my generation of the socialist movement had participated in that liberal capitulation. The activist critics of America's unconscionable intervention in Vietnam discovered that some liberals not only defended that war but did so in the name of liberal principle. They then overgeneralized their understandable disgust. The entire 1950s Left, they said, had given in to McCarthy and only the Communists had kept the faith. The liberal rationale for Vietnam, then, was just one more example of how anti-Communism inevitably drove people into the camp of reaction.

My article is documented proof that this was not the case. There were anti-Stalinist radicals like me who were outraged by the liberals who did indeed turn their backs on civil liberties in the name of anti-Communism. And there were liberals who shared our view and who worked with us in defense of Communists and in principled opposition to Communism. We socialists referred to the Soviet Union not as Communism but as Stalinism, for we wanted to emphasize that it was the systematic repudiation of Marx's emancipatory vision, rather than its realization.

My critique of the ACCF appeared in *Dissent*. *Dissent* was not simply a magazine; it was the center of a socialist political tendency that criticized both East and West in the name of a single standard. It was edited by Irving Howe, one of the most decent and thoughtful men of my times. Indeed Irving is one of the few people to have written an autobiography that understates his own virtues. By honestly and candidly confronting all of his doubts and hesitations about his own political ideals he fails to communicate the incredible commitment, the passion, of his dedication to that ideal. With great personal sacrifice he founded and maintained *Dissent* in the dark days of McCarthyism.

As I look back on my article, I am quite satisfied with its basic thrust but bothered by some of its overgeneralizations. In his marvelous analysis of James Burnham, George Orwell had said that the characteristic intellectual sin is to assume that the present will continue into the indefinite future. Insofar as my piece attempted a grand theory of why so many liberals caved in to McCarthyism, it took some real tendencies—bureaucratization and the new role that intellectuals could play in the emerging "knowledge society"—and chiseled them into stone.

The fact is, as so often in the past, the liberals survived their disgrace and played an honorable role, not simply in the civil rights movement, but in the antiwar struggles of the sixties, where they provided most of the rank and file and many of the leaders. I will never forget marching in a huge peace demonstration in New York in 1967 and observing the laughter and applause that greeted a little group of activists with the picket sign, "Middle Class Americans Against the War in Vietnam." Lenin would never have dreamed of such an event.

Moreover, there was, in the 1960s and 1970s, a greater social space for independent radicals than I had anticipated. One reason was an enduring accomplishment of the New Left. It had legitimated the discussion of socialism and Marxism in the academy and, not so incidentally for me, had made it possible for an open radical to be appointed a professor at Queens. In 1953, that would have been unthinkable; in 1973, it happened. Of greater political significance, a group of extremely talented militants from the student movement of the sixties kept their values and acquired Ph.D.'s. So it is that I suddenly discovered in the eighties that the

American Left had more technical competence on economic issues than ever before in its history.

On a more personal level, I am dissatisfied with the references to the "Stalinists" in the article. At that time, I really didn't know any Communists—when we met at meetings it was to intrigue against one another, not to communicate—and my epithet was an abstraction. Later, in 1956, when the Khrushchev revelations about Stalin and the Hungarian Revolution created turmoil in the Communist world, I had my first truly personal contacts with the Communists. They were, I was surprised to discover, complex and often decent people who had served the wrong cause for right reasons while fighting courageously for social change in American society.

In short, what I learned by taking sides in this period was somewhat ambiguous, a mix of truths that I maintain to this day and of half-truths that I had to outgrow. My attack on the liberals who cut and ran before McCarthyism is as true today as it was when I wrote it (and it was partly reprinted twelve years after it first appeared, when it was revealed that the CIA had played a role in the Congress for Cultural Freedom). And my principled anti-Stalinism, even as I defended the rights of Communists, real and alleged, was right, too.

But there were complications, and the young man in the first, exhilarating flush of a new radicalism did not see them. The humanity of the Communists, we have just seen, was one. Of greater political significance, and danger, was the antiliberalism these events inspired. It confirmed me in a sectarian view that, even though we worked on common projects with the liberals, there was a chasm between them and us. In fact, as I was later to realize, there was a continuum and some of the best of the liberals were social democrats without knowing it.

Ironically, when I tried to explain that point to the first generation of the New Left a mere seven years after my article came out, I got into trouble because they were in the grip of the same antiliberal emotions that had once stirred me. I could not, as it turned out, exorcise my own ghost. Intellectual breakthroughs are handed down to those who come after: the zero concept, once a magnificent discovery, is now a grade-school subject. But the political learning process is more complex than that, and my young friends of the sixties insisted on their right to make my error.

But, for all the qualifications, I am proud that I was hostile to both Stalin and Joe McCarthy; and the article is, among other things, documentary proof that my generation of the anti-Stalinist Left did not panic in the face of a vicious assault on freedom. We took the side of freedom, East and West.

# 2
# The Committee for Cultural Freedom

*Dissent, 1955*

That the American Committee for Cultural Freedom (ACCF) is a grouping of some significance in our intellectual life is not to be disputed. Its well-publicized statements are often taken as the quasi-official opinion of intellectual liberalism. It counts among its members, most notably on its masthead, the names of many intellectuals with a long history of devotion to cultural freedom. Nonetheless, this organization has recently suffered—and so far as one can determine, continues to suffer—a severe political crisis on the very issue of cultural freedom which is its presumable reason for existence. The immediate occasion for this crisis we shall describe later; for the moment we need only say that it concerns statements by its leading officials so compromising to any libertarian spirit that a number of prominent ACCF members have publicly protested. Behind this immediate crisis, however, lurk the larger problems that beset those American intellectuals who are sincerely devoted to cultural freedom yet are simultaneously involved with a politics that prods them to qualify, weaken, and sometimes even negate this devotion.

Though it had a previous embryonic existence, the American Committee established itself after an International Congress for Cultural Freedom held in Berlin in June 1950. This meeting was attended by intellectuals from 21 countries and was followed by the formation of national groups. The basis of the international organization was a manifesto signed by a wide spectrum of intellectuals, from Ignazio Silone to Sidney Hook, from David Rousset to Jacques Maritain. Consisting primarily of rhetorical affirmations of freedom, the politics of this statement were as unexceptionable as they were vague, save perhaps for a sideswipe against "neutralism."

The International Committee was conceived as a kind of "united front." Answering the question of "whether a real collaboration between Socialists and right-wing parties is possible or desirable," it declared: "This collaboration is desirable if its objectives are limited to the task of uniting each free nation against threats to its freedom from within and without and thus acting as a deterrent against aggression."

Now the concept of the "united front" has an honorable as well as dishonorable past. Almost always it has served a useful purpose only when it led to various groups or individuals acting in common for delimited ends while not pretending to dissolve their larger differences. Nor is there any reason why a "united front" in defense of cultural freedom should not be possible and useful—provided, however, that there is a clear understanding as to how cultural freedom can be defended. The statement of the International Committee, one quickly notices, does not provide such understanding; once "the task of uniting each free nation" is raised, the inevitable divisions of politics must come into play or be unhealthily suppressed. The statement—we do not propose to worry this one sentence too much, except for its *symptomatic* bearing—skirts the obvious fact that within the "limitation" it proposes there remains unanswered every question of *how* to oppose Stalinism.

That the point I am making is urgent can immediately be seen by comparing the American Committee and its European counterparts. In the United States the ACCF assumed that the positive task of defending cultural freedom could be achieved primarily through uniting almost every variety of anti-Stalinist. Anti-Stalinism—crude, promiscuous, and often without positive content—became the magic talisman of intellectual respectability, and the result was a curiously ambiguous definition of cultural freedom. The European committees have been more concerned with a living, day-to-day defense of intellectual freedom and have retained a greater degree of political independence vis-à-vis their own governments. By contrast, the American Committee has enthusiastically laid itself open to the pressures and shaping influences of State Department policies and rationales; so that often it has been less an organization devoted to the defense of cultural freedom than an agency propagandizing the American party line. This, in turn, has led to exercises in what might be called intellectual colonialism. For example, it sent James Burnham on a tour in India, with the intention no doubt of having that noted libertarian explain the meaning of cultural freedom to the benighted Indian intellectuals.

The Berlin manifesto was signed by Arthur Schlesinger, Jr.—and James Burnham; by James T. Farrell—and Robert Montgomery. This hodgepodge was to prove characteristic of the inner tension and confusion in the American Committee. When one undercuts its formal pronouncements and examines its actual preoccupations, it becomes clear that anti-Stalinism of the most indiscriminate kind was the only essential requirement for membership. Else how account for the recent election to its executive committee of Whittaker Chambers? Or for the membership of that distinguished thinker and defender of freedom, Victor Riesel? Or for the fact that until quite recently such McCarthyite or near-McCarthyite intellectuals as James Burnham and George Schuyler found it possible to work side by side with Sidney Hook? A committee that could retain such figures (not to mention Max Eastman, John Chamberlain, and John Dos Passos) could hardly be expected to bristle with alertness before the dangers to liberty in the United States, no matter how sensitive it was to the threat from several thousand miles away.

Given the presence of McCarthyite supporters in the Committee—people who were invited, incidentally, with far greater frequency and cordiality than the intellectuals of the anti-Stalinist left—it was almost inevitable that the boast, "We have not allowed this overriding menace [of Stalinism] to blind us to the injustices on our doorsteps," would be understood in extremely broad fashion. The Committee lists the following as points open to legitimate disagreement among its members:

> Was Communism an opinion or a conspiracy? Is there a right to a government job, which even Communists and other totalitarians could claim? Was the fact that a teacher was a Communist to be regarded as professional disqualification or not? What about "guilt by association"? Was the Smith Act a violation of civil liberties? What restrictions could legitimately be placed upon individual freedom in the interests of national security? What was the nature of totalitarianism, of democracy, of liberty?

Obviously, these are questions concerning which honest men can disagree. For a discussion group they would provide an excellent agenda. But such a disagreement can hardly be the basis for common action, even for the limited aim of opposition to Stalinism. The *kind* of anti-Stalinism which follows from supporting the Smith Act, or even from supporting it with numerous qualifications as Sidney Hook does, is fundamentally different from that which follows from condemning the Smith Act. And the problem becomes all the more exacerbated when the announced objective of an organization is not merely opposition to Stalinism (that comes pretty cheap these days!) but rather a positive defense of cultural freedom. What has happened in practice is that the American Committee *has* taken on a political coloration: it has steadily drifted to the right, toward the position of conforming to and apologizing for the intellectual atmosphere in the United States; and this, in turn, must obviously mute its defense of cultural freedom.

In practice the ACCF has fallen behind Sidney Hook's views on civil liberties. Without implying any "conspiracy" theory of history (or even of intellectual intrigue), one may safely say that it is Hook who has molded the decisive ACCF policies. His *Heresy Yes, Conspiracy No* articles were widely circulated by the Committee, which meant that in effect it endorsed his systematic, explicit efforts to minimize the threat to civil liberties and to attack those European intellectuals who, whatever their own political or intellectual deficiencies, took a dim view of American developments. Under the guidance of Hook and the leadership of Irving Kristol, who supported Hook's general outlook, the American Committee cast its weight not so much in defense of those civil liberties which were steadily being nibbled away, but rather against those few remaining fellow travelers who tried to exploit the civil liberties issue.

At times this had an almost comic aspect. When Irving Kristol was executive secretary of the ACCF, one learned to expect from him silence on those issues that were agitating the whole intellectual and academic world, and enraged communiqués on the outrages performed by people like Arthur Miller or Bertrand Russell in exaggerating the danger to civil liberties in the United States.

Inevitably, this led to more serious problems. In an article by Kristol that first appeared in *Commentary* and was later circulated under the ACCF imprimatur, one could read such astonishing and appalling statements as "There is one thing the American people know about Senator McCarthy; he, like them, is unequivocally anti-Communist. About the spokesmen for American liberalism, they feel they know no such thing. And with some justification." This, in the name of defending cultural freedom! As someone remarked, the Committee might better have renamed itself the American Committee for Cultural Accommodation.

We are not, to be sure, dealing with a black-and-white matter. In a number of cases the Committee has acted within the United States in defense of freedom. It protested to Attorney General Herbert Brownell on the treatment of Charlie Chaplin and Arthur Miller; it was active in the Muhlenberg College case where some Chaplin films were banned; it criticized the procedure of the McCarthy investigation of the Voice of America. The Committee also claims to have done good work in ways precluding publicity, and there is no reason to doubt this claim. Currently, it is intervening in the case of Barry Miller, a former member of the Politics Club of the University of Chicago to whom the army refuses an honorable discharge because of his past (anti-Stalinist) associations.

But these activities do not absorb the main attention or interest of the Committee: its leadership is too jaded, too imbued with the sourness of indiscriminate anti-Stalinism to give itself to an active struggle against the dominant trend of contemporary intellectual life in America. What it *really* cares about most is a struggle against fellow travelers and "neutralists"—that is, against many European intellectuals; but it fails to see that even in terms of such an objective, it could be effective only if it fought with vigor and passion against the violations of freedom that have mounted up in the United States, instead of querulously minimizing their extent and gravity.

One of the crippling assumptions of the Committee has been that it would not intervene in cases where Stalinists or accused Stalinists were involved. It has rested this position on the academic argument, advanced most systematically by Sidney Hook, that Stalinists, being enemies of democracy, have no "right" to democratic privileges and that, consequently, no threat to civil liberties or cultural freedom is involved when they are deprived of these privileges. But the actual problem is not the metaphysical one of whether enemies of democracy (as the Stalinists clearly are) have a "right" to democratic privileges. What matters is that the drive against cultural freedom and civil liberties takes on the guise of anti-Stalinism. Thus, for example, such an outrage as depriving the veteran anti-Stalinist radical Max Shachtman of a passport with which to travel in Europe—a State Department act one may assume the ACCF would not approve of—is made possible or at least much easier by the precedents created in prosecutions and persecutions of the Stalinists. Given such facts, it becomes extremely difficult, if not impossible, to defend civil liberties without clearly defending the civil rights of Stalinists (which has nothing whatever to do with spies or sabotage). And this the Committee has failed to do.

But it has gone even further. In December 1952 it published a "Memorandum on the Visa Problem." This document was concerned with the entry of foreign intellectuals, trade unionists, etc., into the United States. The cases that gave rise to the memorandum were, of course, those of Stalinists. In the course of the analysis, Section 212 (a) (28) of the McCarran Act, which bars visas strictly on the basis of political criteria, is discussed.

In this discussion the Committee assumes as a matter of course that it is perfectly legitimate to bar Stalinists (or members of the Communist Party) from visas. There are recommendations for exceptions, for a sophisticated use of criteria, in the case of Stalinist-front members, but the assumption is always that the mere holding of Stalinist *opinions* is automatically a sufficient ground for refusing a visa. The Committee objects, on the ground of vagueness, to a definition for exclusion based on adherence to "economic, international, and governmental doctrines of world Communism or . . . of any other form of totalitarianism." It finds "adequate," however, the criterion for exclusion of those who "advocate or teach or who are members or affiliated with any organization" that advocates or teaches the "violent overthrow" of the government. In effect, thereby, the Committee proposes its own version of the Smith Act, and abandons the long-standing and honorable position of American liberalism that such phrases as "violent overthrow," besides being vague and misleading, are insufficient grounds for political discrimination.

This curious defense of cultural freedom is capped with an even more curious statement: "We know that the visa problem was not created by arbitrary malice on the part of congressmen or State Department officials. It is but one reflection, and not by far the largest, of the stresses and strains which this free country is suffering as a result of its determination to resist Communist totalitarianism."

As a piece of apologetics this statement is fantastic. As a description of reality it is far more accurate with regard to the stresses and strains within the Committee itself than within the United States.

Perhaps the most important—certainly the most scandalous—incident revealing the inner bent and bias of the Committee has occurred quite recently. In the December 27, 1954, issue of the *New Republic* there appeared, under the pseudonym Brian Gilbert, a discussion of the Lattimore case. In the February 14, 1955, issue, Sol Stein, executive director of the ACCF, came to the defense of cultural freedom in a long communication that is certain to become a classic document for the history of the collapse of American liberalism. This document, which contains an endorsement of the McCarran Committee, was given the approval of the executive of the ACCF.

Mr. Stein's first point verges on the incredible. He writes:

> If Mr. Gilbert's article expressed his displeasure with the perjury case now pending against Owen Lattimore, readers may question the propriety of such interference with judicial process and the appropriateness of such pressures upon a judge and jurors who will have to maintain objectivity in weighing the answers.

This statement, let it be remembered, appears in a context of a long juridical and extrajuridical harassment of Lattimore—and to deplore this harassment in no way depends upon any sympathy with Lattimore's opinions. Had there not been public discussion of the case, it is very possible that the vast "pressures" from the right that were quietly exerted might well have succeeded. Yet, in defense of "cultural freedom," Mr. Stein begins with the suggestion that such cases are not a proper subject of discussion. He then proceeds to discuss them.

(In passing: Mr. Stein's concern for the sanctity of juridical processes does not seem to have kept the ACCF-sponsored book *McCarthy and the Communists*, by James Rorty and Moshe Decter, from several times characterizing Lattimore as a "skillful, effective and influential party-lining propagandist." This statement is, of course, substantially in agreement with one of the counts of the perjury indictment against Lattimore. If one accepted Mr. Stein's notions about what is proper to discuss, the Rorty-Decter book could thus be read as an attempt to exert "pressures upon a judge and jurors.")

In another section of his communication, Mr. Stein writes:

> Congressional committees, however, when they function responsibly, perform a valuable service in furnishing the public with evaluated information concerning the work of apologists and agents of the Soviet Union who *have not—or cannot be proven to have—broken* existing laws. [Italics mine—M.H.]

Perhaps the most extreme of the current interpretations of powers of congressional committees claims the right of exposing general "situations." But Mr. Stein, speaking for the cause of cultural freedom, goes further and suggests a competence to deal with "apologists" (not, mind you, spies or saboteurs: simply apologists!) who "have not—or cannot be proven to have—broken existing laws." The remainder of his communication, a crass and vindictive justification of the prolonged harassment to which Lattimore has been subjected, is entirely in keeping with the totally antilibertarian—and indeed, in this case, downright inhumane—spirit of his ideas about cultural freedom in America.

It is to the credit of several ACCF members that they have not kept silent about the Stein scandal. A series of letters from ACCF leaders appeared in the February 28, 1955, issue of the *New Republic*, and these are worthy of close scrutiny. Herbert J. Muller, in a blunt attack on Stein, wrote:

> It is humiliating that a nation confronted by literally life or death issues should still be distracted and embittered by an

hysterical search for scapegoats . . . it seems unfortunate to me that [liberals] should dissipate what little influence they have by . . . feeling obliged to prove their 100 percent liberality of spirit by springing to the defense of a McCarran.

Arthur Schlesinger, Jr., wrote to say he thought the ACCF "ought to find better things to do than to harry Lattimore." Richard Rovere caustically referred to Mr. Stein's "satisfied-customer view of the McCarran Committee"—an indictment that not even a hostile critic could improve upon. Mr. Rovere cast further light upon ACCF when he remarked that the majority of its Executive agreed with Stein's views "and looks upon mine as eccentric."

But by far the best and most impressive letter came from David Riesman. Since Mr. Riesman's views on American society have been subjected to a good deal of criticism in *Dissent*, it is only just that his position receive here the praise it deserves. We reprint his letter in full, and particularly invite attention to its final sentence:

Sirs:

I recently resigned from the Executive Committee of the American Committee for Cultural Freedom. My decision to do so was taken long before the letter on the Gilbert article, though letters such as this, which appeared to me to demand the entire Committee's attention for the vindictive pursuit of the shrinking minority of "liberals who haven't learned," was one of the reasons for my resignation. (I had delayed resigning at the urging of friends who hoped that the Executive Committee could be reconstituted, so as to become more representative of the concerns of the membership at large, but I eventually became convinced that this was not the case and that, at any rate, I did not have the time, energy, and capacity for the effort.) The Committee, it goes without saying, has accomplished many good and valuable things, in clarifying the nature of Communist totalitarianism and in exposing the apologetics of its fellow travelers, and in defending, as an aspect of cultural freedom, civil liberties in the academic and intellectual community; many activities of the latter sort have, in the interests of the individuals involved, not been publicized. Still, what appeared to me as a disproportionate amount of the Committee's limited energies has gone into the drafting and discussion of such things as Mr. Stein's letter—a task that can be left to individuals (and congressional committees!) and one that does not require a Committee for Cultural Freedom.

Just before resigning, I had written a letter to Mr. Stein asking to be dissociated from the letter on the Lattimore case, and suggesting that whoever wrote it sign it and speak for himself. [This letter is referred to in the previous paragraph.] In writing Mr. Stein about the draft letter, I once more emphasized my feeling that there were more important issues demanding the Executive Committee's consideration, and that in any event (irrespective of the factual accuracy of the letter, which I did not question) to put the whole weight of the Committee for Cultural Freedom behind the pursuit of an already beleaguered man, living in limbo and not permitted to teach classes, was an act of inhumanity.

David Riesman

It is sad—indeed, humiliating—to report, however, that the official ACCF position found its only supporter in . . . Norman Thomas, the leader of the Socialist Party and also active in the ACCF. A good part of Thomas's long letter consisted of a blustering attack on the author of the original *New Republic* article for using a pseudonym—as if Thomas had not associated during his lifetime with numerous socialists who, for good and sufficient reasons, also used pseudonyms. Thomas then went on to say that "lawyers, devoted to civil liberty" have praised the McCarran inquiry into Lattimore as "something of a model in congressional investigation." And again: "One can stand up for Owen Lattimore's rights when he is threatened with criminal proceedings and yet believe intelligent opinion in and out of Congress was the gainer of the inquiry conducted by Judge Morris" (i.e., the McCarran committee).

In the same issue of the *New Republic* there is an extremely effective answer to Thomas by the magazine's editor, Michael Straight, in which it is demonstrated at length that the McCarran committee did not follow the rules for fair investigation set up by Thomas himself in his book *The Test of Freedom*, and that it did not aid public understanding of anything. That Norman Thomas, identified in American eyes with the cause of socialism, should have let himself be put in the position of defending Sol Stein's outrage—this tells us a great deal not merely about the ACCF but about the debacle of American radical and liberal politics in general.

It would be easy to adopt a simple tone of anger against the ACCF. Yet the point in analyzing it cannot be a mere denunciation, if only because its membership includes good and honest people; it acts as it does not out of malice or because it is manipulated by a secret caucus, but from what is evidently free choice. Why then has it drifted into such an anomalous position?

Part of the answer is supplied by the general development of American society. In *White Collar*, C. Wright Mills assigns considerable importance to the rise of the intellectual technician and the parallel bureaucratization of society—with a consequent loss of independence on the part of the intellectual who is absorbed in this process. Another description of the same process (although with a totally different—indeed sympathetic—judgment of the result) was made by Lionel Trilling in the *Partisan Review*: "Intellect has associated itself with power as perhaps never before in history, and is now conceded to be itself a kind of power."

And indeed, in going over the roster of the American Committee one does find intellect associated with power, in the successful journalists, editors, union functionaries, and the like. Certainly this process of the loss of independence and the rationalization of the intellectual life plays a part in the creation of a phenomenon like the American Committee. It indicates an almost complete reversal of the traditional estimate of the intellectual as a focus of opposition toward the status quo; it marks an abdication of critical function.

This general point gains in concreteness when it is related to the Cold War. The feeling of betrayal that developed out of the increase of knowledge with regard to Stalinism was reinforced by the tremendous polarizing effect of the Cold War. Together, the two events hastened an either/or kind of philosophy; the very mood of American intellectual life in recent years has become increasingly that of "critical support" (with the inevitable emphasis on the second term gaining the ascendancy) of American foreign policy. Here, the loss of independence is intensified by the polarities of the international situation. And when this is combined with the more basic social process of bureaucratization of the intellectual life, the result is the kind of ambiguity embodied in the American Committee.

Finally, certain speculations are possible with regard to the reasoning of some ACCF leaders. In a way, the ACCF is organized along lines rather similar to the select social club or, if one wishes to be more kindly, a self-appointed and self-perpetuating "academy." Members are co-opted after sponsorship; one must be *chosen.* A good number of its active leaders are people who have had bitter and scarring experiences with Stalinism, whether through party membership, front association, denunciation as Trotskyists real or assumed, etc. Some of them are people with a feeling that *only they* appreciate the urgency of combating Stalinism, a feeling of vast and even violent impatience with those "ritualistic liberals" who cling to the traditional pieties of civil libertarianism. This feeling is rather similar, though it is not quite the same, as that which has been described by Hannah Arendt as the "ex-Communist" syndrome—*only they* can know the cunning and power of the enemy. It is not a feeling likely to make for either a supple politics or a firm defense of cultural freedom.

These elements of social and personal motivation may put certain ACCF leaders in an understandable light, but they do not, and cannot, excuse the political basis and actual practice of the Committee. With increasing velocity, the ACCF has moved toward the position of embracing "pure and simple" (which is to say, not at all pure) anti-Stalinism, while maintaining a great deal of silence on the state of cultural freedom in the United States. In the 1930s many a Stalinist front group was for freedom here and not in Russia. In the 1950s there has been a certain reversal of terms, a drive for absolute freedom in Russia (where the ACCF does not yet have any influence) and an ambiguity with regard to freedom in the United States (where it does have influence). Neither point of view adds stature to American intellectuals.

Meanwhile, the exchange in the *New Republic* has served to bring implicit disagreements into the open. David Riesman's letter poses a challenge that neither the ACCF leadership nor its members can ignore. We do not think it an exaggeration to say that the issue involves far more than the attitude of intellectuals toward Lattimore: it involves nothing less than the future of cultural freedom. That is, it involves the question faced by all the accredited institutions of American liberalism: will they, in a situation where every social pressure makes for accommodation and retreat, be able to remain liberal?

# PART 2

# 3
# Culture and Society

There was a moment in the mid-fifties that would have had great comic potential were it not part of a national tragedy.

I was working for the Fund for the Republic, a civil liberties foundation headed by Robert Hutchins, who had been the boy-wonder president of the University of Chicago. The Fund was under bitter attack from the Right, and Fulton Lewis, Jr., a key McCarthyite broadcaster, had devoted part of his program each night to exposing the subversive character of the foundation.

I happened to be in California, working on a study of the blacklist in the entertainment industry, when the Tenney Committee, the state's imitation of the House Un-American Activities Committee, released a preposterous report that the Young Socialist League, which I chaired, was in the forefront of an international plot to reunite the socialists and Communists of the world. Never mind that we would have been opposed to such an effort had it been real. Even more to the point, never mind that we had fewer than 200 members in the United States at that time—hardly an Archimedean point for a global conspiracy. I waited for the witch-hunters to document my links to the Fund.

At that very moment, the anti-Communism expert of the *New York World-Telegram*, Frederick Woltman, published a front-page article about finding a Marxist at the Fund for the Republic. The evidence was a lengthy article I had written in *The New International*, an anti-Stalinist Marxist magazine of minuscule circulation, on . . . Marxism and art. As it turned out, Woltman was persona non grata with the orthodox McCarthyites since he had deplored some of their hero's methods while endorsing his aims. So Lewis and the others refused to take a lead—even a lead about a dangerous Marxist aesthete—from a heretic.

But why, in any case, did a Marxist journal bother to print such an article—or the analysis of politics and the novel that follows? And even if that can be explained, what significant learning experience, relevant to American culture, was involved?

That first question might be reframed in terms of the *Partisan Review* paradox. *Partisan Review* was the quintessential anti-Stalinist intellectual journal of the 1930s and continues to this day. It has puzzled some people as to how it could have been simultaneously Marxist in politics—with a Trotskyist tilt—and deeply appreciative of the poetry and literary criticism of T. S. Eliot, the self-proclaimed monarchist, Anglo-Catholic, and classicist.

For Joseph Stalin, a man who wanted music that could be hummed and art that inspired people to follow his politics, the *Partisan Review* paradox is indeed outrageous. Art is defined, and evaluated, politically, and the art of a reactionary is therefore reactionary. But that is neither Marxist nor serious.

Marx had insisted in the opening pages of the *Grundrisse* that there is no simple relation between art and society, no way to explain how Greek tragedy had, from within a rather simple and underdeveloped society, achieved a greatness that much more economically "advanced" societies could only envy.

Trotsky had written fairly complex appreciations of literary modernism (indeed the fact that he wrote so well was one of the reasons why he had such an impact upon intellectuals). Antonio Gramsci told in the thirties of how the socialist task was to win cultural "hegemony," not just political power, that the revolution was moral and psychological as well as economic and political (his ideas were not widely published until after World War II, when they had a significant impact on the largest Communist party in Western Europe). For one who knows the history of Marxism there is no *Partisan Review* paradox: it is not strange that a young radical in the McCarthyite fifties would be writing about the novel.

In a personal sense, as my political commitment deepened, my literary concerns fused with my new awareness of society. I retained the Chicago Aristotelian respect for the text, the insistence upon a close reading as the foundation of literary interpretation. But now I connected the text and the society, always insisting upon the complexity of their interrelationship. There was one period when I spoke every year at Antioch College: one talk on politics as such, one talk on culture and politics. And I began to discover the Marxist underground, the deviants like Karl Korsch, the closet deviants like Georg Lukács, who stressed a dialectic in which the artistic and the spiritual had an independent value of their own and were not seen as the "reflection" of what was really important, the economic.

Eventually, I wrote two books in that mode, *The Accidental Century* (1965) and *The Politics at God's Funeral: Spiritual Crisis of Western Civilization* (1983). All well and good, it might be said. But what is it that raises this little history above the level of a Marxist footnote with an autobiographical twist?

Herbert Marcuse and the 1960s are part of the answer.

When I was first groping my way into the Marxist underground I came upon a tremendously important book by Marcuse, *Reason and Revolution.* It talked of what was revolutionary in Hegel and how Marx had integrated a great deal of that German idealist into his "materialist" thinking. I had had intimations of that fact, primarily from two volumes on Marx's intellectual development published by Sidney Hook in the thirties (that Hook has since become a neoconservative with a soft spot for Marx does not, of course, diminish the value of his earlier accomplishment). But Marcuse now made me see these things more clearly than ever before.

Much more to the present point, it was Marcuse who became a New Left guru in the sixties. But then, he was not alone. Gramsci's heritage was at work and so was the influence of the Frankfurt School of both the older (Adorno, Horkheimer) and younger (Habermas) generations. There were Eastern European dissidents, like Kolakowski and Kosik, and they, like Marcuse, rejected that simpleminded economic determinism that had so impoverished the Left, insisting on the relevance of culture to social and political struggles.

It is, of course, true that some of these developments were faddish and superficial, that Marcuse was cited much more often than he was read, that the concept of alienation quickly went from being an unknown term in Marx's unread early writings to the status of a boring cliché. Still, the idea of the politics of culture—and the culture of politics—had a significant impact on mass movements. It was, for instance, a force in the United States among feminists, environmentalists, gays, and lesbians. In France in 1968, it became an incitement to the creation of a youthful commune that almost toppled Charles de Gaulle from power.

Indeed, one cannot understand the political victory on the Left in France in 1981 without seeing that François Mitterrand and his Socialist Party were the heirs—the improbable heirs, in some ways, but the heirs nonetheless—of those heady days in May when the radicals behind their barricades in the Latin Quarter cried, "Imagination to Power!" It was not for nothing that, in the campaign of 1981, Mitterrand was presented with a red rose at every stop.

As I write, Mitterrand is in deep economic and political trouble (a situation explored in chapter 24). But, whatever happens to the socialists in France, the underlying theme of the fist and rose—of the way in which the social affects, limits, and even subverts the spiritual and aesthetic—is clearly on the agenda of the late twentieth century—and of the twenty-first.

It would, however, be wrong to give this introduction an unambiguously happy ending. On the literary side, my prediction that the novel was finished as an art form makes me one of a rather large company of gravediggers who watched the corpse come back to life. I guess I could salvage a bit of my honor by pointing out that the most exuberant—and political—novels of these times are to be found in Latin American societies, which went through a much different evolution from that of the European countries and the lands of European settlement.

I prefer not to make that plea. I thought at that time that the novels that have come since from the pens of geniuses like Gabriel García Márquez and Mario Vargas Llosa would never be written. I was, after all, a young and enthusiastic man under the spell of a soaring theory and that often leads to overarching generalizations that do not exactly hold up. So even though I find much of what I said valuable and true, my prediction was simply wrong.

And on the political side there are some other ambivalences. True enough, the cultural Marxists, like Marcuse, enormously deepened their methodology and, in the spirit of Marx, extended it to regions of the human spirit that he did not have the time to explore. This is a gain and so was the political-aesthetic critique of capitalism made by the young—and sometimes excessively anarchist—revolutionaries of the sixties and seventies. But this Marxist trend is to be found mainly in the universities and among the "new class" of the college educated. It is hardly a vibrant force among the workers and other popular movements. Indeed, Marxism is schizophrenic in the 1980s in much the same way that I argue in my essay that the political novel was split in two. Where it has gained in cultural depth, it tends to be politically irrelevant; where it still has something of a hold on the masses, it tends to be culturally simplistic. The major exception would be the Italian Communist Party.

Still, this essay is a case of taking sides and the basic choice it represented was, I think, quite right. Underlying it is a rejection of the notion that one had to be either a Baudelairean dandy contemptuous of the masses or else a militant simplifier who reduced cultural to a mere "reflection" of the truly basic economic structures. I continue to think that and, more to the point, in the years since this discussion of politics and the novel was published, more than a few people have come to agree.

# 4

# Is There a Political Novel? The Artistic Limits of the Political Novel Today

*The New International, 1958*

Has there ever been a novel in which a character is as politically motivated as Koestler's Rubashov in *Darkness at Noon* and, at the same time, is a round, complicated person like James's Princess Casamassima? Has there, in short, ever been a really successful political novel?

If we want to answer these questions seriously, our first task is to embrace a certain vagueness. The novel is hard enough to define in itself—and when all is said and done we should be glad to settle for E. M. Forster's masterful imprecision: a novel tells a story. Given this shaky beginning, things get even trickier when we speak of a "political" novel. Since the term does not indicate general style, like naturalism or impressionism, since it is a definition in terms of subject matter, we seem to be faced by a miserable critical alternative. On the one hand, we can define the political novel so broadly that it encompasses almost the whole history of the novel and thus becomes vague and useless. Or else, we can specify our definition more carefully and run the risk of inventing a sterile and artificial construction.

In his provocative study of *Politics and the Novel*, Irving

Howe attempted to cut this Gordian knot. To one reviewer, his definition seemed arbitrary and whimsical, but one suspects that this was because he was unaware of the intricacies involved. Howe wrote, "By a political novel I mean a novel in which political ideas play a prominent role or in which the political milieu is the dominant setting—though again a qualification is necessary, since the word 'dominant' is more than a little questionable. Perhaps it would be better to say: a novel in which we take to be dominant political ideas or the political milieu. . . ."

Let this stand as a working definition. It simplifies, it is highly subjective, and it is probably as well as we will ever be able to do. But once having accepted it, let me state a perspective somewhat bleaker than Howe's: the successful political novel will either be a roman à clef, the charade of a sociological analysis, or else the politics will be swallowed up by the apolitical. The first alternative, the method of *Darkness at Noon*, Orwell's *1984*, London's *The Iron Heel*, may produce works of a limited, though undeniable, genius. The second may result in a masterpiece, as in the case of *Man's Fate*, but the technique is the subordination of the political to some other dominant motive—that is, the book practically ceases to be a political novel.

Why is this true? In part the answer is historical. It is found in the development of the novel; in particular it is the consequence of its complex relation to the fate of bourgeois society. And in part the answer is formal: it involves the intrinsic difficulty of integrating politics into the felt narrative, of marrying Rubashov to the Princess Casamassima.

All of this is a way of saying that politics has bypassed the novel *as a really significant subject matter.*

The rise of the novel was contemporaneous with the bourgeois revolution. In the political order, feudalism was swept away, production was rationalized, the incredible complexity of modern life became a fact. In the aesthetic order, the novel was, in part, a reaction to this fact. As Lukács put it in his study of the historical novel, "The changed relationship between the psychology of men and the economic and moral circumstances of their life had become so complex that a broad representation of these circumstances, an extensive formulization of these interrelationships, became necessary if men were to be shown as the concrete children of their time."

Thus it was that the novel was a revolutionary art form. For it shattered most of the old conventions, it sent literature probing into every corner of human life. In Henry Fielding, for example, there is an exultant, liberating rush of art toward experience, one that burst through the classical canon of the separation of styles. In *Jonathan Wild the Great*, Fielding wrote, "In all, we shall find that there is a nearer connection between high and low life than is generally imagined, and that a highwayman is entitled to more favor with the great than he usually meets with." And in France, Balzac was becoming "the secretary of French society," and probing that incredibly thick and populous world of *La Comédie humaine.*

These novels were soaked in society—for that matter, Lionel Trilling has defined the very essence of the novel in social terms. In Balzac, for instance, there is the careful delineation of the various classes and strata, of the ancien régime, the Napoleonic bureaucracy, the restorationists' impotence, even of the French underworld, for he shared Fielding's notion that the life of the criminal illuminated that of the bourgeois. And yet, the best of Balzac's work was not political in the terms of Howe's definition. When a novel of Balzac's is dominated by the political structure and setting (*Les Employés*), it is a failure; when his romantic spirit dominates, and the political observation becomes the subordinate stuff of his vision (*Le Cousin Pons*, *Le Père Goriot*, etc.) he produces masterpieces.

Balzac is, of course, an almost perfect case, and therefore an extreme one. But much of the same can be said of Walter Scott's historicism and the many novels that it inspired. At the beginning, the novel was almost pervasively social, but not political in the sense of concentrating upon the superstructure of society. The nearest thing to such a vantage point was the ideology of reaction, and that is why a Balzac, with his prejudice for feudalism, was able to create the most finely structured image of the new world to be found in his time.

Thus, the novel began with a social realism (usually mixed with romanticism), with a rush into the complexity and depth of the new bourgeois society. Yet, this did not produce a "political" novel in Howe's sense of the term. (The nearest thing to it was Stendhal.) But, and this is the paradox, the worldview of the rising novel, that of realism, is almost a precondition for the political novel—the only real chance that such a type of literature had for existence was in this period. For then, reality was seen as solid, palpable, as *there*, and in such a world politics is a meaningful subject. Later, when politics became more pervasive, when the ideological critique of society was everywhere available to the artist, this world had disappeared, and this is partly why the most brilliant and insightful analyses of society were to be antipolitical. An impressionist political novel, a surrealist political novel, these are almost unthinkable categories, because there is an irreconcilable contradiction between style and content, form and matter. Thus it was that the two halves necessary to the synthesis of a political novel—a realistic weltanschauung in which politics is meaningful, and a political ideology—were sundered by history.

And here one must dispute Howe's formulation. He writes,

> The ideal social novel had been written by Jane Austen, a great artist who enjoyed the luxury of being able to take society for granted: it was *there*, and it seemed steady beneath her glass, Napoleon or no Napoleon. But soon it would not be steady beneath anyone's glass, and the novelists' attention had necessarily to shift from the gradation within society to the fate of society itself. It is at this point, roughly speaking, that the kind of book I have called the political comes to be written—the kind in which the *idea* of society, as distinct from the mere unquestioned workings of society, has penetrated the consciousness of the characters in all of its profoundly problematic aspects. . . .

My quarrel is with a confusion of society and politics in this statement. Quite early in the development of the novel, indeed, in the time of Jane Austen, the problematic idea of society was present in the novel. Balzac is proof enough. But it was not a *political* idea, and that is the significant dividing line. To develop the question as Howe does is to miss the historical perspective and to tend toward seeing the political novel in its formal aspect, an element that is certainly important but only partially revealing of the actual process. (Incidentally, this criticism is made within a framework of feeling that Howe's book represents a thoughtful, even brilliant, approach to a difficult subject.)

But turn now and look at the second half of the historical situation. The fact is that the main direction of the novel became more and more estranged from politics at the precise moment that ideological movements made the political novel a real possibility, that the formal development of the novel was at odds with a political subject matter.

By the middle of the nineteenth century, the French novel was already moving far away from its beginnings. The liberating, tumultuous force of realism was dividing in two directions. One, via Flaubert, was toward the coldness of realism, and eventually away from society itself toward that magnificent aesthetic accomplishment of our time, the art of the interior self. The other road, that of Zola, was reducing the all-embracing vitality (and romanticism) of realism to a more mechanistic view, which ended up in the dead end of the "slice of life." Both movements were a reflection of the loss of élan in bourgeois society, of the new threat from the rising socialist movement. That they were simultaneously antibourgeois in content, and soaked in the spirit of the bourgeois world, is only one of the paradoxes that result from the intricate relationship of art to society.

Franz Mehring wrote somewhat prophetically of this situation before the First World War (that his method was somewhat mechanistic does not destroy the validity of his conclusion). He saw that naturalism was only "halfway," that it was simply representing, but that it had not achieved a really critical standpoint. And he felt that unless it did gain a new vantage, it would go over to the side of decadence. His disjunction, it turns out, was sound —and the fact is that naturalism was unable to rise above itself. The truly great works of the novelistic imagination in the twentieth century have thus been produced by those bourgeois antibourgeois who were the magnificent, creative victims of decadence. And the high road of the novel has not been toward a new synthesis of the old naturalism and the new politics, but rather along the way of the disintegration of society. The characteristics of the best novels *entre deux guerres* are as Erich Auerbach recorded them: "multipersonal representation of consciousness, time strata, disintegration of the continuity of exterior events, shifting of the narrative viewpoint. . . ." In such a tendency, there was little that was conducive to the development of a political novel.

This is not to say that the novel had escaped politics. That is impossible. Rather, the political criticism was not expressed politically, for it was not merely society that the crisis of the superstructure called into question—it was all of reality. As Philip Rahv put it in his *Image and Idea*, "[The] artists are no longer content merely to question particular habits or situations or even institutions; it is reality itself which they bring into question." Thus, on the one hand, naturalism had become so constricted that it could not rise above its narrow view of the world and achieve a political novel; and the antinaturalistic trend, the method of greatness in our time, had gone *beyond* politics.

Two apparent exceptions should be noted. The first is that magnificent flowering of the second half of the nineteenth century, the Russian novel. Here there was a greater concern with politics. This higher consciousness was partially a function of the same situation that so politicalized the Russian working class: the pervasiveness of czarist backwardness and autocracy. And yet Dostoevsky at his most political—say, in *The Possessed*—has also gone beyond politics; that is, the political question is viewed, not primarily in terms of power or social class, but as it relates to the individual pathos, above all, to the problem of religion. That, among other things, is why his most political novel, *The Possessed*, is inferior to *Crime and Punishment* and *The Brothers Karamazov*. In the masterpieces, there is no real pretense at political analysis, and the other element is clearly dominant.

The second exception concerns a series of contemporary novelists, most of them veterans of the revolutionary movement: Malraux, Silone, Camus, Sperber, etc. But here again, I would argue that their books either are an unfleshed political analysis (Orwell's *1984*), or else they are concerned with issues more ultimate than politics (Camus's *Plague*, Malraux's *Man's Fate*.) The real synthesis, the image of the political novel with which I began—the hypothetical marriage of Rubashov and the Princess Casamassima—is not achieved in the work of these writers.

But finally, there is the one real exception, the work of genius that forces us to cast all of this in terms of general tendency and historical fact rather than as a literary law: Conrad's *Nostromo*. In this book, there is the feel of social life (almost Balzacian in its force), political vision, even political prophecy. Perhaps nowhere else in the art of our time is there such an image of capitalism and imperialism. And at the same time, *Nostromo* has a wealth of deep characterization, a world of individual human beings.

And yet . . . even here, in this magnificent exception, the process we are describing is visible. For in *Nostromo*, and particularly in the person of its hero, that deeper theme of alienation and loneliness is always present. This novel, richer than *Lord Jim* or *Victory*, still displays a real continuity, a focus upon the problem of the anguish of failure; the modern, slightly blurred hero seen at his supreme moment. *Nostromo* is a synthesis, and this makes it one of the finest works of the political novel—or, in a sense, the *only* achieved political novel.

Thus, history played a trick on the political novel. When the realistic view of the world—essential to the incorporation of political ideology into the novelistic imagination—was present, the ideology was not. When the ideology had emerged, the novel, in its main tendency, had moved away from a solid, objective concern with the external world. Both changes are complexly related to the rise and decline of bourgeois society, but their brunt is unmistakable: they made the political novel, as a serious art form, an exceptional case, they exiled it from the mainstream.

But the historical development of the novel does not, all on its own, account for the lack of political novels. We also must take note of an important formal consideration, one that casts a great deal of light on some of the attempts to write political novels in our time.

In the last volume of *Remembrance of Things Past, The Past Recaptured*, Marcel Proust wrote, "True art has nothing to do with proclamations—it completes itself in silence." And, a little later, "A work that contains theories is like an object upon which one leaves the price tag." There is both truth and paradox in these comments. The paradox resides in the fact that Proust's polemic against ideas in the novel occurs in a section, some seventy pages long, devoted to critical theory. But the truth is that there is at least a tension between the novelist's task of portraying the felt human world and any attempt on his part to engage in ideological discussion. Indeed, this section of Proust's own book, valuable as it is in itself, is unquestionably a flaw, not so much because it is an abstract discussion, but because it is much too long, and has no organic unity with the rest of the book.

If, then, we abstract from the overly formalist bias of impressionism that Proust brings to his subject, we can recognize not a contradiction but a tension between the fictional purpose and the discursive idea. In the novel itself, this tension has expressed itself in two forms. On the one hand, there are the books in the tradition of the roman à clef; on the other hand, there is the tendency of the perception of reality itself to overpower ideology in the novel, to shatter any real possibility of a synthesis.

It would be wrong to dismiss the first type of political novel out of hand. But we certainly have to admit that it is characterized by a certain thinness, that it never reaches the really profound. Evelyn Waugh's political satires, such as *Black Mischief*; Orwell's *1984*; London's *Iron Heel*; and Koestler's *Darkness at Noon*—these represent the wide range of possibility for the genre. Yet all have this in common: their characters tend to be "flat," defined less by a complex of human and social interrelationships than by their function of acting out a political theory. We do not feel, for instance, that Rubashov is motivated by his unique and distinctive personality, but rather he acts according to Koestler's analytic conception of the old Bolsheviks during the Moscow Trials.

Lukács was greatly concerned with this problem of the typical, and made a sharp distinction between two approaches to it. He wrote, "Thus, the type, according to Marx and Engels, is not the abstract type of classical tragedy, nor the figure in Schiller's idealistic generalizations, and even less that which Zola and the post-Zola literary theory have made of it, the Average. The type is rather characterized as that striking personality in whose dynamic unity true literature reflects life, comprehending in its contradictory unity the most important social, moral, and spiritual contradictions of a period, bringing them together in a vital unity." If we accept this distinction—as I do—then it is obvious that the authors of the novels we have just been discussing fail to create "types." And even in their politicalization of character they are thereby cut off from a genuine and moving profundity.

This is not to say that such books are valueless. When they are well done, as in the case of *1984*, they can be deeply moving. But when they cut themselves off from a certain human complexity, they lose a feeling of depth and interrelationship that has been the particular genius of the great novel.

On the other hand, there are "political novels" that are filled with the intricacies of personality, in which the characters move, not according to an analysis or as the charade of an ideology, but as unique personalities. And here, we can see the formal problem of the political novel in all its acuteness. For when this is attempted, the almost inevitable result is that the book actually subordinates the politics to other values and motivations—the novel becomes less political.

The classic case of this process is André Malraux's *Man's Fate*. Some time ago, William Empson wrote of it, "The heroes are Communists, but they are frankly out of touch with the proletariat; it is from this that they get their pathos and dignity and the book its freedom from propaganda." I would go much further than Empson, for the ultimate values, the motivational spring of *Man's Fate* is not political at all. The Chinese Revolution is the setting in which Malraux approaches the theme of death that has been central to his writing from the very first. And the real point of the book is not the interrelationships that arise in the course of a revolutionary attempt to emancipate man from exploitation, but the drama of the aristocratic hero's fight to transcend his own mortality. (In Malraux's later art criticism, the painter was to function in the same way as the politicals of his novels: Malraux's Goya is, in a sense, Kyo from *Man's Fate* in another guise.)

Why does this de-politicalization of the novel happen? In part the answer is historical, along the lines we have already discussed. Malraux, Silone, and Camus are the children of bourgeois culture even in their hatred of the bourgeoisie. They have the consciousness of modern man, and this is their general vantage point. And rather than being unique and separate authors, the representatives of a distinguishable genre, they are contemporary novelists who deal with the modern concern *in terms* of politics, in a political setting, and not *as* politics.

But there is also a formal consideration (though it is, of course, related to the historical). Politics is not "ultimate." It is, however intricately, a reflection of more basic realities of human existence. This means that under the most favorable historical circumstances there will be a tendency to go "beyond" politics. And in an age such as ours, when it is precisely the basic realities (indeed, the very reality of reality) that have been brought into question through an unprecedented and total crisis of society, it is almost inevitable that the most political of realists will go beyond politics. In short, the formal difficulty, the one that Proust discussed, has been made all the more effective by the specific cultural conjunction of our time.

Under the very best of circumstances, then, there would be many difficulties in writing a masterly political novel. In our time, the actual situation has led to a bifurcation of the political novel into its two parts, and has inhibited a genuine synthesis. On the one hand, we have provocative, stimulating books (all the more personal because of their journalistic immediacy) that are political but by that fact miss the fullness and complexity of life that is characteristic of the novel at its best. And on the other hand, we have novels written by politicals, even with political settings, but there the politics tends to be stagecraft and not the real substance of the book.

It is wrong to think that there is any simple and single literary category of the "bourgeois novel." Such terms are the invention of a sterile, mechanistic determinism. And yet, we cannot utter a really complex judgment about the novel unless we understand its relation to the rhythm of bourgeois culture.

In part, what we are dealing with here is the persistence and pervasiveness of bourgeois culture, *precisely* at the moment of its decline. It was one of Trotsky's more flashing insights to note, in *Literature and Revolution*, that the most characteristic cultural expressions of a society occur at the moment of its decline, during the imminence of its downfall. The political novel is, quite literally, impossible today in the sense of a real synthesis. So is the social novel. For that matter, one can cogently argue that the novel itself, as an art form, is nearing dead end.

For the object is gone, culturally speaking. The tactile, palpable external world that was at the center of centuries of Western art is no longer there. And the trend in literature for over a century has been toward subjectivity. In the process, we have received magnificent works of the imagination, the various, eclectic, exciting, and probing gift of decadence. We cannot deny Thomas Mann's insight: our sickness has been creative. It goes without saying that the price is too high, monstrously so, that our beauty, warped and deformed but beauty nevertheless, is the consequence of a social agony and that a human being must prefer an insipid peace to a hundred Guernicas. Yet the major point that I wish to make here is not political or moral, but critical.

As long as our present cultural situation lasts—and in all of its permutations it will continue as long as our social situation does—we are cut off from a whole series of literary creations. Among them is the political novel. But that is not so serious, for that is a subclass of a subclass. The disturbing question is the one posed and answered by Orwell in his essay, "Inside the Whale." Are we now in a plight where we can say, as Orwell did, that there is the "*impossibility* of any major literature until the world has shaken itself in shape"? Is the situation of the political novel, its dead end, the symptom of a much deeper malaise that infects all our literature? I would not be as aggressively pessimistic as Orwell—nor so optimistic as to rule out the possible truth of his grim insight.

# PART 3

# 5
# Unlearning Experience

In these chapters, I do not appear as a precocious social critic who anticipated political and cultural trends before most people knew that they even existed. Rather I am the victim of my inability to take my own excellent advice: an unlearner.

Since the fifties were so conservative in every sense of the word, there were only a handful of us who had been the left-wing youth of that decade, to greet the new radicals of the student movement of the sixties. I was one "generation" older than the New Left, a grizzled veteran in my early thirties when they appeared in their late teenage and early twenties. At first I was even something of a guru to them. There are only three Americans over thirty whom we respect, Tom Hayden wrote in an article in *Mademoiselle*: Norman Thomas, C. Wright Mills, and Michael Harrington.

I have described at some length, in *Fragments of the Century*, how I then forfeited that trust. But what surprised and even shocked me when I was going through my essays and articles to prepare this volume was that I had warned everyone, myself included, against the stupidity I committed. In the 1962 analysis of the student movement I had very shrewdly warned against taking the errors, the sloppiness, the inconsistencies, of the young radicals as if they were considered "positions" of a longtime leftist cadre.

My failure to listen to myself occurred within the most dynamic white student movement of the sixties, Students for a Democratic Society (SDS). The black rebels were, of course, mainly organized in the Student Nonviolent Coordinating Committee (SNCC, or, as we pronounced it, "Snick").

For a variety of improbable reasons the youthful radical activism of that decade first manifested itself in one of the oldest social democratic institutions in the country, the League for Industrial Democracy (LID). I was a young Turk in the LID and joyously greeted and worked with the new generation that announced itself at the University of Michigan at Ann Arbor in 1959–1960. At that point they were members of the Student League for Industrial Democracy but by 1962 they had decided to call themselves Students for a Democratic Society. The first essay in this chapter was written shortly before the fateful meeting at which SLID became SDS. It was held at a United Automobile Workers educational center at Port Huron, Michigan, and it produced one of the most important radical political statements of the times.

At Port Huron, I disagreed with my youthful new friends on two related issues: how explicitly anti-Communist the Left should be, and to what degree one should dismiss American liberalism as a hypocritical front for the establishment? On the latter question, the SDSers adopted an antiliberalism similar to my own during the McCarthy period—a position I had then abandoned as I realized that liberalism ranged from people on the left wing of conservatism to those who were socialists without knowing it. In a beery discussion that lasted well into the night I attacked my former self—and I was right to do so.

When it came to the issue of Communism, a mere ten years' difference in age turned us into the representatives of two different epochs. When I declared myself an anti-Communist I identified with the general strike of the Hungarian working class against the Soviet invasion of 1956. When they presented themselves as anti–anti-Communists, they did so in rejecting American collaboration with the partisans of Batista in the attempt to overthrow Castro at the Bay of Pigs. Intellectually, we could agree; but emotionally, viscerally, we talked past each other.

It was at this point that I carefully ignored the good advice I had given in my 1962 article. I became a tough faction fighter, treating sincere young radicals, who were at worst confused—and understandably so—as if they were the implacable foes of any criticism of Communism. I left Port Huron early on the next day and shortly afterward received an inaccurate report on what happened next. I was told that my advice had been totally ignored, which turned out to be untrue, and a bruised ego thus became an incitement to compound my initial mistake. At that point, I briefly joined in with the older generation of the LID and supported locking the youthful heretics out of the office. I took the wrong side.

I came to my senses within a matter of weeks, congratulating those on the LID board who had voted against me. I then tried to make amends—but it took years to effect the final reconciliation, and I remain ashamed of my actions. The third chapter in this part, chapter 7, "The Mystical Militants," was written well after that break with the founding sons and daughters of SDS and was part of my attempt to reach out to them, but without becoming an uncritical sycophant (there were not a few devotees of the sixties cult of youth who did that). My comments on the romanticism, and sometimes the self-indulgence, of that generation stand—but so does my enormous admiration for their energy and idealism. They helped remake the university and the culture; they played a catalytic role in the antiwar movement (particularly in the earlier, "teach-in," phase); they put their lives at risk in the civil rights struggle.

Strangely enough, the denouement of this self-critical hindsight is actually happy. There was a handful of SDS activists who followed a mad argument to its logical conclusion and turned to terrorism. There were others who became careerists. But there was a third group, numbering in the thousands, that continued to work, in the most diverse ways, for the values that had inspired their youth. They became community organizers helping working-class families fight city hall on prosaic issues like zoning, mortgage money, and utility rates; some turned up as trade-union organizers even though SDS had been quite suspicious of the official labor movement; many of the women played important roles in the feminist movement, some of them as union organizers trying to sign up that vast, underpaid constituency of female workers; and so on.

In the mid-seventies, roughly ten or so years after my spectacular performance at Port Huron, I offered one of the SDSers we had barred from the office—a "Red-diaper" baby from a Communist family, one of the best organizers and speakers I have ever known, Steve Max—a major organizational job in the Democratic Socialist Organizing Committee (DSOC), which I chaired. And twenty years after Port Huron, I was elected national chair of the Democratic Socialists of America, the merger of DSOC and the New American Movement, the principal successor organization of SDS. In an extraordinary development on the American Left, there was a unity rather than a split and some of us who would have found it difficult to talk civilly to one another in 1962 worked together in sorority and fraternity.

We had all learned from experience, but whether that is of any importance to the culture remains to be seen. Perhaps it was all a bittersweet drama on the irrelevant left-wing margin of the society. I obviously do not think that—and have wagered a good part of my life on my judgment. When the next turn to the left comes in American society—and I think it will occur somewhere between 1986 and 1992—the prospects will be much better than they were in 1960 when the New Left first began to emerge. For there is a movement, with its focus in the Democratic Socialists of America, that spans generations and the quarrels of the past in the most extraordinary way.

In any case, I hope the militants of the future may learn from my unlearning experience. I certainly have.

*Historical note*: Some of the events referred to in the two chapters that follow are now ancient history, so an explanation is in order with regard to some of my references. The Washington peace demonstration took place in 1961, demanding an end to nuclear testing; in a minor gesture of major significance, the young president sent coffee to the pickets. The remark about the "Berkeley Zengakuren" uses a fashionable tag of the times that linked the new American youth movement with the Japanese student organization whose demonstrations helped force President Eisenhower to cancel a trip to that country. The *barbudos*—the "bearded ones"—was a friendly way of talking about Castro's guerrillas during, and immediately after, the struggle for power in Cuba. The "sociology that sees the breaking of eggs to make an omelette as a guiding political analogy" is a reference to the pro-Soviet thesis that Stalin's violence and repression, unfortunate as they may have been, were necessary means (the breaking of eggs) to the happy end (the omelette) of socialism. Leo Huberman and Paul Sweezy were editors of an influential magazine, the *Monthly Review*, which was at that time critically supportive of the Soviets. Huberman died some time ago; Sweezy, whom I liked personally even when I disagreed with him, now more or less shares my analysis of Communism as a new form of class society, anti-socialist as well as anticapitalist. The allusion to a conservative with an "I Like Nike" picket sign has to do with the Nike ballistic missile. Finally, *Operation Abolition* was a film praising the House Committee on Un-American Activities that was widely shown, and debated, on campuses in the early sixties.

# 6
# The American Campus: 1962

*Dissent, 1962*

I am writing this from New Haven. Last night I debated a retired general on the House Un-American Activities Committee before about two hundred students. The meeting was sponsored by Challenge, an organization at Yale that brings controversial speakers to the campus. A contingent from the local Young Americans for Freedom showed up, though they were not in costume (sometimes they come to peace meetings in ROTC uniform; on their last outing everyone wore dark glasses). I would guess that the audience was at least two-thirds on my side and rather demonstratively so.

Ten years ago, when I first came here to speak, the meeting was held in a student's apartment off campus. Our mood was that of catechumens. This contrast in New Haven could be extended all over the country, for during the past decade the campus has opened up. There is a spirit of debate and concern working among the students.

I have been traveling the country throughout this period (for several years, I thought I should have been billed as the "oldest young socialist" alive; now, alas, students sometimes call me "sir"). In that time, I have been privy to an endless number of bull sessions about the nature of the "student movement." For that matter, one of the characteristics of the reawakening on campus is a sort of frenzy of introspection and self-consciousness, with groups spending almost as much time in front of a mirror as on the picket line.

This experience has convinced me that it is next to useless to propose some general theory of the campus. The generations succeed one another with a rapidity almost like that of the tsetse fly; the departure of a few key students can change the look of a college within the span of a summer vacation.

So let me set down a few impressions. The change on the campus began around 1956 or 1957, it was enormously accelerated by the sit-ins and the sympathy demonstrations they evoked, and it is still moving forward. Its mood has been more radical than liberal, oriented toward single "issues" rather than finished ideologies (but conscious politicals have often played a decisive organizational role). Its tone is moral, focusing on questions like peace, capital punishment, and human equality, ignoring economic conflict and social planning.

If the year 1960–61 was under the sign of the civil rights movement on campus, 1961–62 was dominated by the reaction to the Bomb.

Indeed, the most striking recent development has been the growth of the Student Peace Union. The Washington peace demonstrations were probably the most spontaneous expression of student feeling since the thirties. At Earlham College in Indiana not too long ago, students told me that some of those who went from other midwestern schools were under heavy administration pressure to stay home. The very fact that these schools, so long out of the student mainstream, were involved at all is a sign of how powerful is the emotion produced by the Bomb and the issue of testing.

Throughout the darkest days of McCarthy there were always the predictable colleges of the New York underground where a few sophisticates held the line. Now student politics is becoming more indigenous, less of a New York graft.

The SPU is particularly important in view of the vague, almost moody character of the peace sentiment. Its leadership contains a fair number of politically astute young people. Thus the Washington project had a clarity often lacking in student actions today. Yet it is precisely the political diffuseness of the rank and file that gives the organization a broader appeal than any student group of recent memory.

So it is that one finds students motivated by religious considerations, students from small schools, students who have never belonged to any group, working together. In Berkeley last November, I went down to the "Veterans' Day" demonstration. Several hundred pickets demonstrated silently as the legionnaires marched past (the dignitaries in open automobiles didn't know what to do when they saw us: some waved; some froze; and one beauty queen took an SPU button). The young people there were not the seasoned pickets of the "Berkeley Zengakuren," that informal group that had developed out of the Chessman walks, the House Committee demonstrations and civil rights projects. They were younger, less sophisticated, new to political life.

If peace has come to the fore during the last year, the question of Cuba has receded. This reflects in part a disillusionment brought about by the obvious growth of the Communist apparatus in that island. The improvised, irreverent mood of the barbudos having been replaced by the hard maneuvers of the aparatchiks, there is little basis for student sympathy. Yet the Cuba sentiment is still worth a comment or two.

To veterans of the radical movement, student attitudes on Cuba, or Russia, seem to have a familiar fuzziness. But it would be a mistake to think that one is confronting a finished ideology of support to totalitarian capital accumulation, a resurrection of that discredited sociology that sees the breaking of eggs to make an omelette as a guiding political analogy. These attitudes have a different basis and once again they are more mood than program.

Students today distrust adult leaders and organizations (and particularly the liberal establishment). They are radical, bent on working out their own ideas. The initial sympathy for Castro came more from Sartre's version of him as a revolutionary existentialist than from the apologetics of Huberman and Sweezy. And often, the break with the hypocrisy of American society generates a suspicion of anyone who comes down hard on Communist totalitarianism. In the first radical flush, these students fail to distinguish between the official anti-Communist slogans of the status quo and the critique of a democratic Left.

The point is, these attitudes must be faced and changed. But they cannot be done by regaling the newly radical students with the facts of the past. It cannot be done from a lecture platform, from a distance. Rather, the persuasion must come from someone who is actually involved in changing the status quo here, and from someone who has a sympathy for the genuine and good emotions that are just behind the bad theories. I do not want to give the impression that there is a wave of pro-Communism in the student movement. Not at all. I simply want to emphasize that there is a complex feeling here and that it cannot be dealt with through a recital of the old categories or by a magisterial act.

One of the main impulses for the present student surge came from the sit-ins in the winter of 1960. That event set off sympathy pickets, conferences, and Freedom Rides. Since then, the Southern Negro students have made tremendous advances; the Northern students have, in many cases, gone back to the books or to other causes.

It is very difficult to convey the flavor of the student movement in the South. When I went to the meeting of the Student Nonviolent Coordinating Committee in Atlanta in the fall of 1960, I was convinced that the initial force had been spent. It all seemed to be marked by a sort of amiable, parliamentary chaos, and there seemed to be no basis for the emergence of a concerted, organized drive. I was mistaken. In the ensuing year and a half the Southern students have produced a full-time, dedicated cadre, and all the old theories about "professional revolutionists" seem to have found a somewhat curious practical incarnation.

Yet the tremendous gains of the Southern students pose a problem. These youth share the distrust of adult leadership with their counterparts in the North. Experience has taught them that the older, established spokesmen are prone to reconciliation and compromise. As a result, there is a mood of the youth "vanguard" that has serious consequences (youth alone cannot transform society or even a region of it) but that also corresponds to the immediate reality (youth, in fact, *is* the vanguard in the South).

In any case, one now meets the full-time activist from the South. As one student at Howard told me, "Sitting in has become like going out and getting a pack of cigarettes." At times there are glimpses of a new status order based on how long one has been in jail. (I thank God for my one comfortable night as a guest of the New York City police. That is a bare minimum. Otherwise, one would be as déclassé as a virgin in a street gang.)

Perhaps the most hopeful sign in the South is the way in which the students have committed themselves to voter registration. That inevitably means the development of a broader movement, of bringing adults together with the youth. Still, the accomplishment of these students is already the greatest achievement of the youth movement in decades.

From reading the journals one might think that there is a wave of campus conservatism. As far as I can tell, that is simply not true.

I have been North, South, East, and West, and I have yet to find a chapter of Young Americans for Freedom that is playing a really vital role on campus. Here at Yale (the YAF national chairman is a student in New Haven), the group might have fifty duespayers and far fewer activists. Generally speaking, YAF is less of a force on the big campuses than the Young People's Socialist League—and no one has been writing about a socialist sweep among the young.

The young conservative publications are slickly edited and expensive. One gets the impression that some adults, probably the Goldwater people, have decided to build a sort of Stevenson movement on the Right. However, they are certainly not leaving the direction of it to the young. Events like the Madison Square Garden rally are created by professionals like Marvin Liebman, the defender of Tshombe and Chiang, and have all the spontaneity of the Komsomols marching in Red Square.

Sometimes I get the feeling that part of the conservative student reaction, limited as it is, involves an emotion quite similar to that of the democratic radicals. There are, of course, the prematurely old YAF-niks with vests and a measured arrogance. But there is also a kind of student who has a genuine hatred of the rottenness of the establishment. At Harvard, several YAF students helped raise money for the Southern students (they were, it seemed, opposed to the state in Mississippi as well as in Washington—and even though their own organization has smeared groups like CORE). At Chicago, the center of a conservative radical wing, at least one leader has joined SANE (how else get the state out of the military sector?), and their theoretical journal has attacked the House Un-American Activities Committee in the name of libertarian values.

In general, though, the young conservatives are the product of some good copywriters, not of the campus scene. There are student bodies with a fair amount of right-wing opinion—Nixon did fairly well in the polls in 1960—but most of the young fogies are too busy with pan-Hellenic affairs to worry about "I Like Nike" picket signs.

Yet there is one source of conservative politics that is important: the Catholic college. In the course of the past few months I have had a fair amount of encounters with Catholic college students (at Albertus Magnus, Manhattan, Notre Dame, Fairfield, and before a regional meeting of the National Federation of Catholic College Students). The impression that comes from this experience has been curiously contradictory.

On the one hand, the bulk of the Catholic students are much more conservative on civil liberties than the youth of the secular colleges. The normal reception to a debate over *Operation Abolition* at a big school has one-third of the audience in favor of the House Committee and at least two-thirds vociferously opposed (I might add that the Committee's film fantasy on San Francisco has done more to promote campus discussion of the issue, and to create sentiment for the abolition of the Committee, than anything in years). At the Catholic colleges I found the proportions reversed.

Yet the Catholic liberals and radicals I met were, as a group, much better than their non-Catholic counterparts. Precisely because they were living in a generally conservative milieu and come from a tradition historically hostile to the Left, their views seem to have more intellectual substance than those of their non-Catholic similars. They come to their conclusions, not as a matter of accepting dominant values as the New York liberals do, nor even by sharing in a widespread mood. They work through to their convictions and they must be prepared to defend them.

The campus has awakened in recent years and is continuing to do so. The revolt is not, as in the thirties, a product of sympathy with mass union struggles. It is quite often uninterested in the problems of the economy. There is, rather, a radical mood in the midst of a semi-affluent society, and the key terms are the Bomb, the racist, the executioner. As a result, there is a freshness and élan and more than a little ignorance born of innocence. Yet it would be a terrible mistake if the adult radical concentrated on what seems to be the classic repetition of old errors. The dominant emotion is good, it is a witness to the idealism and courage of the young. If the adult reaction is one of preaching, it will simply reinforce all of the hostilities to the establishment, and no one will listen.

What the adult radical must do is attempt to bridge the gap between the generations, to understand that the students need political advice, that they must become part of a larger, post-college community—and to understand that, with all their problems, they bring to us a gift of freshness, enthusiasm, and élan.

# 7
# The Mystical Militants

*New Republic, 1966*

The young radicals whose personal statements have appeared in the *New Republic* these past weeks are marvelously, and problematically, American. They are mystical militants, articulating the authentic miseries of the poor while maintaining some of the attitudes of the middle class. They are also one of the most significant, hopeful developments in recent American life. I do not emphasize their importance as an uncritical compliment. They have already been subjected to quite enough journalistic flattery, and some of the mass media would probably like to package them as they did the Beats. Moreover, I have differences with the young radicals and have on occasion been puzzled, exasperated, and even saddened by them. Yet the happy fact remains that the emergence of a personally committed generation seeking basic social change is momentous. They are a minority of their age group, to be sure, but a creative, activist minority who should place their stamp upon the times. Eventually, and it will probably try the anarchist spirit of some of them, they are going to lead adult movements and change this society. Whatever their shortcomings, the New Leftists hold out the hope for a renewal of American social criticism and action.

I do not intend to respond point by point to the *New Republic* series. Rather, what follows is an interpretive, discursive reaction to some of the themes the young radicals raise.

First, there is the Americanism of these rebels against American society.

When I became a radical in 1948 (the last year of the politics of the thirties), it was taken for granted (on the Left) that the Fourth of July was really a front for the four hundred families. In part, this was a heritage of European socialist theory, in part a legacy of the American experience of a Depression that had demystified so many clichés. One did not get angry that the powers that be lied and cheated and manipulated. That, after all, was their function in life, just as it was the task of the Left to create a society that would not need to corrupt its avowed values.

The young radicals of today, it seems to me, did not start with this inherited cynicism. They became teenagers during the American celebration of the Eisenhower years and were, for the most part, not really conscious until after both Korea and McCarthyism. They seemed to have believed what they were told about freedom, equality, justice, world peace, and the like. They became activists in order to affirm these traditional values with regard to some ethical cause: defending civil liberties against HUAC, picketing for the life of Caryl Chessman, demanding an end to nuclear testing, fighting for civil rights. The shock generated by the society's duplicity in this or that single issue then opened their eyes to larger, and even more systematic, injustices.

It is, I suspect, this unique fifties-sixties experience that gives the New Left its distinctive flavor: a sense of outrage, of having been betrayed by all the father figures, that derives from an original innocence. And it is also the source of the young radicals' insistence on sincerity and community. They begin, not with an image of the future that was received, in one way or another, from Europe and involves theory and history, but from a sense of the immediate contradiction between democratic posturing and the undemocratic reality. They descend from the Abolitionists and Wobblies, not from Marx.

This intense, even painful, consciousness of American hypocrisy has led the young radicals to people who do not, or cannot, play the national rhetorical game: the left-outs, the outcasts. And it has involved them in a contradiction between mysticism and militancy.

In the iconography of the thirties, the proletarian was a figure of incipient power and a Puritan sense of duty. The lumpen proletarian was despised because he did not belong to a conscious class, because he floated; and he was feared as a potential shock trooper of fascism. By the fifties, much of the old élan had left the labor movement and, with an overwhelming majority of the people satisfied with Eisenhower, there did not seem to be much of a political perspective for insurgency. At this point a cultural rebellion took place among young people. It was expressed among the Beats who contracted out of the system; it informed Norman Mailer's vision of the white man who aspired to the cool and the hip that white society provoked in the Negro.

As disestablishmentarians, the young radicals continue this tradition of the fifties. They identify precisely with the lumpen, the powerless, the maimed, the poor, the criminal, the junkie. And there is a mystical element in this commitment that has nothing to do with politics. By going into the slum, they are doing penance for the sins of affluence; by sharing the life of those who are so impoverished that they are uncorrupted, values are affirmed. It is honest and moral and antihypocritical to be on the margin of society *whether the community organization works or not.* Indeed, there is a fear of "success," a suspicion that it would mean the integration of the oppressed into the corruption of the oppressors.

But, on the other hand, the New Leftists are not fifties Beats (and, by the way, I do not use the term Beat pejoratively). They are angry militants who see the poor as a new force in America, perhaps even as a substitute for the proletariat that failed. So Stokely Carmichael, one of the best of the breed, insists that the

Mississippi and Alabama sharecroppers can choose for themselves. He understands that ultimately, to paraphrase an old labor song, no one can abolish poverty for you, you've got to abolish it yourself. And from this point of view, it does make quite a bit of difference whether the community organizing campaign works or not.

An analogy from the thirties might illuminate the political hope that is here asserted by the young radicals. In 1932 or 1933, many polite Americans believed that if you gave a worker a bathtub, he would put coal in it. And the skilled AFL members thought it preposterous that mass-production machine operators could form *their own* union. On paper, the right to organize was proclaimed by the Wagner Act. In fact, it took at least five tumultuous years of picketing, striking, and sitting in before the CIO turned the brave words into something of a reality. Similarly in 1964, America declared war on poverty; and most of the well-bred citizenry did not intend by that to have field hands and janitors speaking up for themselves; and the young radicals, who have this knack of taking America's promises seriously, sought a surge from below to give meaning to the phrasemaking on high. But, as I think the New Left realizes, this analogy is faulty in part. The mass-production workers were, just as radical theory had said, forced by the conditions of their existence (thousands of men assembled at one miserable place with common problems and interests) into a solidarity that became the basis of union organization. The poor, as Tom Hayden noted in his *New Republic* contribution, are not grouped into incipient communities. A slum street fragments and atomizes people; the two largest groups of the poor, the young and the old, have little to do with one another; and even if they could get together, the poor are still a minority of the society. Therefore it is going to take even more creativity to help the outcasts into their own than it did to build industrial unionism.

## What Hope for the Poor?

For a number of reasons the New Leftists shied away, until quite recently, from thinking through the problems posed by their own militancy. For one thing, they are indeed "American" in the empirical, activist, antitheoretical sense of the word. For another, they rejected the scholasticism of some of the traditional Left formulae (as well as the genuine profundity of the Left's intellectual heritage) and they were imbued with the spirit of the civil rights movement of the early sixties, where the willingness to go to jail was more important than political abstractions. This winter there have been signs that the young radicals are moving into a phase of discussion and debate (at a Christmas vacation meeting at the University of Illinois, the SDS militants discussed political strategy, ideology, Communism, the role of women in the movement, etc.). And this is necessary if the conflict of mysticism and militancy is to be resolved. For if the poor are seen as Dostoevskian peasants whose beauty is their suffering, then politics and the inevitable alliances with others is a contamination; but if they are to be a social force, then coalition is a necessity.

The New Leftists regard the welfare state, rather than the economic royalists, as the incarnation of the status quo. This is an almost inevitable result of trying to look at America with the eyes of the poor. It is very right—and it is a dangerous half-truth.

The welfare state developed in the thirties was created by, and for, the "middle third" of American society: the liberal middle class and the organized workers. The poor were, and still are, those who were left behind in the Depression because of bad geographical, occupational, or political luck: migrants, farm workers, full-time laborers at poverty jobs, racial and ethnic minorities that came into the economic mainstream at the time of the computer rather than of the assembly line. In addition, the poor include all those who have suffered from a *relative deterioration* in various social insurance and income maintenance programs (social security, unemployment compensation, etc.).

The visible enemies of the poor are not the captains of industry but the landlords, shopkeepers, and, often enough, the agents of the welfare state. For the welfare state is, of course, ill-financed and bureaucratic, and thus distorts the good intentions of many of the fine people who work for it and reinforces the vices of the bad. So for the poor the welfare state means a humiliating dependence and fear, and requires a constant, cunning battle against authority. The young radicals attempt to articulate these fierce resentments that they discovered in the slums, and the experience does not leave them in a mood for sociological nicety. The welfare state is, they say, a fraud. And the liberals, who actually boast of having created this monster in the name of humane values, are therefore the worst hypocrites.

In formulating this attitude, it is not simply that the New Leftists overlook some history, which youth always does, but that they ignore some *relevant* history. The welfare state did not come out of the thirties as a result of a liberal plot to manipulate the dispossessed. It was created over the violent resistance of most men of property and wealth, and its creation required a major upheaval on the part of the workers, from the bottom up. Business did not begin its conversion to welfare statism until the World War II discovery that a federal agency staffed by corporation executives was not exactly a class enemy of the rich; and its final conversion to "tax cut" Keynesianism waited upon the persuasiveness of Lyndon B. Johnson. There was, and is, a very real element of buying off the restless natives in business acceptance of welfarism.

The relevance of this history is that the current welfare-state consensus is not quite so homogeneous as President Johnson and some New Leftists sometimes think. For the apparent agreement conceals the latent conflict between the sophisticated conservatives on the one hand, and the liberal–labor–civil rights forces on the other. One can rightly accuse the liberal welfarists of having been too nostalgically proud of *their* upheaval to understand the terrible urgency, as seen from the bottom of society, for more change immediately. But it is something else again to *equate* all present supporters of the welfare state with one another.

## Acting Out a Morality Play

And here I think I come to my most serious criticism of the New Radicals: that they sometimes expect the poor to act out the moral values of the middle-class radical who has come to the slum.

I find, for instance, a genuine poignancy in Tom Hayden's realization that a coalition of the outcasts will not really be able to change the society and that radicalism can only give itself up to, and become part of, "the energy kept restless and active under the clamps of paralyzed imperial society. Radicalism then would go beyond the concepts of optimism and pessimism as guides to work, finding itself in working despite odds. Its realism and sanity would be grounded in nothing more than the ability to face whatever comes."

This attitude is a logical deduction from theory that all the welfare staters, from Henry Ford to Walter Reuther if you will, are the same kind of manipulative bureaucrats. For if everybody but the poor and outcast are "them," then "we" must inevitably lose, for by definition "we" are not strong enough to transform a fraud and scandal supported by 60 or 70 percent of the society.

The conscious and committed radical can find his solace in such a vision; most of the poor, I suspect, cannot. Indeed, one of the things that has made the poor so inarticulate, so unorganized, so hopeless, is precisely the conviction that they can't win. Are they now to be told stoically to treasure their misery, which, though permanent, is at least not corrupted by the hypocrisy of affluence? That will be cold comfort. And it will not move them to action, but rather reinforce their passivity.

The danger is that the poor will thus be assigned roles as abstractions in the morality plays of the disenchanted middle class. To fight this possibility, the New Leftists must come up with a strategy that offers real hope to the other America. And this means making a more sophisticated analysis of the coalition that supports the welfare state.

For the liberal wing of this consensus certainly did not start with the intention to build a manipulative bureaucracy, and it maintains values that *could* provide a basis for transforming the present structure. If the social-change movements of the previous generation must be shaken up by the poor, they must be shaken up in order to be made allies. To do this requires an intensification of the efforts to organize the slums and ghettos and backwoods as an independent political force. But if there is to be honest hope, that organization must be thought of as the catalyst of a new political majority in the United States, and not as a doomed last stand of noble savages.

There is reason to hope that these new directions will be taken. An incredibly American generation in our midst has become radical by taking the house platitudes seriously. Its hatred of hypocrisy and its identification with the outcasts are magnificent; its empiricism and its middle-class mysticism are sometimes troubling. Now that New Leftists are becoming more reflective, their anger and their activism should become even more effective, their radicalism that much deeper and more profound.

# PART 4

# 8
# Listening

In 1952, Middlebury College sent Dorothy Day of the Catholic Worker an invitation to speak at a major conference. Dorothy simply assumed that our movement had been asked to have a representative address the meeting, which was most certainly not the case, and sent me in her place. But when I got off the bus in Vermont, wearing the hand-me-down pants from the stock we had to give out to alcoholics on the Bowery—they ended about three inches above my shoes—the Middlebury people were nice enough to let me speak.

I have been doing that for the thirty-two years since I went to Middlebury. In the fifties and early sixties, it was hitchhiking and buses and trains, with occasional plane flights paid for by the Fund for the Republic where I worked as an intellectual handyman. Later on, it was mainly jets. But even then, there were often two or three hours on the road from the airport to a college campus or a union hall.

Those trips, which let me listen to people all over this enormous country, were as important to my learning experiences as the hours I spent poring over books. In my brief career as a writer trainee at *Life* magazine in 1950, I met a reporter in the Washington bureau who had actually predicted that Harry Truman would win the 1948 election. While the other journalists were interviewing one another about the coming landslide for Thomas Dewey, that man had actually talked to some of the people who were flocking to Truman's enthusiastic meetings. When he told the editors that Truman was going to win, they laughed at him—until the morning after the election.

In the 1950s there were two propositions that almost every serious thinker in the United States knew to be true: that mass society and culture were homogenizing the nation, that there were really no differences left in the country; and, a related point, that there were no Americans who were poor since everyone clearly shared in our glorious abundance. I knew from my eyes and ears that both of those notions were false—more precisely, they were dangerous half-truths—long before I turned to the official statistics to give the only proof that our credulous age will accept: impersonal numbers (which are often generated on the basis of prejudices but which appear to be "mathematical," "scientific").

As I encountered the two essays reprinted here as chapters 9 and 10, I discovered something else. I was doing research on my first book on poverty in the United States for a long time, only I didn't know it. In "Granville Hicks's Small Town" there is a passing reference to the "hill folks" living just off the beaten track in upstate New York. When I heard of that little enclave of poverty, I didn't generalize about it. It is not even central to the article. Yet it clearly entered into my intellectual unconscious; it was part of a knowledge I possessed without knowing it, a knowledge simply waiting for me to make the connections.

The article from *Commonweal*, which was my most important literary outlet throughout the fifties and to which I owe an enormous debt, is not simply a part of that same process. It is an ironic illustration of how the writer works. I wrote in that spring of 1960 about "The Other America" and meant by that phrase, not the poor America that outrages the conscience, but the good

America, the decent America, that survives even in the age of mass culture.

But at the very same time, there is material in that article—the description of the California migrants—that was to become part of my book *The Other America*, but in a totally different context. And yet, I am not surprised that there was such a 180-degree reversal of the meaning of that phrase. What I had heard, what I had seen, on the road was that the mythic America of the fifties with a single culture and no social classes or poor people did not really exist. In the *Commonweal* article, I stated that proposition in terms of what was positive in the culture and called it "the other America." In my book, I put the idea in terms of what was negative in the economy and social structure and used the same name. The meanings, strange as it may seem, were linked.

Finally, it was through these experiences on the road that I became a deeply patriotic man. It was then that I first formulated a concept that is with me to this day: If you are a radical, you must love your country, for you are asserting that, beneath all that is wrong and unjust, there still survives a human potential for good, for a new and different kind of society.

# 9
# Granville Hicks' Small Town

*Dissent, 1957*

The Capital District is an urban complex around Albany, New York. It includes Troy, a winter-beaten sort of city, with shops and factories, a city old enough to have a downtown section with much of the architectural charm of Louisburg Square in Boston. Twenty miles to the east, after Route 2 has risen through rolling hills to a height over 1,500 feet, there is Grafton.

Approaching the town, there is a Slow Down sign. And almost before you can obey the law, you are told to Resume Speed. In between there is, at best, a mile of houses. Around a little square on Route 2, there is the general store, and on the catercorner a one-room schoolhouse, and set back from the road a row of houses, among them the Baptist Church. At first glance, Grafton is one of the thousands of American towns where you Reduce Speed: a bend in the road, a clump of life, and not much more.

But Grafton is different. Or rather, perhaps, all the small towns are different from the image that develops in the urban imagination—whereas what really distinguishes Grafton is that it has its chronicler. Granville Hicks, one of America's most active intellectuals, a leader in the Communist literary movement of the thirties and currently a frequent writer in the *New Leader*, has lived here since 1932. He has not been an alien sociologist from some great university looking for the stuff of statistics. For twenty-five years he has been an active, partisan citizen, one of the few intellectuals to make good the threat to find roots.

So Grafton is not merely a small town. It is *Small Town*, the subject of a full-length book, written by Hicks in 1946. And it fairly cries out to be a symbol, to be made to stand for a way of life that involves some millions of Americans. That I can't do. For I only passed through. But the unscientific impression also has its use, and even a few hours in Grafton goes deep. My story is of a small town that surely has something to do with the Small Town.

The first thought, after passing through the center of town while still looking for it, is that Grafton could not possibly be the subject of a full book, that one can't stretch a clump of houses into a discussion of several hundred pages. That impression lasts just as long as you don't talk to anyone. But talk—conversation here seems to flow in torrents—and the life that fascinated Hicks fairly leaps out and engulfs the listener. It is not simply that Grafton is some fifty-six square miles in area, that the town is physically more than the little square on Route 2 and the white town hall; it is rather that the community fairly seethes with relationships beneath its clapboard calm.

For Hicks that fact was the center of *Small Town*. His Grafton was not an idyllic place, a retreat for a modern Thoreau. He recorded the narrowness and the bigotry. But he also found a crucial value. Here, Hicks argued, personal relations are of the very essence of existence. Unlike the mass society of the great outer world, the small town does not know its politics and its news as huge impersonal things that happen in the distance. They are part of a daily rhythm. Here, a major decision can begin over a cup of coffee, a basic change can emerge out of a chance meeting at the post office.

Seventeen years later, Grafton certainly communicates the quality that Hicks found; but that quality also seems a little more complicated than his book might lead one to suspect. In a day or so of just talking, one finds quite a bit of neighborliness, of close relations—and also a neighborly hatred, an inbred hostility, the familiarity of contempt.

For all the intimacy of Grafton's life, there still remains the difference between the Native and the Outsider. One man, the former Republican boss of the town, a resident since 1911 and a summer visitor since 1898, confessed that he was still an Outsider. Another, a woman who has been operating the general store for over thirty years, explained carefully that she was not a native. Hicks, with a mere twenty-five years of continuous residence, is of course an Outsider. And the Summer People who cluster around the nearby lakes, they hardly count at all.

Indeed, the way some of the oldsters talk, it is the struggle between the Natives and the Outsiders that has kept Grafton from growing. The town is, as you will learn in a matter of minutes, "the second most healthful in the United States." It has a record of tuberculosis cures, and a long time ago there was a big hotel. But the Scriven family, which owned the hotel, a factory, and much of the property in Grafton, didn't like Outsiders. The former Republican boss had to sneak into property owning back in 1911, and the Scrivens thwarted him when he interested some outside capital in restoring the hotel. Now the factory is long since gone, the hotel has been torn down, and Grafton is without any real industry. Though more and more threatened each year by the Outside, the Natives still maintain their sense of identity.

But the struggle between the Natives and the Outsiders is only one curious aspect of the divisiveness of being neighborly. More important is the political life. And here one has to hark back to the radical sect for a metaphor. The factionalism of Grafton goes far beyond that of the small political group—for here factionalism is neighborly; it does not have the impersonal cover of the city. The town itself is organized from top to bottom. The Republican Party, the traditional focus of loyalty, and the Democrats are the merest beginning of the complicated structure. Factions are defined and redefined around a whole series of immediate questions: whether or not to build a station for the volunteer fire department; how to handle the school problem; what kind of one-hundred-fiftieth anniversary celebration to hold.

I arrived near the end of a bitter struggle. Should Grafton send its children to school in Berlin, to the east, or in Brunswick, to the west? Every person I met had an opinion, a strongly held, thoroughly factional opinion. The worst motives were consistently imputed to the opposition. Within a matter of hours I was told by the pro-Brunswick faction that Granville Hicks supports Berlin because of a marriage tie to the superintendent there. Within a day I was informed that the Catholics favored Brunswick because it would facilitate their getting free bus transportation to the parochial school. There had been several meetings ("They," the New York State education people, were in league with the Berlin faction, and ordered meetings until "they" won, I was told), and there was violent feeling, deep and thoroughgoing hostility.

Or take the question of the sesquicentennial. It will be held this Fourth of July under the aegis of the Veterans of Foreign Wars. There will be thanks from Troy, and much talk, and everyone will know that the anti-Hicks faction, opposed to the Community League, has won a victory. Even celebrating a Hundred and Fifty Years is a divisive problem in Grafton. And the same goes for the new community center. Depending on whom you listen to, you can learn that the new center is either a forty-thousand-dollar pipedream of the impractical reactionaries, or an imminent reality.

All of this is, admittedly, the merest impression—but that is what makes it so singular, so striking. A stranger can enter Grafton and, so intense are the factional arguments, he can learn something about the intricacies of local politics in a matter of hours. Anyone is ready to plunge into the most indiscreet conversation with someone who happens along Route 2. But this situation raises some serious questions about the values put forward by Hicks in *Small Town*.

The City is, to be sure, huge and impersonal, and that is a loss; but it is also private. The Town, if Grafton is in any way typical, is local and personal; but then it is not at all private. The factional disputes in Grafton, as they are reflected in the talk of its people, are so intense as to politicalize social life. True enough, one deals with problems over a chance cup of coffee—but with a co-factionist. Whom one invites over to the house is, evidently, a function of the School Question or the Fourth of July Question. And when this situation is placed in the context of the struggle between the Natives and the Outsiders, it raises some serious thoughts about the value of "neighborliness."

A young woman of Grafton summed up the negative aspects of this intensely personal community life: "Sure, people just stop by for coffee. But they never tell you when they're coming. They just walk in. And sometimes I close the door when I see someone coming down the road; I lock it, because I've got my work to do." In other words, a day in the Town places new value on the impersonal life of the megapolis.

But the intense politicalization of life is not the only surprising fact about Grafton. Along Route 2 you feel the presence of calm and order, but the strange and unorthodox are there just beneath the surface. In this small town, for instance, you can encounter the eighteenth, nineteenth, and twentieth centuries, all side by side.

The eighteenth century is represented by the hill folk. Their hovels are there to see on the back roads, and their life seems to resemble that of a Kentucky mountaineer. There is very little work for the men, and it is possible to live a little off Welfare. According to the "better" Natives, promiscuity, intermarriage of cousins, and drinking are rife. The Town believes that these are shiftless people who only want to work a day or two, until they can get enough money for some food and wine. Most of the people I spoke to felt that the hill folk made up half of Grafton's population, but their figure is probably high. Hicks himself would cut it by half at least.

Still, it is hard to realize that some twenty-five miles from the capital of one of the richest states in the richest nation in the world, there is a social stratum whose way of life dates back to the Revolutionary War. The hill people vote in the major elections, but they are apparently not a real part of the life of the town. And even the old Republican boss is willing to admit that it was a pretty easy matter to vote them, especially after they began to depend on Welfare. They are, it would seem, a reliable part of Grafton's Republican majority.

But then the nicer people are not so simply that. The shadowy existence of the Ku Klux Klan still persists among them. The oldsters can remember their antics in the twenties when they burned crosses: one for the hired hand on a Catholic's place; two for the Jewish family that had moved in down at the general store. In those days, the Klan numbered men who were to become the leaders of the community. One of them was later a Republican Committeeman (along with the Catholic in front of whose house crosses were burned), another was the postmaster. And the Methodist Church, or rather the Methodist minister, was tied in too. The story has it that the minister received three dollars for every Klansman he recruited.

Today, almost everyone seems to regard the old Klan activity as having been prankish and not too serious. Yet one or two people, when asked about the Klan, looked at me significantly and said, "It's still here." In all probability what they meant was not the Klan as a group but the anti-Semitism and racism persist, as part of the narrowness of the town itself. A Negro family that moved in not too long ago didn't have any "trouble," but there were remarks. Yet Hicks is probably right when he says that organized bigotry is not a force anymore.

If the hill folk are an eighteenth-century survival, and the Klan a legacy of the nineteenth, even a day or so in Grafton is enough to surprise one with the twentieth century. Down at the general store, the coasters advertise screwdrivers with Smirnoff vodka—mass society has come to the Small Town. More interesting is Grafton's apparent tolerance for easy living. The hill folk are not alone in their promiscuity. There was a rather large party not too long ago, and one couple realized (more with amusement than shock, to hear them tell it) that they were the only legally married couple present.

Native and Outsider, factions on the School Question, hill folk, the Klan, an avant-gardish attitude on sex: these form an amazingly complex pattern just below the surface of Grafton's curtained calm. That it is so easy to find these things in this Small Town shatters many a stereotype. Is Faulkner's Frenchmen's Bend, one wonders, really such a Gothic and Southern phenomenon? Or have all the judgments been made by city folk living some four hours from Grafton in New York?

What of Grafton's future? Does it have one? Should it? Grafton was never able to find the resources within itself for growth. It fell away from its prosperity of the nineteenth century, when there was a factory and a hotel. Now no one employs more than six or eight workers. The Natives were victorious in the struggle against the Outsiders. One old-timer remembers that the Scrivens fought against a new hotel on the grounds that it would have a liquor license—but then tanked up the hill folk in a shed on every election day. The hotel never came, and the hill folk remained (though now, some say, they are given candy as well as wine).

At the end of World War II, Hicks was hopeful that Grafton could find the power to maintain itself within itself. But now, ten years or so later, that optimism seems to have been the product of an abnormal situation. During the war, Grafton discovered quite a bit of unity, and the civil-defense group (Hicks' faction) was able to accomplish a great many things. But peace in the world brought the factional budget struggle back to Grafton. There have been gains—the fire department has its building, the library testifies to the labors of the Community League—but any real forward movement has failed to develop. And typically, the sesquicentennial is celebrating One Hundred and Fifty Years of existence in an atmosphere of sharp hostility.

And there you have one of the strangest impressions of a day or so in Grafton: almost everyone is pessimistic. "Grafton change?" is a wry question, at least for those to whom I spoke. There is a perverse sort of pride in the intense, fruitless politicking, in the factionalism and disharmony. There is a great readiness to believe a good half of the town "shiftless." (Paradoxically,

Grafton is noted in nearby towns for its community spirit. What *their* politics are like, if the judgment is true, is hard to imagine.) There has been, for example, no attempt to bring an industry to Grafton. Most of the people I spoke to seemed surprised at the idea, but when confronted with it were sure it would never work.

Yet the anomaly is that Grafton is holding its own, and will probably grow. Salvation is not from within. It comes, rather, from the mass society of the Outside, the archenemy of the Small Town. Today, most of the workers in Grafton have jobs in Albany or Troy, and the town is becoming a metropolitan bedroom. It is not suburbia, or exurbia, for those terms imply the presence of the middle class. The commuters in Grafton are, for the most part, workers. They were born here. The town can't provide them with a living. But they can stay, perhaps even keep a cow and a few chickens, and live off the nearby industry.

Only a few miles closer to Troy, the town of Eagle Mills more closely approaches the image of the suburb. Its houses are modern, expensive; its lawns, trim. In time, it is possible that the spread of the suburbs will engulf Grafton itself and completely change its character. But as of today, a curious mixture helps to maintain the small-townishness of Grafton. The economy is based upon the city, but the social relations are those of the country. One worker here spends his forty hours in the shop and then raises chickens and keeps a cow in his spare time. And the Summer People have not made a change, for they cluster around the lake and don't really enter into the life of the town.

Some miles to the east lies Berlin. It is able to exist because of one factory. If that were to shut down, the town would disintegrate, for it has no Troy or Albany to save it. Perhaps, then, industrial decentralization is the only way out; perhaps the towns, except for those that are the centers of a prosperous agricultural life, must disappear, like Grafton, unless they become suburbs of cities.

So Grafton has a new lease on life. But is that good?

In *Small Town* Hicks is quite objective. He does not idealize and put forth the "pastoral" image of a city man dreaming of the countryside. All of the factionalism and the Insiding and the Outsiding are scrupulously recorded. As a result Hicks' case for the small town depends upon one major value: that of neighborliness, of a possibility of personal relations denied to the metropolis. The citizen acts over a cup of coffee, he decides how to vote on the basis of a close knowledge of the candidate who lives down the road and whom he questioned at the general store the week before. But the impressionistic, unscientific feeling that Grafton excites in the rankest Outsider is one that puts Hicks' value in a delicate balance.

For the Grafton that develops out of its own history, on its own power, is provincial, filled with rumors, quarrels, and factions. It accepts the wretched existence of the hill folk with a shrug. And if these attitudes are the dominant values of the town as town, if these are what it develops when left to itself, then perhaps Grafton is an anachronism that can only charm the city man speeding through on his way to Boston, or the Summer Person driving to the lake. And then what good is there in maintaining the character of the place? A case could certainly be made for the destruction of the small-town qualities by the influence of the city, even while the space and the trees and the fine mountain air remain.

I can't pretend to answer my own question. A day or so in Grafton isn't the basis for balancing the neighborly relations and the neighborly hatred and coming up with a judgment. But it is enough to shatter the image of the Small Town, or at least of this small town. Between Slow to Thirty-Five Miles an Hour and Resume Speed Please, there is obviously a complicated, intricate society. By itself, Grafton is dying. As an appendage of mass society, it has a very real hope. That is the obvious paradox just behind the calm, there for the finding of any stranger coming down Route 2.

But then, Grafton is infectious. That also should be mentioned. I myself favor amalgamation of the school district with Brunswick. It sure was a mistake to go in with Berlin.

# 10
# The Other America: Beyond the Neon Signs and the Coke Bottles, Another America Still Survives—as of Now

*Commonweal, 1960*

At twenty, most of us have painfully learned that stereotypes are a way of lying. By thirty, we discover the other side of the coin: that the stereotype is a way of saying a half-truth of expressing the sprawl of reality, the contradictions of experience. To be sure, people and things are frozen, plucked out of time and history in the process, but there is always a wisdom at the center of the distortion.

When it comes to stereotypes of America, there is even more complexity, for all of them are partially true, even though many of them express polar opposites. Dickens's vision of revolutionists devoted to freedom and slavery is accurate; Blake's prophetic image of a liberating nation is too. More recently, the fashionable stereotype has been almost completely negative. "America" stands for gadgetry, rootlessness, in the tyranny of mass-produced kitsch. "Americanization" is the terrible fate that is befalling Europe as it produces an efficient industrial civilization. The symbol of Coca-Cola shall stand over all.

Another America is suggested by Robert Frank in his brilliant collection of photographs, *The Americans*. He has seen a nation of almost tragic spaciousness in which people are glimpsed at a moment of repose: looking out of windows, listening to music, sometimes thoughtful but always waiting, caught in a welter of experience (or, to make the metaphor photographic: riding an endless highway). His camera has defined an older stereotype, one that precedes the theories of mass culture and says the exact opposite of the grim thesis that posits "Americanization" as mechanized mindlessness.

In *The Americans*, one finds two main vantage points: the region and the working people. It is important to remember (or to be reminded) that families need not look as serenely vulgar as they do in a Norman Rockwell illustration, that there are still faces clearly marked by their experience, areas that defy any attempt to erect a huge stereotype. And people still work. The middle-class citizen, so distant from the plant and perhaps hypnotized by automation, can almost come to believe that the commodities of this society are produced invisibly and without human intervention. Frank's camera reminds one that this is not so. For there is an America that has perhaps been out of sight in the fifties. A feeling of helplessness, of frustration in a decade of conservativism and reaction, directed the eyes toward the neon sign and the infinite rows of Coke bottles. But another America remained. It is, to be sure, under the attack of mass culture and it may be destroyed by the incredible incompetence of political leaders. As of now, it survives.

The most obvious, even defining, fact about the other America is its variety, the resourcefulness of its geography. One million signboards can be erected on the highways; hundreds of thousands of vistas can be blocked out of view; but a sweeping magnificence persists.

In Seattle, Washington, the people live in the presence of Mount Rainier. The Indians, it is said, once thought that this solemn peak was God. Their mistake is understandable. Driving in the city, one never knows when the turning of a corner will reveal the aspect of beauty. On a clear day, each hour, each period, is given a special definition by the mountain. And this geography enters into a culture. It is, of course, intermingled with the history of the region: logging, the IWW, the Seattle General Strike of 1919 (in this American city, they spoke of "Soviets" at that time), the weatherbeaten and brawling tradition of a port.

Thus, the coffee cups in many restaurants in Washington are bigger than they are in the East. Their shape developed out of an outdoor, working world and they are part of the texture of life in the area. At the trucker's stop in the Cascade mountains where breakfast is ten strips of bacon, four eggs, and a pile of home fries, these coffee cups are one of the forms defining a history and a way of living. They are related to the towering fact of the mountain.

Then there is a place like Stockton, California. This is the center of lush, profitable farmland that for years has been dominated by huge growers. In the city, one suddenly confronts an unusual sight in contemporary America: a working class defined by its clothes. Someone remarked not too long ago that when the big factories in Detroit put up lockers for the workers, the existence of social classes became harder to see on the city streets. The men no longer went to the shop in their work clothes. Rather, they wore clean shirts and slacks and changed at the plant. This hasn't happened yet in Stockton.

As you drive through the city, the sunburned faces of the lounging men along skid row (where the shape-up for the farm workers takes place early in the morning) are unmistakable. Every field hand wears a hat; the Levis ride low on the hips. The impression is utterly unlike that of a midwestern farm town, for it is dominated by day laborers and not by farmers. And yet, even here, there is a participation in the romance of the métier, the miserable, low-paid, starvation métier: "Picking gets in the blood," a serious face will say. "I've been trying to quit for twelve years, but I'm still here."

And there is an industrial geography, too. Outside of Pittsburgh, there are coal and steel towns with their slag heaps, their company houses, the perpetual shadow of the machine. Yet when the plant gives out (as the mines in West Virginia have), the people cling to their tiny, dirty world. There are friendships, churches, traditions, a fierce way of life within the great world. Here, as in Seattle or Stockton, the region has made a culture. Even here.

One could go on and on, but the point is obvious. The other America is still a nation of regions, of scenic surprise (as the plane lifts over the mountains coming down from Denver, the city of Albuquerque and the desert on which it lies seem almost a Shangri-la). The other America is culturally heterogeneous: its coffee cups are different, so are its politics. Its vitality may well be a matter of cultural lag, of a historic impetus acquired in experiences which predate the era of mass culture. But the other America is real.

And yet there is a point of homogeneity. At its worst, it is a source of arrogant ignorance and bigotry; at its best, it is the persistence of something precious and fine. The other America is not simply a political democracy. It is a democratic culture as well.

Not too long ago, Dwight Macdonald wrote of America in *Dissent*: "*Here*: everybody 'equal' in the sense that nobody respects anybody else unless he has to, by *force majeure*; the national motto should be not 'E Pluribus Unum,' not 'In God We Trust,' but: 'I got mine and screw you, Jack!' or better, 'Brother'—('friend' and 'brother' being used to express extreme hostility and contempt)." Macdonald is quite right, quite fashionable, and quite wrong. Our democratic culture has led to anti-intellectualism, to an incredible egotism, and it lacks a European respect for tradition. All this is true, but this stereotype must have its counterstereotype: the positive, driving force of the egalitarian ethos in the United States.

Take waiters. At the point of table service, a culture expresses its values profoundly. The English waiter "thanks" the patron at every moment in the process. There is a litany of servility. The German customer will call the lowliest busboy "Mr. Headwaiter," but accompanies this by an imperiousness of the voice and, often enough, table pounding. The tone contradicts the form. And in America, waiters are often gallingly independent, slow, poised, and familiar; yet they are not overwhelmed by being waiters, they are as "good" as you are.

On another level, there are thousands of union locals in the other America where workers participate in a living democracy. This is the "other" labor movement (other than the one-sided, and often malicious, image of the union produced in congressional hearings). In it, local presidents are regularly defeated for office, the rank and file produces its own leaders, and a sense of solidarity is real and alive. A famous European socialist once said to a friend of mine, "Your workers walk differently. They seem so confident."

In such an atmosphere, "Brother" is not a word of contempt but a token of a certain community. At times, it is even embarrassing to hear. Not long ago, a rank-and-file unionist in Lansing, Michigan, who had been on the losing side in an election, was shocked at the idea that this should lead him to distrust the union itself. His victorious opponent, he explained to me, was a union brother and despite their differences they were part of a common cause. The moment was, to be sure, sentimental (and consequently not without its irony for the observer), but it happens in the other America.

All of this, of course, is not the product of some mysterious, genetic process whereby Americans were born different—or better. It comes out of our history. The frontier, the immigrant waves, the tradition of opportunity, the struggle of Populist farmers and CIO workers—these are the creative moments of a democratic culture. They have not marked America with those ruins and layers of civilization that make the European tradition so visual. True enough, the other America is constantly tearing down buildings and putting up taller ones. But the continuity does exist in the manners, attitudes, and speech of the people, and this is another sense of the word America.

Perhaps what confuses so many people about the other America is that it is a maze of contradictions. The sense of solidarity can also become xenophobia; the egalitarianism can turn savagely on the representative of high culture. Or, by a peculiar paradox, the American sense of classlessness often becomes a support for the reality of social classes. It conceals antagonisms, it blunts the drive for social justice; the belief that we are "all" middle class is part of a mechanism of domination in which the people are submissive.

Yet these contradictions are but another expression of the expansiveness, the individuality of the other America. And, taking the positive stereotype rather than the negative, this American egalitarianism is a more decent and human way of people meeting people than exists in societies that have impressive monuments to tradition. Indeed, this is probably *the* American monument.

It is important to understand the other America. For if the pessimistic theorists are right, we live in a nation that has been artificially homogenized, and where opinion is infinitely manipulable. That is the pejorative sense of America, and it expresses its own truth. But the inescapable conclusion of such a vision is, at best, the attitude of the benevolent bureaucrat (if only the "good" people could get hold of the means of brainwashing, and manipulate the masses for a "good" cause). On the other hand, there is hope if one can see the other America. Take the Negroes in the Southern sit-ins for an example.

For many years, a great many Negroes in the South conformed to part of the racist stereotype. They were passive, they accepted their own degradation. This was accomplished through a political mechanism of terror, an economic system of harsh exploitation, a social reality of exclusion from the culture of the white man. But even then, the other Negro was developing. First of all, there was the enormous creativity that went into the Negro Church. (To some, this seemed only quaint; in retrospect, it must be recognized that this was a momentous fact.) Then there came the slow contact with a broader world—with the radio, movies, television, the unions, and modern industry. Behind the stereotype, a new tradition was in the making. It burst out in the Montgomery bus boycott; it subsided; it has flared up, all the stronger, in sit-ins.

And what if this would happen, not only among the Negroes,

but throughout the other America as well? The future, if it is to contain hope, is being prepared in the midst of the other America. Here, in that part of the nation that is not dominated by gadgets and mass media, is the source of our creativity. This sentiment, in its gutted form, is the commonplace piety of all the candidates and Fourth of July orators who have ever been. But it may be the expression of a reality, too; the reality of the other America.

# PART 5

# 11
# The War

In the second half of the sixties, I took sides against some of my friends as well as against my enemies. The reason was the debate within the Left over how to oppose the unconscionable American involvement in Vietnam.

The sixties were, for people like me, split in two. From the sit-ins in February 1960 to the Selma-Montgomery march in the spring of 1965, there was a spirit of "good feeling" abroad in the land. Under the inspired leadership of Dr. Martin Luther King, Jr., there was a vast and ecumenical coalition. When we moved down the streets of the black slums in Montgomery on the final day of the Selma to Montgomery march—people on their rickety porches were weeping openly as they watched black and white, trade unionists and priests and ministers and nuns, students and field hands file past—we did not know that it was the last day of the civil rights movement that had surged into life at the time of the Supreme Court decision against segregated education in 1954 and the Montgomery bus boycott of 1955.

We did not know that there were those in that vast assemblage of American conscience who were soon to turn upon one another in the name of hostile moralities. Above all, we did not know that, even as we moved through the streets of a downtown Montgomery that was completely deserted except for the sullen men of the federalized National Guard who had been forced to protect us, President Lyndon Johnson was preparing the escalation of the war in Vietnam and the end of the social hopes of the first five years of the decade.

Indeed, shortly after the Montgomery demonstration, I cried as I watched Johnson tell a television audience, "And we *shall* overcome!" The president of the United States had taken up the words of our civil rights anthem and committed himself to voting rights for the blacks of America. Within less than a month he began the escalation of the American intervention in Vietnam. Everything changed.

In those first five years of the sixties we had sometimes talked of ourselves as the members of a "beloved community"; in the next five years, we were often nasty, querulous. The five chapters that follow date from those unhappy times—which were, nevertheless, years of struggle and genuine moral passion.

But then, I must put these writings in a personal, as well as an historical, context. In the spring of 1965 I suffered a nervous breakdown, which I have described at length in *Fragments of the Century*. For the first year or so it was emotionally very difficult for me to give a speech, to march in a demonstration, or, sometimes, simply to walk down a crowded, noisy street. Over the next several years I gradually fought my way out of that predicament and eventually won the battle with myself.

As I made clear in *Fragments*, I do not think that the polemics of the second half of the sixties caused my problems—the breakdown actually occurred at the end of those happy five years—but they certainly did not help it. The reader should understand, then, that the disputes recorded here carried an emotional charge in my own life that was far from ordinary. And I was, more often than not, arguing with friends.

Except for minor editing changes, chapters 12 through 16 are printed as I originally wrote and published them; in a few cases repetitious material has been excluded. In the case of chapters 12 and 13, which appeared in the *Village Voice* in the fall of 1965, I have substituted initials for the names of those who criticized me because I have no idea whether those individuals still agree with the position they took then. Only Harry Ring remains fully identified and that is because he is still a very public Trotskyist and clearly has not broken with his past.

In those two chapters, there are three basic themes, all aspects of the question of how the antiwar movement should relate to Communism, both as an ideology and an existing system of power. That issue is presented in terms of the tactics of the movement, in analyses of the nature of Communism in general, and as a discussion of the specific characteristics of the Vietnamese Communist movement. The people with whom I argue are, for the most part, my friends on the Left. Had they been disciplined Communists my fight would have been emotionally much easier, for it would have concerned long-standing, fundamental disagreements. But they were people who came out of the same milieu as I and, in some cases, had marched side by side with me in the nascent peace movement of the late fifties.

In one case, I think I was too hard on an opponent. I called William F. Buckley, Jr., "the urbane front man for the most primitive and vicious emotions in the land." This is excessive. Buckley was, and is, a conservative with whom I have the most basic disagreements and in our fifteen or so debates he has proven himself to be a rhetorical street fighter, even if a polysyllabic street fighter. Offstage I find him a more liberal, tolerant, and relaxed person than some with whom I agree. My epithets of 1965 polemicized this complex reality.

The next chapter, "Answering McReynolds," appeared in 1967, when a mass antiwar movement had come into existence and a much smaller group of resisters had committed themselves to nonviolent civil disobedience. Here, too, I was torn. The first radical organization I had ever joined, the Catholic Worker, was committed to nonviolent pacifism and, as I recount in the article, I myself had followed that course during the Korean War. In those years, I had become a friend and comrade of David McReynolds and in this piece I was responding, with evident emotional ambivalence but a clear intellectual commitment, to a "letter" he had written to "his generation" in the *Village Voice*.

As I look back on that exchange, I think I was right on the issues of principle and wrong on some of the conclusions I drew. I had been bothered by what I regarded as the political sloppiness and excessive self-righteousness of some of the antiwar leaders. I have not changed my mind about this one bit. But, in the case of some of the demonstrations, I didn't go because I opposed what I knew I would hear. On other occasions, I marched as a rank and filer because I was so deeply opposed to the war, but I refused to take the podium. I was wrong. When there is a mass movement with a basically just demand, it will almost always include the preachers of nonsense as well as the advocates of truth, and one should not quibble about the small print—or even the large print—of the speeches because they will be forgotten the moment they are uttered. The movement is the message. So one goes, one stakes out a position clearly and ignores the stupidities.

Somewhat similarly, my opposition to nonviolent putschism, to the notion that a moralistic elite can, through civil disobedience, educate the unanointed majority, stands. But I failed to see how the very intensity, the commitment, the personal decency, of most of the resisters spoke more eloquently to the society than some of their own words.

In the last two chapters in this part, both published in 1968, I had to take sides against friends on my right as well as my left. In the political campaign of that year, the liberal-labor movement had split. Most—but by no means all—of the trade unionists and some of the middle-class liberals backed Lyndon Johnson in the name of collective security against Communism. Most—but by no means all—of the middle-class liberals and some of the trade unionists became the core of a mass antiwar movement that now turned from protest in the streets to politics at the ballot box. Both sides had been together when we marched into Montgomery a mere three years earlier.

So now I had to argue, in what I thought were counterproductive ways, with friends who were for the war and with friends who were against the war. I backed Eugene McCarthy, switched to Robert Kennedy when he announced, returned to McCarthy when Kennedy was murdered, and, as the last chapter in this part shows, publicly championed a lesser-evil vote for Humphrey against Nixon.

Most of the bitterness of those years has faded away—but not all. And now I am deeply involved in the nuclear freeze movement and in the struggle against American intervention in Central America. Some of the old differences arise in new forms but, thus far, the Left has been a more tolerant and charitable place than it was in 1965–70. "We who wanted kindness itself could not ourselves be kind," Bertolt Brecht wrote in a haunting—and very Stalinist—poem. I understand that feeling and I am even moved by it. But as politics, it is wrong. The Left is made up of sinners, not saints, but if it does not at least try to prefigure the beloved community in its own life it will be rightly charged with hypocrisy. We didn't do very well at that in the second half of the sixties, when we sometimes took sides against one another with greater vehemence than we turned upon our adversaries.

## 12

# Does the Peace Movement Need the Communists?

*The Village Voice, 1965*

The issue of Communism in the peace movement has been raised on all sides during recent weeks.

On the one hand, the McCarthyite Right has attempted to smear any and all criticism of the Johnson administration's tragic war in Vietnam as Communist "inspired." On the other hand, many in the new rebel generation of the Left have come out for a policy of the "nonexclusion" of Communists in its demonstrations and activities. Indeed, there are some who even regard discussion of the problem as red-baiting. However, since the way in which this question is handled will profoundly affect the fortunes of the American movement for peace in Vietnam, debate cannot be suppressed in the name of such an emotional oversimplification.

I do not write, let it be emphasized, out of a desire to raise the old Left debates of the 1930s, '40s, or '50s—though I happen to believe that those disputes were often relevant attempts to understand the historic social forces of our time. I write because the issue of Communism and peace is being posed here and now, Left, Right, and Center.

First of all, the American Right is behaving predictably. It is not only smearing all of the demonstrators as Communists or as dupes, but it is using the profession of loyalty and support for the Johnson policy in Vietnam as a rallying point for reaction. So it was that the October 29 parade on Fifth Avenue was for the war in Vietnam and for William F. Buckley, Jr., the urbane front man for the most primitive and vicious emotions in the land.

The Right utilizes what might be called the Jehoover method in this undertaking (the name suggests both the director of the Federal Bureau of Investigation and the hero of the Old Testament, and there are some Americans who do not distinguish between the two). The essence of Jehooverism can be summarized in a series of propositions: if a political movement is for a given policy; if Communists are for that policy; if Communists are alleged to be in, or actually are in, the movement; then the Communists must sooner or later—and any Jehooverist worth his salt knows that the moment will come sooner—take control.

The Jehooverist film fantasy *Operation Abolition* immortalized this thesis with regard to the anti-HUAC demonstrations in San Francisco a few years ago. More recently, the international Jehooverists noted the presence of fifty or so Communists in a democratic revolution in the Dominican Republic, and the marines were sent in.

Fresh from this Caribbean success, the Jehooverists have now turned their attention to the student peace movement. There are, they have informed the nation, Communists in these antiwar demonstrations. Since the Communists have practically been jumping up and down in front of the TV cameras like a Johnny Carson audience, waving Vietcong flags and signing their names on public documents, this has not come as a shock to informed people. Then, following the analytical precepts of Jehooverism, the presence of these Communists is said to guarantee that they will take over the movement (the Jehooverists agree with the old-line Stalinists and the Maoists about the inevitability of Communism and the mystical effectiveness of the vanguard party).

In fact, of course, the majority of the protesters are not Communists or Communist-led. The various Communist organizations have, in general, been tailing after a youthful mood of iconoclasm and rebellion rather than creating it. This situation could change, but only if the Jehooverist-Maoist united front succeeds in convincing the young that pro-Communism is the only basis for opposition to the war in Vietnam.

So much for the Right. Now, more seriously, let me turn to those on the Left—and I am speaking of people who are, for the most part, not Communists or pro-Communist—who have defined the terms of the discussion.

To begin with, it should be clear to everyone that we are not talking about a thirties or forties situation, e.g., where a disciplined Communist minority forced the Progressive Party Convention in 1948 to take an anti-Titoist stand on the Macedonian question (it happened). The Communists today are fewer in numbers and organizational resources than in the bad old days. Moreover, a fair number of Communists and pro-Communists today are refreshingly open and unabashed in their beliefs and identify themselves proudly, which is not exactly a way to infiltrate. Finally, the breakup of the Communist monolith has resulted in the emergence of personality types that were unimaginable in the heyday of J. Stalin, i.e., the Communist hipster. (I once heard Norman Mailer convince William F. Buckley, Jr., that Castro could not have been a Communist in his guerrilla days because he didn't talk like a Communist. Mailer's brilliant aperçu will have to be refined, since there is now more than one way of Communist talking.)

Most serious democratic leftists understand these changes in Communism. It is thus somewhat unfair of Arthur I. Waskow to suggest (in the current issue of *Dissent*) that the "old liners" (I think he is talking about me, among others) are primarily concerned with Communist infiltration "control" or that we have an absolute and static theory of Totalitarianism with a capital T. On balance at the present time, I tend to agree with the SNCC activists who feel that their anarchism will corrupt the Communists rather than vice versa. And more than a decade ago, my old Left was making almost a full-time career out of denouncing the thesis that there was no dynamic, contradiction, or national difference within Communism.

It is not nostalgic fear that moves me. It is the present situation and the way in which the peace movement's attitude toward the Communists will affect the possibility of shortening the Vietnam war (a pragmatic, political consideration); and the way in which the same issue might, through careless and emotional thinking, subvert that militant internationalism that is so basic to the radical impulse.

First of all, there are the pragmatics, and here the question is: What is the best way to organize to end the war in Vietnam? For historical reasons, this problem has been posed in a way guaranteed to achieve a maximum of obfuscation. Shall a demonstration or committee, it is asked, have a policy of the exclusion, or nonexclusion, of Communists and pro-Communists?

The reason for putting the question in this way is related to specific experiences of the new generation of radical youth. Their movement began around "ethical," rather than political, demands: abolish HUAC; don't murder Chessman; defy the Mississippi racists; down with in loco parentis, etc. Then, with the Free Speech Movement in Berkeley, the trend was even more toward opposition to our do-not-fold-spindle-or-mutilate society. Personal relations, anti-bureaucracy, and individual rights were thus the watchwords.

And yet the question of "nonexclusion" is, in many ways, a false one. No serious person on the left proposes to require a loyalty oath for demonstrators—or to say that Communists have no right to march in demonstrations. The real issue, then, is not one of civil liberties, but of politics. Of course Communists can come to the parade—but what policies shall the parade advocate?

For the sad, imperfect fact of the matter is that every political movement is exclusionary the moment it adopts a platform. The new radical organizations, for instance, have programs that effectively persuade Goldwaterites, moderate Republicans, and even some liberals to exclude themselves. Yet no one would really argue that an antiwar demonstration has to be organized so as not to offend Young Americans for Freedom. And indeed, the way in which some of the recent demonstrations were organized had precisely and predictably the effect of excluding some anti-Communist leftists. Or, on the other hand, I hope that Students for a Democratic Society will not propose joint action against HUAC with the Ku Klux Klan. The new radicals should effectively exclude the racists by their politics.

We should all agree to defend everyone's civil liberties and right to protest. Here there are no exclusions. We should then ask another question: What democratic political strategy is best calculated to end the war in Vietnam?

There is one answer to this question that says: Let us proceed by way of the politics of the lowest common denominator. We will simply say: End the War! and invite all who agree with this slogan to unite together. In effect, this approach says that the way in which the war is ended is not a basic issue. It proposes that the partisans of Vietcong victory and those who favor a negotiated peace blur their differences, and it allows the American Vietcongers to say that their support for the military victory of one side is a "peace" policy.

I do not suggest that the issue is plain and simple. Some of my friends and most of my enemies on the left marched under the End the War! umbrella in New York. Indeed, in October 1962, during the Cuban missile crisis, I demonstrated behind the simple slogan, Negotiate, Don't Fight! The eyeball-to-eyeball confrontation was on, and there was no time for anything more complicated (or, as it turned out, effective) than an existential political gesture. More recently, I have supported the Berkeley students and their united front—which stretched from Goldwaterites to Maoists and back. The FSM was spontaneous, ad hoc, demanding freedom for all, and under the circumstances everybody joined in.

But these precedents do not strike me as applicable to Vietnam. It is now clear that powerful forces, from the LBJ Center to the McCarthyite Right, are lining up to prevent even a discussion of the war. The immediate counterdemand of the Left, then, is that the issue be made the subject of a national debate. Under such circumstances, those of us who seek to end the war must come up with something more than a picket-line chant like "End the War in Vietnam." Real alternatives and analyses must be offered. But the moment this is done, it is impossible to maintain an attitude of indifference as between those who are simply for the Vietcong and those who are for peace.

In all of this, I am assuming that the peace movement is concerned with changing our tragic policy and not simply with providing individuals the opportunity to demonstrate their morality. If this is indeed the case, then one must at least notice the American people. Most Americans are anti-Communist. Some have the position for the worst of reasons: they are ultra-rightists. Some have it for the best of reasons: they are democrats with a small d. A good number are in the middle, simply accepting a prevailing doctrine. Now, a movement that believes that it is first necessary to persuade the American people to Communism, pro-Communism, or even a-Communism, and only then to get them to end the war in Vietnam, has the civil liberty to promulgate this view. In fact, it will be carrying on an exercise in futility that will give the Legionnaires an excuse to push their Maoist thesis that peace mongering and Communism are one and the same thing.

Others try to escape the American reality by having fantasies about how it would be fine if only the left-outs, the dispossessed, the poor, the unrepresented, would take power in the name of peace, freedom, and civil rights. There are many things wrong with such "radical" reveries. They propose that a minority of the people should establish participatory democracy, which is an impossible exercise in political mathematics. They assume that the unrepresented share the alienation and programs of middle-class protesters when in fact support of LBJ increases, according to all the polls, as income decreases (the poor do not live in a social environment that invites pacifist conclusions).

In terms of political reality, then, the only effective peace movement will be one that dissociates itself from any hint of being an apologist for the Vietcong. Some may say that this is a sad fact about American life (I do not agree)—but it remains a fact. Such people could, on grounds of moral principle, continue in their advocacy of the Vietcong, but that would do nothing to end the agony of the Vietnamese people. But for those of us who want to change American policy and to end the war, the facts of American political life are most relevant and quite clear in this particular case.

In addition to making it plain that it is not a Vietcong apologist, the peace movement should call for: a defense of the civil liberties of all, including partisans of the Vietcong; an immediate end to the bombing of the North and South; a cease-fire; negotiations with the National Liberation Front; the admission of Communist China to the United Nations; a reconvening of the Geneva Conference; and self-determination in Vietnam.

I include the last point—self-determination—with the full knowledge that it could result in a Vietcong electoral triumph. I am not as absolutely positive of this as the pro-VCers in the United States. Georges Chaffard's reports in *L'Express*, which I have found to be a most useful source of information, suggest that in recent years Vietcong taxation, terrorism, and draft policies as well as a simple yearning for peace at any price on the part of the people have made the guerrillas much less popular than before. But I certainly accept the possibility that a free election might result in a Vietcong victory.

However, I would under no circumstances "celebrate" a Vietcong victory. It would be the tragic culmination of twenty years of French and American imperialism, the result of an impossible choice between rightist dictatorship and totalitarian capital accumulation. My attitude here is analogous to my feelings about the Hungarian Revolution of 1956. I believe that the Hungarian October was a democratic socialist rising against bureaucratic totalitarianism. Its program—including democratically elected factory councils—was the most advanced ever offered in Western, or world, history. And yet I did not call for American intervention when the Russians crushed the revolution. I believed that such intervention would have been the prelude to World War III, and if I loved the revolution, I feared atomic annihilation even more. Similarly with Vietnam, I believe that the domestic and international consequences of the war there are so disastrous that we must negotiate even if, tragically, the negotiations would open up the way to a Vietcong victory—and I would regard that victory as a defeat for human freedom.

Thus far, I have emphasized some of the pragmatic political facts of American life. But I don't want it to be thought that my attitude toward Communism is determined by an opportunistic desire to be popular at all costs. I am anti-Communist on principle—because I am pro-freedom.

In the summer 1965 issue of *Studies on the Left*, Tom Hayden and Staughton Lynd reply to an excellent communication by Herb Gans. In the course of their polemic, they write, "We refuse to be anti-Communist. We insist that the term has lost all the specific context it once had. Instead, it serves as the key category of abstract thought which Americans use to justify a foreign policy that often is no more sophisticated than rape." I take this as a fairly typical expression of what I would regard as the confusion that one often encounters among the new radicals. Thus my words are not directed, ad hominem, against the authors but to a certain kind of logic.

To begin with, it is not true that anti-Communism recently "lost" its "specific context" and became a "key category" for the justification of an unjustifiable foreign policy. From October 1917 to this moment, there has always been a reactionary anti-Communism that uses the rhetoric of freedom to support the Batistas, Chiangs, Trujillos, and Francos of this world. Democratic socialist anti-Communists have always fought this kind of anti-Communism. At the same time, there has been an anti-Communism that is not a prop for the status quo, but a worldwide program for freedom everywhere. I can understand the Hayden-Lynd disgust with reactionary anti-Communism—but that does not allow them to ignore all the rest of history.

It was, and is, the McCarthyite logic to argue: Some proponents of a civil rights bill are Communists; therefore all proponents of the bill are Communists, or Communist-dupes. The new radicals have much better values than the McCarthyites, to put it mildly, but their syllogisms are just as faulty: Some forms of anti-Communism are reactionary; therefore all forms of anti-Communism are reactionary.

But I object to this thesis on more than grounds of logic, for I find the Hayden-Lynd argument understandable, a historical product of honest experience, *and* isolationist and anti-internationalist.

I believe that bureaucratic rule and manipulation is a trend in every society in the world (I developed this idea at length in *The Accidental Century*). In the advanced societies of Western capitalism, this bureaucracy is sophisticated, manipulative, coexists with certain democratic freedoms, and attempts to convince the people, as Marcuse has brilliantly argued, that their chains are really fun to wear. In the developing Communist societies, and in the Third World, this bureaucratic rule is much harsher, and in the case of Communism, totalitarian. It is a means for the modernization of these nations through the forced restriction of popular consumption, the superexploitation of labor, and a massive investment in industry.

Now, there are obviously enormous differences between these types of bureaucratic rule. Yet I do not think that one can be in favor of defending the outcasts and victims of Mississippi and Harlem but be indifferent about those in Hanoi and Peking. I do not think it possible to develop a serious foreign policy alternative if, on grounds of revulsion against some of the uses of one kind of anti-Communism, one adopts an agnosticism about the power structure that now rules one-third of the world. Is there not a colonialist aspect to demanding freedom now for every victim of Western injustice and not bothering to think about the victims of Communist injustice?

Some will answer such questions with the worst arguments of the old Communist Left. The developing countries, they say, have so long been plundered and robbed by Western imperialism that they can only achieve self-sufficiency through a totalitarian denial of political freedom that makes the attainment of economic freedom possible. Now, I don't happen to believe that the nonwhite and poor majority of this planet must inevitably be condemned to such a systematic misery, but that is another argument. For now, I would restrict myself to two remarks. If someone wants to claim that beating a surplus out of the hide of a peasant is the only road to progress in the ex-colonial world, that is his civil liberty, but he should not describe this mechanism as the good society or imply that the peasant sings folk songs when he surrenders his surplus. And secondly, it should be remembered that this capital accumulation is not carried out by an abstract spirit but by a human bureaucracy with privileges and elite ideas about itself. And thus, the far side of such economic development will be more sophisticated bureaucracy, a "reformist" totalitarianism, but bureaucracy and totalitarianism nevertheless (as in Russia).

In conclusion, my principled reason for my kind of anti-Communism is that I am for one man, one vote. I do not think there is one man, one vote in Jackson, Mississippi, in Saigon, in Hanoi, in Johannesburg, in Madrid, in Peking, or in Moscow. The Russians are so often for freedom in America, and the Americans so often for freedom in Russia. I think radicals should be for freedom everywhere. And if they ask the peace movement, Are you Communist? it should answer, No; not because it is afraid of capitulating to reaction but because it is for one man, one vote everywhere in this world, because it is for peace and freedom.

# 13
# Harrington Replies

*The Village Voice, 1965*

The Sane March on Washington of November 27 gave, by far and large, an excellent demonstration of how the peace movement should seek to end the war in Vietnam.

The march proposed specific steps toward ending that war: for example, that the United States call for a cease-fire, halt the bombings in the North, and support the principles of the 1954 Geneva accords. Thus, it addressed itself to American political opinion with some hope of changing it rather than raising apocalyptic and utterly irrelevant slogans. Tens of thousands came in response to this approach as it was stated in the march's call. But no one was excluded. Even those who unilaterally "raided" the line of march and attempted, with Vietcong flags or their own slogans, to interfere with Sane's free-speech right to make its own case were there. They were much appreciated by the reactionary press.

In my recent article on Communists and the peace movement I had argued that the issue was not a civil libertarian question of excluding, or not excluding, individuals because of their beliefs or affiliations. "Of course Communists can come to the parade," I wrote, "—but what policies shall the parade advocate?" This essentially political attitude prevailed in Washington. At the Washington Monument, Dr. Benjamin Spock read a statement subscribed to by most of the sponsors of the march. It was the kind of declaration I had in mind when I originally wrote the article in the *Voice*. It said in part:

> It has been said by some of our critics in the United States that the North Vietnamese Government and the National Liberation Front will interpret peace sentiment and demonstrations in this country as effective support for a military victory by the NLF. We wish to make it emphatically clear to our fellow Americans, as well as to Hanoi and the NLF, that this is not the case. . . .
>
> We march for peace through negotiations in Vietnam. Far from supporting the military victory of any side, we believe that anyone who seeks to resolve the issue by a final triumph of arms will prolong the agony of the Vietnamese people, further escalate the war, and thus ultimately threaten the very peace of the world. . . .

It is within the political context of the highly successful November 27 march for peace in Vietnam that I want to respond to the critics of my original article. In doing so, I have not tried a point-by-point refutation of every objection since that would take a book (and I am not even sure that the *Voice* will have the space to print all the letters in any case). I have simply taken the main themes that were directed against me and tried to discuss them in a broad way.

First of all, there were those who misunderstood what I was saying.

I did not call for a purge of individuals, for a policy of excluding demonstrators. I specifically argued that this was not the issue. Harry Ring supports the "nonexclusionists" in their opposition to "red-baiting in general" and in their hostility to "keeping badly needed activists out of the movement because of their views." These are, the reader is told, among the things that "upset" me.

Is it then "red-baiting" for an organization to adopt a political position on how it can best pursue its goal of achieving peace in Vietnam? Is it "red-baiting" if a demonstration dissociates itself from the Vietcong? Is it "red-baiting" to say that those activists who carry Vietcong flags are not exactly mobilizing American opinion for peace in Vietnam? Mr. Ring certainly implies a yes to all of these preposterous positions. And is it wrong for an open political organization (note, we are not speaking of an employer or the government, but of a voluntary political group) to define its politics in such a way that it will discourage those who do not share them from joining? Scrape away the tired rhetoric and that is the real content of Mr. Ring's insinuating formula about keeping people out "because of their views."

A second major theme of the letters concerned Communism itself.

R.F. is happy that a good part of the peace movement has stopped taking the issue of anti-Communism seriously. That may or may not be a factual description of the present situation. If it is, it represents a disaster. The power structure of one-third of the world is Communist. It is the most dangerous unradical isolationism to say that a peace movement—whose concerns must be global—has no obligation to think about whether this enormous concentration of political, economic, and military power is for good or for bad. Indeed, how can one seriously propose a peace policy for America without having some analysis of the Communist response? And this is true whether one is pro- or anti-Communist, for it simply indicates that one cannot be a political agnostic about regimes that control more than a billion people and thereby affect the very destiny of mankind.

I am further convinced of the need for serious thinking about Communism by people in the peace movement when I see the confusions on this topic in many of the letters. And here, the issue of one man-one vote looms large.

For Mr. F., C.H., and others, there is a counterposition between political freedom and economic and social freedom. As Mr.

F. writes, "The existence of economic security and intellectual opportunity is more desirable than voting; in fact they are ends while voting is a means. . . ." In the same vein, Mr. H. points out that there are "different versions of real political freedom" in the world: "The Communists believe people are only free, free of class domination, when they structure their political action through their version of socialism; we believe they are free, free from immediate coercion, when they use voting machines."

The Communists do indeed believe as Mr. H. says. I think they are wrong. Some democrats believe that voting machines are the totality of democracy. I think they are wrong too.

One man-one vote is not the only freedom, but it is, in the modern world, an essential freedom. Where the state owns the means of production, as under Communism, the decisive issue is: Who owns the state? For the "owners" of the state will make it serve their ends—including, Mr. F., their economic and intellectual ends. In a stratified society, the people can "own" the state in only one way: through the political freedom to change its policies and personnel, i.e., through political democracy, or one man-one vote. If, as under Communism, a bureaucracy effectively "owns" the state that owns the nationalized means of production, that fact will give it title to class privileges as surely as a stock certificate does under capitalism. And the mechanism of this class domination by the minority bureaucrat, I would suggest to Mr. H., is precisely his dictatorial monopoly of political power, i.e., the absence of one man-one vote.

Thus, if there is any hope for freedom—in an economic and social, as well as a political sense—in Communist society, it will come when the people successfully assert the principle of one man-one vote. Only then can they own the state that owns the means of production. This analysis, and these rights, "even" apply to North Vietnamese peasants.

Under capitalism, things are different. Social and economic coercion is not, at least under "normal" conditions, the direct political function of the state. But though there is formal recognition of the principle of one man-one vote—and even the imperfect practice of it—economic and social inequality mean that some people are "freer" than others. Henry Ford carries more weight than you and I. Therefore, there must be a determined struggle for economic and social democracy. In the pursuit of this end, the principle of one man-one vote offers the possibility of nonviolent social transformation. It is therefore precious.

The Communists are wrong when they say that they have dispensed with political freedom (one man-one vote) in order to abolish class oppression. They have abolished this freedom in order to modernize and to establish, through a political dictatorship, the economic and social hegemony of a new exploiting class. The capitalists are wrong when they say that the simple right to vote ipso facto makes a man equal, since that right can coexist with enormous social and economic inequalities.

Thus it is wrong to put civil liberties, the right to political organization, and one man-one vote on one side and economic and social security and freedom on the other. For in the bureaucratic, centralized, and technological modern world, political democracy is not a mere formal matter but the very—and only—means by which people can transform the power structures of the East and West and make them responsive to their economic and social needs. And "even" the people of North Vietnam and of China and of Russia have a place in this vision of things.

Now let me take some remarks of Mr. Ring's as a point of departure and intrude a little recent history into the discussion (my main sources for the latter are Phillippe Deviller's *Histoire du Viet-Nam de 1940 à 1952* and the revised edition of Bernard Fall's *The Two Viet-Nams*). Mr. Ring says it is false to equate "communism with totalitarianism." Marx and Engels called themselves communist: I would not call them totalitarian; therefore communism is not totalitarian. In fact, I do believe that Marx and Engels were revolutionary socialists and impassioned democrats. But I do not believe that the various Communist regimes are carrying out their program: e.g., Marx's advocacy of the principle of the immediate recallability of all elected officials—an extreme version of one man-one vote—does not exactly apply in Russia, China, North Vietnam, etc., where even the basic right of independent political opposition is denied.

Secondly, and more specifically, Mr. Ring tells us that the North Vietnamese regime has "Stalinist features in both its politics and method of rule." I propose to spell this out a bit since the conquest of political power in the North by Ho Chi Minh's Vietminh provides, I think, an anticipation of the probable consequences of a Vietcong victory in the South.

The "Front for the Independence of Vietnam"—the Vietminh—was founded under the direction of Ho and the Communists at the beginning of World War II. On October 25, 1941, the Vietminh issued the slogans of its first manifesto: "Union of all social classes, revolutionary organizations, and ethnic minorities. Alliance with all the other oppressed people of Indochina. Collaboration with all the French antifascists. One goal: the destruction of colonialism and fascist imperialism." The Vietminh proposed universal suffrage, the democratic rights of a free press, assembly, etc., the nationalization of the property of fascists and collaborators.

Throughout its history, the Vietminh was always careful to have non-Communist but sympathetic elements play a prominent, if not a decision-making role. Those who did not go along with the Communists were murdered. R.M. says he does not know of any democratic anti-Communist force in South Vietnam. This, I suspect, is the case. In part, it is a function of French and American imperialism, which preferred puppets like Bao Dai or reactionaries like Diem to genuine democrats. And in part it is a result of the effectiveness of Ho Chi Minh in physically eliminating his political opponents.

For example—and Mr. Ring might take particular note here—Tha Thu Thau, the Vietnamese Trotskyist leader (the Trotskyists had a mass following in Saigon in the 1930s and early 1940s), was murdered by the Vietminh in 1945. The study of Vietnam by Anh-Van and Jacqueline Roussel, published by the Trotskyist Fourth International, bears the dedication, "To the memory of Tha Thu Thau and Tran-von Trach and all the Bolshevik-Leninist comrades who fell under the blows of Stalinism in Indochina." In the light of these events, I find Mr. Ring's formulation on Ho's movement somewhat mild: "There is considerable evidence that the North Vietnamese regime has Stalinist features in both its politics and methods of rule." The Trotskyist movement, to which Mr. Ring adhered the last I knew, has more than "considerable evidence" of this fact; it has the dead bodies of its martyrs.

More broadly, as Bernard Fall describes the situation in 1945–46: "While Ho was negotiating with French Government officials in Fountainebleau, his ablest deputies . . . were liquidating the 'internal enemies of the regime': leaders of religious sects . . . mandarins . . . intellectuals . . . Trotskyites, and anti-Communist nationalists." In the summer of 1946, Fall relates, Vo Nguyen Giap, the Vietminh minister of the interior, neutralized the nationalist groups, forced their (anti-French) leaders into exile, and, on July 11, 1946, closed down the newspaper *Vietnam*, the only remaining organ of the nationalists.

All this was done while the Vietminh were proclaiming a constitution that provided civil liberties for all citizens—and was claiming to be a broadly based movement, "democratic" rather than Communist in function. When, however, this "united front" of Communists and non-Communists took power in the North, they proceeded to the establishment of a totalitarian Communist state. In 1956, during a "land reform" program that Ho himself later admitted to have been wrong, Bernard Fall estimates that 50,000 North Vietnamese were executed and 100,000 sent to labor camps. Indeed, on November 2, 1956, the peasants of the old Vietminh bastion of Interzone IV in Ho's native province rose against the Communists—as had been done twenty-six years earlier in protest against French colonialism—and were put down by the 325th Division of Ho's army with the deportation or execution, Fall estimates, of 6,000.

I would suggest to R.M. that this seems to have been a democratic anti-Communist movement.

Now all of this relates to one's attitude toward the Vietcong. I do not think, as R.M. suggests, that the Cold War can be reduced to a struggle between democracy and dictatorship. I had no illusions about Bao Dai and Diem; I have none about Ky. But I suspect that Mr. M. and others have an illusion or two about the VC. For the evidence is clear that the VC was initiated by veterans of the Vietminh and that the National Liberation Front is the same kind of "broad" "united front" as its predecessor in the North. I do not pretend to know the exact degree to which the VC takes orders from Hanoi or from Peking or is autonomous. That is not relevant to my argument. What is relevant is that the VC, whether indigenously or externally controlled, is clearly modeled on the Vietminh, and there is every reason to believe that its victory in the South will lead to a regime of the North Vietnamese type, i.e., to a Communist and totalitarian regime.

This is why I would not celebrate a Vietcong victory if it emerged from that self-determination that I advocate. No, R.M., there probably is no viable, democratic anti-Communist movement in the South—and that is a tragedy. The police, executioners, terrorists, and various other agents of France, the United States, the Vietminh, and the Vietcong have effectively seen to that. Those who will pay the price for this situation will be the people of South Vietnam. For myself, I am as concerned with the rights of the peasants of Interzone IV in the North as I am for those in the Mekong Delta in the South.

Finally, there is the issue of negotiations and the withdrawal of American troops.

Mr. H. says, "To call for negotiations between invader and invaded for any other purpose than agreement on the details of the immediate withdrawal of the invader's troops is to add a cloak of legitimacy to the idea that nations have a right to invade other nations whenever they can get away with it. . . ." Would that the categories of moral legitimacy ruled the world and were a guide to political strategy! I do not think that the millionaires of Western capitalism have a moral right to their fortunes. However, I do not restrict myself to the simple demand, "Give up your money!" for those same millionaires hold tremendous power and are not going to surrender their wealth simply because I ask it. Similarly, judged by morality, I suspect that all of the contending parties in Vietnam are guilty to one degree or another and that the only true innocents are those peasants over whose bodies the fighting takes place. But I want to end the war in Vietnam as well as make ethical judgments about the situation there.

Mr. H. asks if I would have advocated negotiations between the Russian invaders and the Hungarian revolutionists to determine how much of Hungary the Russians would control in 1956. Of course! If despite their superior military force, which permitted them to take over the entire country, the Soviets, who were totally immoral in what they were doing, wanted, for whatever Machiavellian reasons, to negotiate and allow the freedom of one Hungarian province, or one city, or one neighborhood, I would, under the miserable circumstances, have leaped at the chance.

Secondly, as Marcus G. Raskin and Bernard Fall point out in their own proposals in the *Vietnam Reader* that they edited, "There seems to be surprisingly little disagreement as to the type of negotiations to be undertaken. Both sides . . . have referred to a Geneva-style conference. . . . Both sides also have agreed that both zones of Vietnam would continue to operate as separate states for a fairly long period after a cease-fire and that both would be free of foreign troops and bases."

But then, there is the American-political aspect of all this. Mr. Ring writes, "Why can't you simply say: The simplest, quickest, and most effective way to end the war in Vietnam is to bring the GIs home?" I would answer that the simplest, quickest, and most effective way to keep the GIs in Vietnam is to persuade the American people that the only choice is escalation or immediate withdrawal.

Let me conclude by returning to the November 27 march. The march rallied serious political sentiment for ending the war, and it did so by proposing thought-out political ideas in a context of advocating peace through negotiations and opposing the hawks on both sides.

When I saw a VC flag introduced into the line of march, the nasty thought crossed my mind: Were I an agent provocateur for the CIA I would get a VC banner and join the demonstration. The more such flags, the more plausible the McCarthyite-Maoist thesis that the partisans of peace must also be apologists for Communism. The flags, I believe, were not the work of agents provocateurs (though the government has had its plants in such enterprises before, e.g., in the Cuba trip that wound up before

HUAC). Sadly, I suspect that these ultra "militants" are the unwitting enemies of the very Vietnamese people they want to help. In the future, I fervently hope that they have the courage of their convictions (assuming that they cannot, alas, be rationally persuaded from them) and that they will hold their own demonstrations instead of trying to disrupt the activities of groups like Sane.

But precisely because Sane made its position so clear, the VC flag wavers were only able to harm the march in the most reactionary sections of the press. And here, to me, is the key to the problem of Communism (or any other ideology that comes on like a raiding party) in the peace movement. The crucial thing is that the peace movement be clearly and openly political; and that it oppose the partisans of military victory on both sides on the ground that escalation will torment Vietnam even further and threaten World War III; that it advocate peace through negotiations. Then anyone who wants to rally behind such an approach should be made welcome in the line of march.

# 14
# Answering McReynolds: A Question of Philosophy, a Question of Tactics

*The Village Voice, 1967*

David McReynolds's letter to "my" generation—to "those who were part of or were influenced by the democratic Left between the purge trials and the Twentieth Party Congress"—is a thoughtful statement of some of the agonizing issues posed by the tragic war in Vietnam. This answer is intended in the same generous, unpolemical spirit in which he wrote.

I begin with a personal anecdote, not to flaunt a venerable credential, like an American Legionnaire of the antiwar movement, but to make a point about my own ambiguities.

In 1950, when the Korean War broke out, I joined the Army Medical Corps Reserve, thinking that noncombatant status would satisfy my conscientious objections to American participation in that conflict. When I enlisted, both the Army and I thought I was to be sent to Korea, but there was one of those sudden changes in policy and I was required only to go to biweekly training sessions. In 1951, I went to live at the Catholic Worker house, a spare-time soldier dwelling in a pacifist community. When I had to go to drill, I waited until everybody was at dinner, since I didn't want to be seen uniformed in the livery of my compromise. Eventually, I went on the annual two weeks of active duty with a firm promise from the officers that my principles would be respected. As soon as we got to camp, I was sent to the infantry; next day, they tried to give me a rifle and march me to hand-grenade instruction. I refused the gun and the grenade lesson and, after some very anxious moments and due to good luck and sympathetic superiors, was sent back to the medics.

After all the turmoil—and fear—of thus defining my position (I later severed all my connections with the Reserve, but that is another story), I was walking along a road in the camp. A column of marching men came by, and suddenly, even though I had fought grimly for my right not to be among them, I felt lonely and left out and wanted nothing more than to get into step.

That is how I often feel these days when I watch, or read about, the antiwarriors in some new confrontation. My heart, my emotions, my instincts are with them; but, in a good many cases, my head will not allow me to join up. I truly wish that I could see the issues as sharply defined as Dave McReynolds does. But I can't. My ambiguities are in no sense a function of doubts about the wrongness of the evil war in Vietnam. On the contrary, I believe that politics and morality require that all our energies be devoted to ending this abomination in Southeast Asia at once. That is precisely why I cannot participate in some of the demonstrations.

At the beginning of his letter, I think Dave McReynolds introduces something of a red herring. I am talking about the issue of Communism. Since I have written so extensively on this point, I would just as soon leave it alone, but McReynolds puts it first among his comments and uses it to explain the failure of my generation to respond with sufficient militance to the war. So I have no choice but to deal with it once more.

His meaning is clear enough: that some of us on the democratic left mute our opposition to the war because of an obsessive concern with Communism ("We see the NLF and North Vietnamese not as living creatures but as abstract symbols holding guns, ideological puppets directed from Moscow and/or Peking"). Yet I do not know of anyone on the democratic left who views the struggle in South Vietnam as the result of a Russian, Chinese, or any other kind of conspiracy. That is a view that is still entertained in the State Department and on the American right, but it is not to be found anywhere that I know of among "my" generation of the Left. . . .

But then, how does one face up to the issue of Communism in Vietnam itself? McReynolds writes, "We must recognize that the struggle of the Vietnamese has long since transcended politics and even its own violence and has become an existential statement about man and his willingness to suffer and to endure." This is a tragic half-truth, and I can sympathize with the emotion that led both to the perception and the distortion it contains.

The average Vietnamese wounded, maimed, or killed probably knows little of the great ideological struggles of this century. Many of the cadres of the Vietcong are moved by a genuine nationalism and thirst for social justice and not by admiration for totalitarianism or the ambition to become privileged bureaucrats. The peasant caught in the fate of war is a witness to the indomitable resilience of man; and the militant, however much one disagrees with his politics, is touched with heroism. Given the technological savagery that the United States has loosed upon these people, I can understand Dave McReynolds's reaction: to forget all the ideological disputes in the presence of their suffering, rebellious humanity.

I can sympathize with this response—but I cannot agree with it. For even the sacrifice of blood in Vietnam has not exempted that land from politics. Indeed, I think that McReynolds is not existential enough, for he does not carry the tragedy that he evokes to a quite possible, brutally ironic, conclusion. Suppose that finally peace does come to Vietnam and that the Vietcong take over, and the new government then turns upon the peasantry, as it did a decade ago in the North, to force collectivization; suppose that the dying leads to a betrayal of what the men—and the women and children—died for.

In saying this, I am not arguing that one should, therefore, support the war because the peace might—or probably will—end in a Communist regime. Two years ago, in the *Voice* (November

11, 1965), I advocated self-determination for Vietnam, even though this involved "the possibility that a free election might result in a Vietcong victory." The point I made then, and repeat now, is that French and American imperialism have created a situation in which a peace that will probably lead to dictatorial Communist rule is preferable to an "anti-Communist" war that ravages the land and people of the country we are supposed to be protecting, threatens World War III, and corrupts the moral fabric of American society. (I put "anti-Communist" in quotes because Paris and Washington have since 1945 been the most effective recruiting sergeants for Vietnamese Communism. Somewhat similarly, I did not favor armed Western defense of the Hungarian uprising of October 1956 against the Russians, even though I regarded the revolution as democratic socialist. Magnificent as that uprising was, its destruction was a lesser evil than the nuclear war that intervention would probably have provoked.)

But, even though one could thus conclude that a policy that would probably lead to a Communist victory in Vietnam is a lesser evil, it must be made clear that such an outcome is still an evil. And an emotional solidarity with a people that has been subjected to almost a quarter of a century of war must not blind us to the fact that, even after all that misery, they have not escaped from politics. I insist on this point not out of scholarly fanaticism but because understanding it is the prerequisite to struggling for a world in which peasants will have more meaningful alternatives than submitting themselves either to Western domination or to the totalitarian accumulation of capital.

The analogy of Algeria might make this point even clearer. During that country's struggle for independence, there was no serious issue of Russian or Chinese involvement, since the Algerian Communists never really recovered from the fact that their French Communist comrades supported the repressive colonial policy in North Africa right after World War II. There were romantic revolutionaries in the West—and particularly in Paris, where some of them risked their lives for their convictions—who were so outraged by French brutality and humbled by Algerian courage that they viewed the National Liberation Front (FLN) as the vital cell of a new socialist society. Those of us on the democratic left who campaigned in support of the Algerian demand for independence were often asked if the FLN would set up a dictatorship (rather than a socialist utopia) once it triumphed. We answered honestly that it probably would, in considerable measure because the French had made democracy impossible. But, we said, even though the right of self-determination would lead to this unhappy conclusion, it was preferable to the continuation of French rule.

Five years after Algerian independence, the bourgeois leaders have been purged by the militant politicals, the militant politicals have been overthrown by the army, and many of the young Frenchmen who engaged in the clandestine struggle would probably be deported as subversive from the nation they helped to create. The point is not simply that we were right and the romantics wrong. It is that the Left cannot ignore these complexities if it wishes to transform them. And that means that the Communist leadership of the national movement in Vietnam must be recognized and analyzed so that we might someday offer the poor of the Third World a positive good rather than a lesser evil (in the September–October 1967 issue of *Dissent*, I described at some length what this might mean).

But, as a final word on the Communist issue, I hope that Dave McReynolds's letter is not a sign that he is buying the newly fashionable devil theory of an international anti-Communist conspiracy. This view notes that the most right-wing, vicious elements in the country are anti-Communist, sees that democratic leftists are anti-Communists too, and then proclaims that these antithetical political tendencies are, therefore, part of a single, sinister movement. Joseph Stalin once operated on a similar illogic, declared that the German Social Democrats of 1932–33 were really fascists in disguise, and thereby made a major contribution to Hitler's rise to power.

But the issue of Communism is really not the central one I want to raise. For, in his defense of the tactics of nonviolent resistance, McReynolds is talking about the best tactics to employ in ending the killing. For me, as for him, that is the crucial point:

How can we stop the war in Vietnam? And it is from the standpoint of this common goal that I disagree with at least part of his analysis.

In the December 7, 1967, issue of *The New York Review of Books*, Noam Chomsky put it this way: "Resistance is in part a moral responsibility that cannot be shirked. On the other hand, as a tactic, it seems to me of doubtful effectiveness, as matters now stand. I say this with diffidence and considerable uncertainty." Basically, I agree with Chomsky's assessment of the practicalities, but this leads me, as will be seen, to conclusions that differ from his.

To begin with, there is the individual, moral level of draft resistance. On this count, I have the same attitude as McReynolds, Chomsky, and other advocates of resistance. I was a conscientious objector during the Korean War and was willing to go to jail rather than to serve in the army, and that would be my position now, were I of draft age, but with even greater emotional certitude. I think that the young men who are voluntarily giving up their (middle-class) deferments and handing in their draft cards are making a courageous witness. I would, incidentally, like to put the public prosecutor on notice, in writing, here and now, that I support them in their conscientious decision, and if this is a violation of the law on my part, so be it.

At the same time, I do not believe that such a highly motivated form of resistance is going to create a mass movement that will end the war. The great bulk of the draftees, as Dave McReynolds notes, come from working-class and impoverished backgrounds and, for a number of reasons beyond their control, are simply not able to take such a stand. On this level, then, draft resistance is a moral imperative by which the individual conscience enjoins a man to refuse to take part in violence he considers immoral; and it is a moral and political witness by a minority, which could possibly touch the hearts and minds of some of the uncommitted. But it is not, as Chomsky notes, an effective method of winning peace.

Dave McReynolds then proposes a certain way of implementing our support of these young men—by closing the doors of the induction centers—and here we part company. This tactic is urged with the greatest seriousness, yet I think it contributes to a confused, self-indulgent, middle-class, and even antilibertarian tendency that is coming more and more to the fore in the peace movement. I am not, as will be seen, heaping all of these adjectives upon McReynolds's ideas for action—but I am asking him to see where his strategies could lead.

In the struggle to end the war in Vietnam, political effectiveness is a major determinant of morality. The activist who maximizes his own sense of dedication, exhilaration, and righteousness *and* alienates his fellow citizens from the cause of peace is immoral (I judge here objectively; whether he is actually guilty depends, of course, upon his individual subjectivity). If a person is commanded to kill in an unjust war, I believe he must refuse no matter what the political consequences; but if he undertakes a demonstration against the war, he is morally obliged to act with a view of how he affects others.

Thus, when Dave McReynolds proposes to block the induction-center door in support of the draft resisters, the relevant question is not, "Is draft resistance right?" but rather, "Will this action hasten the end of the war?" In my opinion, the rising sentiment against the war has come about in spite of, and not because of, tactics of civil disruption. The horror and ugliness of what is happening in Vietnam, not the kamikaze tactics of a minority of the protesters, have incited revulsion.

But, McReynolds might reply, "What should a good German do, knowing he and his children are safe but knowing that the Jews are collected every day from the ghettos of the cities?" This analogy, as McReynolds himself admits earlier in his letter, is dangerously inexact. In a fascist dictatorship where there are no other means of changing a murderous policy other than illegal opposition, that is, in Germany under Hitler, the good German uses all available means to fight genocide, including nonviolence, guns, bombs, poison, and so forth, but not including nuclear weapons. In a country that, for all its obvious, tragic faults, is still democratic enough that the government negotiates details of a protest march with organizers who call that government's leaders moral monsters, it is still possible to change policy democratically and nonviolently. Under such circumstances, an elite minority cannot impose its will upon the nation.

I can understand youthful impatience toward my insistence on democracy and democratic forms. The war is daily more monstrous and the political process seems so insensitive, slow, and indifferent to basic moral issues. I cannot here detail all of the reasons for my advocacy of democracy, but let me state only the most pragmatic and least transcendental: If the Left leads in an assault upon civil liberties and democratic norms, it will unleash the Right, which is much more skilled in and has much more support for such tactics. George Wallace is every bit as fervid as the peace activists, and he has a simple answer to their protests: Jail the dissenters. There are, to be sure, some militants who are under the impression that America is already a fascist country. They lack, of course, any sense of what fascism is (the armed dictatorship of the Right does not confer with opponents who have announced the intention of carrying on civil disobedience; it shoots them), but even more than that, they have no sense of how real and tough the American power structure is. Even Senator Joseph McCarthy was only a despicable, demagogic reactionary, not a fascist, and I shudder to think what would happen if the paranoids of the Right really armed themselves and took to the streets.

In short, I believe that a leftist attack upon democratic legality, a leftist championing of elite decision-making by students and professors, would prolong the war in Vietnam and push domestic American politics even further to the right. It is a responsible tactic to block a door as a witness as long as it is done without any intention of really depriving others of their civil liberties to enter a building (I did exactly that when I was arrested on the opening day of the New York World's Fair) and quite another thing to try to "close down" an induction center. Does Dave McReynolds really think that his demonstration will move the uncommitted? Or might it not make them more sympathetic to Johnson?

In McReynolds's case, I am quite sure that the door-closing tactic is urged from within a democratic perspective, even if, from my point of view, mistakenly. But an ugly tendency toward anti-libertarianism and elitism is developing among some of the resisters.

For instance, Jerry Rubin urges "a nationally coordinated strike [that] will paralyze the major knowledge factories of the nation—shut them down for good with one national demand: America, dismantle your massive murder machine" (*Voice*, November 16, 1967). The dumb workers, the stupid farmers, the ghetto dwellers, the overwhelming majority are not going to be consulted; the pure, moral, "leftist" youth are going to decide. Instead of the dictatorship of the bourgeoisie or proletariat, we are to be treated to the dictatorship of the graduate students, the knowledge-factory hands.

In all of this, there is a strain of youthful middle-class petulance and self-indulgence. "The worst thing you can say about a demonstration is that it is boring," Rubin says. (The worst thing you can say is that it does not bring people to oppose the war, I would say.) "Good theater is needed to communicate radical content." And, most precisely, candidly, and exactly, "The youth movement should not judge actions on the basis of whether or not they will alienate the American middle-class mass, but whether or not the actions liberate the imagination and energy of youth." A Vietnamese peasant who is being shot at because of the policies supported by the American middle class might disagree.

Rubin concluded that article with a proposal to disrupt the Democratic National Convention: "Bring pot, fake delegate's cards, smoke bombs, costumes, blood to throw, and all kinds of interesting props. Also football helmets." On the most superficial level, I wonder, if it were shown that *not* smoking pot, wearing costumes, throwing blood, and so forth, would hasten the end of the war, whether Rubin and his cothinkers would subordinate their free middle-class spirits to the necessities of a political struggle.

On a more serious level, I am disturbed when the Left proposes to break up public meetings. For Lyndon Johnson and Dean Rusk—and even the Joint Chiefs of Staff and General Westmoreland—have a right under the Constitution of the United States to peaceable assembly. One of the many reasons I am in favor of their right to advocate their wrong ideas is that I want them to respect my right to advocate my (to me) right ideas. There used to be a militant antiwar socialist slogan, "Those who begin this war shall not end it." I would suggest to the social disrupters that if they take a calm look at the relationship of forces in America today, and particularly at the control of the forces of repression, they will see that they are creating a logic whereby "those who break up meetings will not be able to hold meetings." Mark you, I support the right of people to gather together to discuss disrupting meetings. I am just not sure that the power structure will be quite so libertarian as I am.

Finally, let me take up the famous opposition of "negotiate now" and "withdraw now." Dave McReynolds says that the slogan of "negotiate now" is a "politically expedient solution" to the tactical problem. Of course it is! And I would add, in terms of my previous distinction, that antiwar activity that is not politically expedient, that is, that does not mobilize Americans to end the war, is objectively immoral in the light of the tragic urgency of Vietnam.

When I went down to Washington with a Negotiation Now delegation to present some hundreds of thousands of signatures to a meeting of congressmen and senators, the chairman was Bishop Shannon, a Roman Catholic ecclesiast from the Midwest. In his statement, the bishop, while saying that he was forced to oppose the war, commented that he prayed nightly for the president. To a good many of the militant confronters, such a sentiment would probably seem either funny or obscene. But to the corny, dialectical, and very human American people, I suspect it had the ring of authenticity. I even think that such a quiet statement coming from a Catholic bishop who is against the war might even have more political effect than resisters pissing on the Pentagon steps.

But finally, Dave, I confess once again to being emotionally dissatisfied with my own position. This war is so ugly and horrible that I want to do something more personal, more involved than simply being rational and political. But I can't participate in demonstrations that will alienate people from the antiwar cause: I can't condone "leftist" attacks on the First Amendment freedoms;

I can't endorse middle-class elitism or regard middle-class psychodrama as a substitute for serious politics. In a way, it would be a relief to get arrested again and feel that I had put my whole being, and not just my political thinking, on the line. But I insist that every action be related to the supreme task of ending the war. If I have an obsession, that is it.

# 15
# Voting the Lesser Evil

*Commentary, 1968*

Ending the war in Vietnam must be the aim of any liberal or radical strategy for 1968.

The tragic character of the American involvement in Southeast Asia is, for me, so obvious that I will only note it rather than argue it. Our commitment to this hideous conflict threatens World War III through a military confrontation with Chinese Communism. It has already reversed many of the hopeful trends toward a Soviet-American détente and even a liquidation of the Cold War. And last but not least, it ravages an innocent land that has already undergone a generation of bloodshed. America acts as the heir of French imperialism, supports a government led by officers who fought against their own countrymen on behalf of a colonialist army, and thus continues a tactic that, for over twenty years, has driven nationalists into a Communist-led movement.

Moreover, and this is not so obvious, the American involvement in Vietnam constitutes the strongest right-wing force in our domestic political life. There will be no solution to the crisis of the cities, no response to the economic, social, and psychological outrage of racism, and no positive answer to the hysteria about "crime in the streets" as long as the war goes on. Since this is the case, any strategy that seeks to mute the issue of Vietnam in order to forward the struggle against injustice within the United States is self-defeating.

A dedicated, brilliant liberal like Leon Keyserling would challenge the above thesis. In this, he is an able spokesman for a point of view that has significant influence in the American liberal movement, particularly in its labor wing. Keyserling argues that, in terms of economic resources, America is so wealthy that it can simultaneously fight the Vietcong abroad and the slums at home. That is quite right. He also insists that the poor, both black and white, must not be required to pay a disproportionate cost of the war. That is quite right, too, and therefore doves should unite with hawks in the battle for civil rights, antipoverty funds, and all the rest. Those opponents of the war who refuse to work on such issues with, say, the AFL-CIO leadership because of the latter's support of Johnson's Vietnam policy are not being militant. They are simply imposing the heaviest burden of a war that the middle-class peace movement has not succeeded in stopping upon the backs of people in the ghettos and the backwoods.

But where Keyserling is, to my mind, quite wrong is in thinking that there is any *political* hope to push forward with social programs as long as the commitment to Vietnam continues. The effort must be made, to be sure, but, given the right-wing impact of Vietnam upon American life, it will be a holding action at best. Since 1965, the administration has de-escalated the struggle against poverty and racism every time it has escalated the attack in Southeast Asia, and the Great Society no longer survives even as a phrase. The president has not simply shifted trillions of dollars from construction to destruction. He has appropriated all the intangible resources at his command—human energy, intelligence, and imagination—in support of his Vietnam policy as well.

As a result, Mr. Johnson has helped to create the conditions for what Bayard Rustin has termed "the politics of fear and frustration." The poor were promised an "unconditional" war on poverty in January 1964. The beginnings of the campaign were exceedingly modest—a reconnaissance rather than a battle—but there were reasons to hope. So black America, the most dynamic, aspiring part of the other America, gave massive support to Johnson in the 1964 elections. But then, having raised up the spirits of the poor, and particularly of Negroes already in political motion, Mr. Johnson dashed them down. Out of this bitter experience, a sense of frustration swept the activists. Some turned to an angry, and even racist, militancy; others sank back into a despairing nihilism. The whites were fearful of this aroused frustration, and professed reactionaries therefore received more and more support. In 1967, they successfully mounted a savage attack upon the Aid for Dependent Children program and, in effect, passed an anti-Negro law (actually, *all* of the young receiving help under ADC were harmed—it was an anti-antipoverty law—but the blacks among them suffered the most grievously, as usual).

In other words, the domestic political consequences of the Vietnam policy have canceled out the economic possibility of waging two vigorous wars, one tragic and one happy, at the same time. I will certainly join with Keyserling and his cothinkers in insisting as loudly as possible that this *should* not be so. But a political strategy has to be based on the sure knowledge that it is already a fact.

In this perspective, every major issue in America today is a function of the war. Those who argue, for instance, that the real debate in the coming campaign will be over "crime in the streets" and not Vietnam, fail to understand that the first issue depends on the second. When Mr. Johnson's commitment to Southeast Asia made it impossible for him to redeem his sweeping promises to the American ghetto, he lost the chance to deal with Negro frustration in a positive way. Since the president is thus unable to remove the fundamental and outrageous causes of black desperation, he has no effective answer to the white backlashers who demand the rule of the nightstick. Were it not for Vietnam, it might well not even be necessary to have the discussion over "crime in the streets," for vigorous programs would deal with basic causes; but, thanks to Vietnam, Mr. Johnson finds it so difficult to answer his critics on the right that he is apparently going to try to steal the issue from them.

In saying these things about Johnson, let me dissociate myself from some of the more hysterical antiwarriors, in part out of a sense of simple fairness, in part because of the politics of the future.

I see Lyndon Johnson as more tragic than malevolent. In 1964, I suspect he honestly and genuinely wanted to complete Franklin Roosevelt's New Deal. I was convinced then, as now, that he did not understand the radical departures that his goals implied, but at least he was pointing to the real problems. In Washington in those days, and on the very campuses that are now most disenchanted and angry with the president, there was a sense of hope and possibility. But slowly, in tiny increments of error, through carefully phased and counterproductive escalations, Mr. Johnson led this nation into the most morally disastrous war in its history. And among the many victims of this policy were his own best intentions.

It is also politically important to maintain a sense of the complexity of the issue. If this horrible war is ended before an ultimate escalation, then the only hope for progressive social change will be a reunification of the liberal and labor forces now so bitterly divided with regard to the administration's foreign policy. There exists no political majority for democratic structural reform without the trade unionists—who represent the largest organized force for such domestic innovations—the Negroes, the liberal middle class, and others. The efforts of various New Left theorists to discover a new "proletariat," be it among the poor, the blacks, the alienated, the youth, or wherever, have all failed. Now, it is conceivable that it will even be impossible to construct the kind of coalition I describe here. But it is certain that this represents the only chance for humane transformations of America and, eventually, of America's role in the world.

When the war is over, the Council of Economic Advisers tells us in its 1968 report, $30 billion will become available in eighteen months ($15 billion through cutbacks in Defense spending; $15 billion through the normal fiscal dividend that an expanding economy provides). How will it be spent? The Council mentions a number of possibilities, the very first among them a tax cut. And there is no question that there will be powerful conservative forces pressing for such a reactionary Keynesian intervention to stimulate the postwar economy. On the other side in such a debate will be those who will seek to use this money for direct public investments to meet vital social needs. For this latter view to prevail, the factions of the democratic Left that are now bitterly split over Vietnam will have to come together again.

For this reason, I would urge my point of view against that of Keyserling and the labor liberals in a certain way. I believe that they are quite wrong in failing to understand that, so long as Vietnam continues, America will move to the right on all fundamental social questions. One fights the trends, and there might even be a victory here and there, but the political economics of 1968 are such that the administration cannot, and will not, supply the resources both for the wrong war there and for the right one here. And this fact, more than any speech by Rap Brown [a militant SNCC leader], will incite some black Americans to desperation and white Americans to fear. But in thus insisting that Vietnam is central to every major question in the campaign, I want to act so as to promote cooperation now on immediate social issues and between doves and hawks, and thus lay the basis for the coalition of the future.

So my criterion for judging political strategies this year is this: How will a candidate, or a tactic, help to end the war in Vietnam? And I take this position not simply because of what that conflict is doing in Asia and in the world, but also because of what it is doing in America.

Given this standpoint, the various "resistance" strategies are not an effective means of bringing the war to a close, though they may well be transcendental obligations that bind the individual conscience. For the most part, resistance is an attempt to give political meaning to the moral anguish of young people faced with the impossible choices of serving in a war they consider to be profoundly unjust, going to jail, or fleeing to Canada.

But the fact remains that, however morally necessary some form of resistance may be to the individual, it is not an effective political tactic against the war. It is largely confined to the middle class, particularly when it becomes a matter of risking jail, and to a tiny minority at that. Moreover, when resistance takes the form of *épater les bourgeois*, of subordinating the struggle to end the war to the battle for pot or groovy clothes, it becomes a contemptible act of petty, bourgeois self-indulgence in which "doing one's thing" is more important than the agony of the Vietnamese. Finally, when the resisters do not simply witness their own convictions but try to stop others in the exercise of their democratic rights, they are not simply antilibertarian but are running the risk of provoking a McCarthyite repression.

If I were Lyndon Johnson, I would hope that the "Yippies" have a marvelous campy happening at the Chicago Democratic convention and identify the antiwar cause with the East Village and Haight-Ashbury. In American political terms that would constitute the most effective prowar demonstration imaginable.

Then there are the various third-party strategies on the left, the most serious among them being the Peace and Freedom Party, which has qualified for the ballot in California. These efforts will, I believe, lead many committed and excellent people to a political dead end. For such groups have taken a principled, programmatic position in favor of being a marginal minority—and that is not going to end the war or prepare for the peace.

In California, for instance, prominent Peace and Freedom leaders have made it clear that unmasking Eugene McCarthy is one of their main functions. And indeed, the tactic of persuading liberals and radicals to switch their registration out of the Democratic party will make Mr. Johnson's task all the easier during the primary. But this is not a simple aberration of tactical judgment. It flows from a long-range strategy that is current among many New Leftists. It is worth taking seriously, not because it has any serious political substance, but because it speaks to the emotions of many young people who must eventually be won to a democratic left coalition.

The basic premise underlying the Peace and Freedom tactic is that there is a chasm that separates radicalism and liberalism. Thus in San Francisco last year, the Vietnam referendum had to be phrased in terms of immediate withdrawal; dividing the antiwar camp in this way, it allowed the president a gratuitous victory. Thus, too, I heard a young militant at a Berkeley meeting last October (it was in violation of an antilibertarian injunction) denounce the main enemy of the peace movement: Senator Robert F. Kennedy. And thus, too, they argue that Eugene McCarthy is really prowar.

Here is how Carl Oglesby, writing in the February 1967 *Ramparts*, defined "the historic mission of American liberalism": "bridge all the old contradictions and close the wounds of America." Now there is no question that liberalism, which is nonrevolutionary and proposes reform within the system, can be used to prop up the status quo. There are indeed corporate liberals who, having learned from Marie Antoinette, are happy to "social engineer" some bread for the masses so that the elite can keep its cake. But there are also liberals whose main concern is reform, not the system reform is supposed to ameliorate. These are the ones who stood firm against McCarthyism and defended the rights of Communists, who struggled for the social changes that allowed so many of the New Leftists to go to college, who risked their lives in the civil rights struggle, and so on.

But in the Peace and Freedom view, this contradictory, changing phenomenon of mass liberalism has been reduced to the worst aspects of its most conservative wing. And in one stroke, the organized American working class (which stands for a domestic liberal program), most of the Negroes, most of the middle class, are placed beyond the pale. There is no understanding that America will move to the left only when these people, acting out of what is best in their liberal commitment and in response to overwhelming events, turn in a radical direction. Instead, there is an emotionally satisfying proclamation of radical righteousness that appeals primarily to college students and graduates.

So I would reject the Peace and Freedom approach on two grounds. First, its long-range strategic orientation is a blueprint for irrelevance and contains elements of elitist contempt for the democratic potential of rank-and-file Americans. And second, in terms of the overriding necessity to organize for ending the war in

Vietnam, this tactic would reduce the antiwar movement to a moralistic fringe.

Therefore, in this election it seems to me that political efforts to stop the war must be directed toward one of the two major parties—or both.

Between now and the Democratic convention there is no question in my mind that Senator Eugene McCarthy's campaign provides the most effective way of challenging administration policy. McCarthy has a position in favor of negotiations that might both win the support of the majority of the American people and actually provide the basis for ending the Vietnamese agony. His efforts are concentrated in the party that already commands the allegiance of those who are concerned both about Vietnam and about social change in America.

I certainly wish McCarthy's record on several domestic issues were better than it is, but the fact that he provides a rallying point for effective antiwar sentiment is a much greater contribution to the cause of domestic transformation than a perfect voting record in the past. For Vietnam, once again, is the determinant of our domestic possibilities as well as a hideous event in its own right. The McCarthy style has been much criticized, and I am not sure on that count who is right: perhaps an understated approach may produce more lasting eloquence than the flamboyant psychodramas that some of McCarthy's critics on the left demand. But in any case, Eugene McCarthy is the only Democrat who, at this writing, has taken a courageous and audacious stand against the war in the form of a direct challenge to the president. That makes up my mind.

McCarthy, I assume, will not win the nomination. But if his movement can command significant, committed minority support within the Democratic party, it will provide the most effective way of registering antiwar protest. Lyndon Johnson will hear about such strength; so will the Republican party.

But the Democratic party will nominate Johnson. What then? At that point it will be necessary to follow a rigorous lesser-evilism that, in most cases, will point to an emotionally unsatisfying, and even repugnant, vote. For the claims of the suffering people of Vietnam and the threat of World War III posed by a continuation of that war are so urgent that gestures that are merely moral become immoral.

In a contest between Lyndon Johnson and a Republican superhawk (Ronald Reagan certainly, Richard Nixon possibly), I would vote for Johnson on lesser-evil grounds. It has been somewhat fashionable in recent years for opponents of the war to apologize for voting for Johnson in 1964 because he turned out to be a Goldwaterite on Vietnam. I make no such apology. Johnson was, and is, a lesser evil than Goldwater on Vietnam and, in comparison, a positive good when it comes to domestic questions. For all of my anger at Johnson's violation of his campaign promise of '64, for all my suspicions that he was planning escalation even as he talked peace, he has not yet turned over the conduct of the war to the Joint Chiefs of Staff. Perhaps he will do so in the future. But Goldwater, I am convinced, would have done it four years ago. And Reagan would do it next January, and perhaps Nixon would. And since I believe the Joint Chiefs are, whether wittingly or not, objectively advocates of World War III, I would vote for Johnson as against a superhawk.

If a Republican dove ran against Johnson, or even a somewhat dovish Republican who was trying to take advantage of the popular antiwar sentiment, I would, with great reluctance, vote for him. I say this even though I am convinced that the election of any Republican, no matter how liberal, would further conservatize the Congress. For the Republican party is certainly going to be to the right of any of its doves, and the coattail effect that always takes place in presidential years would be reactionary in this case. But, once again, four more years of Johnson's war policy would have an even more rightward effect than would be produced by a dove Republican with a conservative Congress.

Moreover, I am convinced that one of the main reasons that Johnson does not really seek negotiations (I believe that every one of his peace offers has announced American willingness to accept a Vietcong surrender in one form or another) is that once they are concluded he will have to explain why he spent all that blood and treasure on the venture. And since a political settlement of the war will inevitably involve concessions to the National Liberation Front, Johnson cannot find a rationale that would justify the high human and material price of his policy. Therefore, I believe that a Republican dove, even a somewhat opportunistic one, would be able to end the war where Johnson could not.

But if the choice is between the president and a merely hawkish, but not superhawkish, Nixon, I would vote for Johnson on the grounds that he is clearly to be preferred on domestic questions. At the same time, I would make it quite clear that this eventuality strikes me as a failure of the democratic system—that at a moment of high peril and profound issues there is no significant choice with regard to the fate of the nation and of the world as it is posed in Vietnam. For there would be no serious way to vote effectively for an end to the war.

Finally, a few general comments: I assume that the foregoing is as depressing to read as it was to write. Yet I think it important, even in these rather dark days, not to jump to apocalyptic conclusions as some on the left have done. There are, for instance, those who think that democracy has broken down because they have not been able to persuade a majority to agree with an antiwar position. Now, this may well show that the democratic majority is capable of being tragically wrong under certain conditions. But it does not prove that there are no longer ways of changing men's minds and creating new majorities. Therefore one must insist, and particularly to the young in these disenchanting times, that the struggle is going to be a long one, that it might conceivably even be lost, but that it is by no means over yet.

So if a certain conservatism of American social structure and political habit results, in one way or another, in an endorsement of this terrible war, it is hardly the moment to flee into revolutionary fantasies in which the poor misguided people are really radical if only they'd listen to the spokesmen of their true interest. Neither is it a time for withdrawal, either into a hippie ghetto or into a suburban inwardness.

There are congressional and senatorial elections of enormous moment on the ballot and, should the Wallace candidacy succeed in winning a balance of power for segregation, it would be of great importance. Even if the most obscene consequences of the Wallace tactic do not come to pass, there is still the battle over social legislation. Therefore, it seems to me that, no matter what an opponent of the war might decide to do on the presidential line, it is of the utmost urgency to participate in all of the other campaigns where there are significant choices. For eventually, once this war is over, there must be a new majority in America and it will number in its ranks those who now differ on the war. That is why it is so important to seek to end the war in such a way as to make it possible to win the peace: that there will never be another Vietnam; that there will be a new America.

# 16
# Straight Lesser-Evilism

*Dissent, 1968*

After having participated in the dynamic mass movements of the new politics in 1968—both the Kennedy and McCarthy campaigns—I intend to vote for a candidate of the old politics, Hubert Humphrey, even though his nomination was a triumph of the machine over the political realignment that I have worked for in recent years.

Humphrey's position on the most decisive issue of the year, Vietnam, is unconscionable. He has either been the enthusiastic booster of the horror in Southeast Asia, or else the vacillator hinting, but never quite saying, that he is a dove in hawk's clothing. On the other main question in the election, "law and order" (otherwise known as "get the blacks, hippies, and welfare chiselers"), the vice-president had shamelessly kind words for Mayor Daley after the police lawlessness in Chicago; and his support of the war precludes him from proposing the massive social programs that are an alternative to the nightstick.

In terms of political structures, Humphrey won the nomination by relying on moderate racists, the machines, and, alas, most of the labor movement. In the process, he managed to turn back a youthful reform surge that is the most exciting, and perhaps most significant, thing to have happened in American politics since the industrial workers of the CIO became an electoral force in the thirties.

The previous paragraphs do not exactly constitute a positive endorsement of Humphrey. My reason for casting a ballot for the vice-president is, of course, straight lesser-evilism. Where there is a difference between presidential candidates, and where a protest or third-party strategy can neither affect the present choices nor even prepare for decent options in the future, I believe there is a moral obligation to vote for the better man even though he inspires no confidence. In 1968, the middle-class puritan who refuses to soil his hands in this way is helping to condemn the American people—and particularly the black, the poor, and the young—to four years of Richard Nixon. Hubert Humphrey is clearly preferable.

In making this argument, I do not base it upon a virulent personal antipathy to Nixon. I am appalled by the sorry history of Tricky Dicky over the years, and I am hardly comforted by the soulless, opportunistic technician who proclaims himself to be the "new" Nixon. But my position is not primarily based on such personal, visceral considerations. Nixon is the political incarnation of a drift to the right. If he becomes president, it will legitimate the forces of repression, including the police militants. Moreover, a Nixon victory would result in a Congress even more reactionary than the present one.

Even if Nixon's economic policies are only as bad as Eisenhower's, the resultant stagnation, unemployment, and poverty will either provoke minority risings and majority terror or else it will drive tens of millions of Americans into a passive, nihilistic, corrosive despair. If, as I think likely (since the Republican party of 1968 is to the right of 1952's), Nixon's domestic leadership will be even more catastrophic than Ike's, the situation will be worse.

On the most crucial issue of the day, Vietnam, Nixon is the institutional leader of the Cold War party. Given the fact that the

Soviet imperialist crime in Czechoslovakia has strengthened the American hawks, this could have consequences well beyond Southeast Asia.

However, there is one outcome of the election even more disastrous than a clear-cut Nixon victory: an ambiguous Nixon triumph in the House of Representatives in which the presidency is won through a deal with the Wallaceite South. For Wallace is the nearest thing to a genuine American fascist since the days of Father Coughlin; i.e., he has a demagogic social appeal as well as the mentality of a prison guard. If his racist politics make a significant showing outside the South—and particularly among union members—that would be a blow to every democratic hope.

It is, therefore, impossible to say Tweedledum/Tweedledee. And it is reprehensible and idiotic to advocate a policy that puts the Right in power on the grounds that the consequent repression will "radicalize" its victims. In the first place, that is inhuman and manipulative, and vulture politics; in the second, it doesn't work —as the ghosts of the German Communists of 1932–33 can attest.

But having made a rather depressing argument for my Humphrey vote, let me conclude these remarks on something of an upbeat. The Kennedy-McCarthy forces managed to win about one-third of the Democratic convention in a campaign of nine months' duration. Indeed, they had achieved such a momentum that, had there been any alternative candidate not named McCarthy or McGovern, the delegates at Chicago probably would have nominated him rather than the vice-president. But that alternative did not exist.

I do not think that this phenomenon is confined to "kids" or is transitory. It reflects the growth of a college-educated constituency in which quantitative expansion may well have turned into something qualitatively new: a mass base for "conscience politics." If that movement retains a certain cohesiveness, if it eschews fourth-party adventures and self-righteous gestures and concentrates on assembling a new majority in the mainstream, I think it can transform American politics.

# PART 6

# 17
# Dee-Sock

In 1973, about two hundred socialists, veterans of a grueling faction fight in the Socialist Party over the war in Vietnam—we fought a majority that took George Meany's interventionist line in that horrible conflict—started a new organization. It was called the Democratic Socialist Organizing Committee and its nickname was an imaginative reading of the acronym, DSOC: "Dee-Sock."

At the founding convention I delivered a keynote speech that had been circulated to, and been approved by, most of the two hundred. We wanted, we said, to put an end to the divisions of the sixties. There was no reason for people to perpetuate organizational differences that were determined by what should have been done in the past. If democratic socialists agreed on the present and the immediate future, they should join together and then discuss their old quarrels over a beer after the demonstration or the day's political campaign was over.

We had exceedingly modest expectations for ourselves. We had decided to begin anew in the period right before and after the McGovern defeat of 1972 and we anticipated that the immediate future would be dominated by reaction. We did not, of course, know that Watergate would interrupt, and muddle, the trends. We thought that we would succeed if we managed simply to survive. We were then pleasantly surprised when we grew from 200 to about 5,000 members in 1982.

When we started DSOC, one of the most distinctive things about us was that we were committed to coalition politics and electoral work in the liberal-labor wing of the Democratic party. The dream of a homogenous "proletariat"—be it the traditional working class, or the underclass of the minorities and the poor that some of the radicals of the sixties had seen as the new agency of radical change—was abandoned. We understood that within the context of late capitalist American society the Left would have to take on a prosaic, extremely difficult job: to unify labor and minorities and women and environmentalists and peace activists and all of the rest of the progressive constituencies. Together they might prevail; fighting one another they would lose.

That was easier said than done. Environmentalists, for instance, sometimes simply said, "Shut down the polluting plant!" without giving a thought to the workers who would lose their jobs as a result. And there were unions so concerned to keep those jobs that they allied themselves with management in fighting against valid environmental demands, some of them actually designed to protect the health of their own members. We tried to make ourselves a bridge, to talk of union concerns in the environmental movement and of environmentalism in the unions, to seek a common ground.

For the majority of the Left in 1973, our notion of building such coalitions in the Democratic party was rank heresy, a sellout to a "bourgeois" institution that contained many racists, sexists, union busters, corporate lobbyists, hawks, and every other species of reactionary. Yes, we said, right-wingers are in the Democratic party—but so is the entire politically organized American labor movement, 90 percent of the blacks and 75 percent of the Latinos, the best of the feminists and the antiwar activists, and so on. We were, we said, on the "Left wing of the possible."

We enjoyed a modest success, recruiting trade unionists and Democratic party activists, developing dynamic groups centered on socialism and feminism and socialism and religion. In 1978, Democratic Agenda, a liberal-left coalition focused on programmatic issues in the Democratic party that had been initiated by DSOC, persuaded 40 percent of the delegates at the Democratic party midterm to vote against the budget cuts of Jimmy Carter, an incumbent Democratic president. And in 1982, when DSOC merged with the New American Movement, the main organization to survive from the New Left of the sixties, we did in fact help to liquidate the heritage of backbiting on the left, that goal we had identified nine years before.

The new, merged organization is called Democratic Socialists of America. It counts between 7,000 and 8,000 members, and perhaps 1,000 of them are activists regularly committed to the work of the group. It is a chastened boast to write that it is the largest democratic socialist movement in the United States in fifty years. But DSA is also a refraction of social history with an importance out of proportion to its numbers.

It is one of the worst ironies of socialist history that a movement that seeks to create a society of sisterhood and brotherhood, of genuine community with a profound respect for differences, has been, more often than not, intolerant, unsisterly, unbrotherly, consumed by internal hatreds. Perhaps the greatest single accomplishment of DSA is that it has brought together people who, not too long ago, would not talk to one another and would even find it difficult to be in the same room. There are deeply committed anti-Stalinists and former Communists who have become democratic socialists but refuse—rightly, I think—to simply denounce their past; there are Zionists and people quite critical of Israel; unabashed Fabians and unabashed democratic Marxists; and so on. Of enormous importance, there is an extremely strong feminist contingent and an active gay and lesbian group. These 1960-ish social movements do not simply introduce a new politics into American socialism; they bring with them a way of looking at the personal implications of the political, a sensitivity to style. Machismo, they correctly say, is not simply a characteristic of individual males; it is a cultural, political, military dimension of the society as well.

So we created a nicer socialist organization than had ever been. But what about the pretensions in the chapter that follows, published in *The Nation* in the mid-seventies? How does my insistence that one take sides for socialism hold up?

The crisis I defined in this article is still in progress. Moreover, there has been a radical political response to it in the mainstream of American life, just as I said there would be. Only the radical who leads it is Ronald Reagan, a man who was willing to make innovative—cruel, ultimately unworkable—departures in economic and social policy.

I will not repeat my critique of Reagan here for it is spelled out in some detail in the essay on the crisis of French Socialism in chapter 22. I will simply reassert my conviction that there is a future for American socialism, that it is relevant to these times.

My hopes are extremely modest. I see no possibility that socialists will play a major role in leading a mass movement in the foreseeable future. What I do envision is that the collapse of the Reagan economic recovery—when, and how profound, that crisis will be, neither I nor anyone else knows—will once again put the issue of alternative policies on the agenda. The traditional liberalism that ruled in the Democratic party from Roosevelt to Carter is not, I think, capable of responding to the structural transformation of the world economy that we are living through. There could be new solutions in the center—top down, technocratic planning, for instance—but there will be a need for, and a relevance of, the ideas of the democratic Left in general and its socialist wing in particular.

Generals, the cliché says, always fight the last war. And there is no question that I am deeply marked by the experience of the sixties when there was a new, and powerful, surge to the left but no older generation with the capacity to give it some sense of continuity and tradition. So the wheel was reinvented, sometimes well, sometimes badly. But this time when history turns the corner—and I am deeply convinced that it will—there will be an organization that just may be able to help give a greater focus, a greater effectiveness, to the new energies.

The ideal remains as it was in this article: to take socialism from the margin of the society and to make it a factor in the mainstream; to broaden the political discourse for all Americans by helping this nation discover solutions that are a commonplace in every other advanced industrial democracy and still anathema here.

# 18
# Say What You Mean—Socialism

*The Nation, 1974*

What attitude should liberals take toward radical, structural change? Should they stick to their eminently pragmatic and very successful tradition and focus upon serious increments of reform while refusing to generalize about historic epochs and social systems? Or should they make a new departure and speak in terms of alternate forms of society, of socialism as against capitalism?

I have been putting these questions to liberals for a good twenty years, suggesting that it is time for them to consider the transformation of the system rather than its improvement. I have not, I am afraid, persuaded nearly enough people. But now events are posing the same issue, and if it is possible to ignore a socialist intellectual argument, it is rather difficult to overlook an energy crisis, or some other tumultuous happening, that shatters the peace and quiet of the status quo. So there is now some hope that America will finally grow up and join all the other advanced industrial democracies in which discussion of socialism is a commonplace.

I noticed this hopeful tendency during the height of the energy consciousness last winter. Academic friends who had regarded my own socialist commitment as an idiosyncrasy began to say that perhaps the economic system itself had something to do with the catastrophe. Small wonder. For a few brief months the disastrous consequences of the normal state of affairs in the United States—that the government follows the priorities of the corporations, with expensive, antisocial results—were writ large on the very surface of everyday experience.

To be sure, people tried to forget the energy crisis the minute the waiting lines vanished from the gas pump. As soon as the OPEC embargo was over, the nation tried to pretend that the winter of its oil discontent had never happened. The difficulty is that the issue will not go away. Assuming the most reassuring of projections—that everyone can get plenty of gas at the corner station (which is not at all certain for even the immediate future) —$50 billion will flow from the affluent West to the OPEC powers this year, a fact that establishment organs like *The Economist* of London understand will change the whole world market. There are possibilities of both recession and further inflation in that incredible transfer of funds, and the $9 billion loss imposed upon the Third World as a result of higher energy prices this year is certain to exacerbate the danger of famine.

So let us assume, as realistically we must, that the United States will continue to be reminded of the perverseness of its economic system, not by clever socialist insights but by brutal economic and social facts. In that context, is there a serious political possibility that American liberalism might be forced (as British liberalism was in the early part of the century) to consider basic alternatives to the fundamental structure of this society? And if so, how is that promising development to be encouraged?

Before turning to that specific political issue, let me be a bit more precise about the late capitalist system in America by making a very summary analysis of the energy crisis, which has been forcing some people to think about the issue. Our plight is not primarily the result of the Yom Kippur War and the OPEC boycott that followed upon it. It stems, rather, from the federal socialization of private, corporate goals in the oil industry. In 1950, as part of the anti-Communist strategy in the Middle East, the

National Security Council and the Treasury Department secretly decided to allow the American companies to deduct 100 percent of the taxes they paid to oil-producing powers from their American taxes. This was better than twice the deduction that a normal corporation received; it meant that the industry and the oil-rich governments could raise taxes per barrel and send the bill to the American taxpayer; it laid the basis for a collusive relationship—at first utterly dominated by the companies; now much less so—between the OPEC nations and the oil giants.

President Eisenhower climaxed a generation of oil *dirigisme* in 1959 by imposing oil import quotas. In the name of national defense, we effectively "drained America first" at a cost to consumers—in higher prices for protected American crude—of as much as $4 billion a year. Eisenhower initiated a federal highway program, the most momentous social measure of his administration, which helped destroy the railroads, mass transit, the orderly and planned development of urban space, and which reinforced the evils of poverty and racism in the isolated central city. The nation was thus made dependent on the increasingly expensive and increasingly efficient private car and is still paying in the neighborhood of $5 billion of federal subsidies a year for this destructive inanity. Finally, a whole series of special deductions—for depletion, intangible drilling costs, etc.—were worth billions and turned the profit-and-loss statements of the big oil companies into exercises in creative writing.

All the outrages that are so plainly visible in the energy crisis are, I would argue, to be found throughout the rest of society. The internal revenue core is a labyrinth of special privileges, providing about $80 billion in tax savings per year, mainly for the rich; all industry is dependent upon governmental management of the level of effective demand in the economy, a project that is almost always carried out by giving corporations carrots, but that rarely takes to them with a stick; and so on. This is the picture of a capitalist—or corporate collectivist—society, with a governmentally planned economy maximizing the interests of wealthy individuals and big companies.

The result is an incredible maldistribution of wealth. In 1974, so Nixon's Council of Economic Advisers told us this year, the lowest 20 percent of American families received 5.4 percent of the national income; the top 5 percent got 15.9 percent. That was a slight rise at the bottom (0.3 percent) and a slight decrease at the top (1.6 percent) but even that token redistribution falsifies the reality, because the figures omit the imputed rental value of owner-occupied homes and capital gains. A more accurate and shocking computation is the analysis of the distribution of wealth included in the government's recently published Social Indicators. Though the figures date from 1962, there is not the slightest reason to think that there has been any substantial improvement. We are told that the bottom fifth of America owns 0.2 percent of the wealth, while the top fifth owns 76 percent. That means that the top fifth possesses three times as much as the other four-fifths!

I have cited these figures and made my summary comments on the energy crisis to stress two propositions: the federal intervention into the economy is ordinarily antisocial because it follows corporate priorities; this intervention results in a continual and probably increasing maldistribution of wealth. On both counts, there are reasons to believe that something is radically wrong with the system itself. It is true, as Marx pointed out, that modes of production do not simply produce goods and services but also perpetuate themselves and their social relationships. That was bad enough when it took place in a relatively laissez-faire economy of the nineteenth century (the model of capitalism in *Das Kapital* is roughly the same one to be found in *The Wealth of Nations*); it is much more intolerable when such oligarchic results are carefully promoted by the power and technology of the democratic state.

Moreover, if my version of the American reality is accurate, the consequences for the liberal approach to reform are serious. For the long-range tendency of the system is antiliberal, and that means that after every surge of social creativity—say the New Deal of the 1930s or the Great Society of the 1960s—the forces of the old order flow into and dominate the new institutions and turn them to their own purposes. Thus Richard Nixon, the onetime free marketeer, is now a Keynesian president who has used wage and price controls (to benefit the rich), run the highest peacetime deficits in our history, and in general employed liberal techniques for conservative ends. The serious pursuit of liberal aims requires that one go beyond liberalism.

All this, I submit, has been objectively true for some time. Now, however, it may be becoming subjectively obvious. That is why it is particularly important to probe the resistance, not simply of American society or of its corporate rulers, but of liberalism itself to a philosophy of structural change—i.e., toward what everyone else in the world rightly calls socialism. Putting aside for a moment the obvious antisocialists (businessmen, big and small, and all those under their ideological influence), I call attention to a paradox: if one examines the official positions of Americans for Democratic Action, or the New Democratic Coalition's statement of principles in 1972, they are seen to be socialist in all respects save one—they do not mention socialism. They are for the redistribution of wealth, for government intervention on behalf of the poor, minorities, and working people, and for the extension of public ownership. Why is it, if these liberal organizations urge essentially social democratic programs, that they have so steadfastly refused any social democratic identification? And, much more to the point, does the use of the term "socialist" make any difference at all? Why bother with nineteenth-century nomenclature if the late twentieth-century substance is satisfactory?

First of all, why do the best of liberals advocate socialist programs that do not speak their own name? The obvious and compelling answer is politics. In America, with the exception of a few unusual constituencies, the socialist label is a hindrance in mainstream electoral politics. Socialism is associated in the popular mind with totalitarianism, foreign ideology, atheism. These associations are not true, but unfortunately truth, particularly complicated truth, is no defense in a political struggle. Therefore, the extremely difficult question that must be answered before one can seriously propose to introduce the idea of socialism into American life is: Why should any candidate take the risk? If it is possible to campaign for socialist ideas, as long as they are not so described, why bother with the idea of socialism?

American business supplies the beginnings of an answer. It

has taken the idea of socialism with dead seriousness over the past three-quarters of a century, investing considerable time and money to repulse an ideology that never achieved more than 6 percent of the presidential vote. Why did the corporations bother so much about the label? In part because businessmen, for all their pride in their pragmatism, are among the most dogmatic ideologues to be found in the nation. Even as sophisticated, informed, and empirical a paper as the *Wall Street Journal* becomes in its editorials absolutely metaphysical in its devotion to the free-market panacea. The Committee for Economic Development is much more shrewd and worldly than the National Association of Manufacturers—that is the difference between the haute and petite bourgeoisie—but I suspect that even the magnates of the CED dream of those marvelous supply-and-demand curves intersecting in a Newtonian, frictionless space to assure the most efficient allocation of resources and happiness. In short, one reason for the antisocialism of big business is sincerity.

But there is another, more cynical, reason. Antisocialism is an extremely effective weapon for opposing liberal reform, and that has been its realistic political function for generations. Norman Thomas used to tell of the Chicago ward boss in the 1930s who gathered his precinct workers together. "Do you remember," the boss said, "that we told you last year that Social Security is socialistic and we are against it?" They did. "Well, we're for it now. It isn't socialistic anymore." In the 1970s that ward boss metamorphosed into Richard Nixon, the Keynesian, the proponent of a guaranteed annual income, the advocate of a form—the cheapest, most private-sector-oriented form, to be sure, but a form, nevertheless—of national health insurance, and so on. Policies that he would have denounced as "socialistic" when he came to Congress in the mid-1940s were now part of dynamic free enterprise.

The point is that as long as the antisocialist prejudice is widespread it is an effective barrier to incremental reform. It is not an accident that the Tennessee Valley Authority has never been imitated, though, despite its environmental sins, it is an obvious success. All of that fantasy so expensively and assiduously promoted by the business-owned and -operated power companies—all that antisocialism—had its effect. Indeed, Senator Adlai Stevenson's proposed federal gas and oil corporation, based on the TVA model, was introduced with the specific disclaimer that its sponsor remained absolutely loyal to the American economic system meaning: to the American economic myth.

American antisocialism also helps create self-fulfilling prophecies that are extremely useful to the conservative cause. If the public is persuaded that the private sector, with its managed desires, its built-in obsolescence, its enormous, unpaid social costs, is the realm of freedom, the politicians will see to it that the public sector is as underfinanced and shoddy as possible. Which, of course, then proves that the public sector is bad, the private sector good. So, when there is a desperate need to expand the public sector—as there is now in the energy industry—we may be sure that the nation will not act, or that, at best, it will act in a timid fashion calculated to give the edge, and even the control, of the public undertaking to the private sector.

So liberals have a very real interest in making the rational discussion of socialism possible in the mainstream of the society; for until that is done liberal reform will be crippled and even blocked. Furthermore, if it is true, as I believe, that this society is being forced willy-nilly to structural change, the persistence of antisocialism in the major parties will guarantee that the nation will either not respond to the challenge or will do so on terms dictated by the corporate ideologies. Only those structural changes will be allowed that are certified as non- or antisocialist, as in the case of Nixon's use of "Left" techniques for "Right" purposes. Thus, even though a liberal organization can propose (though not enact) many of the individual components of a socialist program, the basic animating spirit that must accompany each of those components—that there must be a fundamental change in the distribution of wealth, in the mode of economic decision-making and in the very character of our dominant corporate institutions: in short, a wholesale democratization of economic power—will be lacking.

In sum, it is a bitter fact of late-twentieth-century life that socialist ideas without the idea of socialism can be, have been, and will be used for reactionary purposes. As the energy crisis, the specter of famine in the poor parts of the globe, and all the other basic, structural issues rush in upon us, it is of utmost importance that there be a response as powerful and integrated as the problems that provoke it. That could mean employing Left techniques for Right purposes; but it could, and should, mean socialism.

But how, then, can this last possibility be made political in the America of the mid-1970s?

One cannot begin by either converting or defeating incumbent liberal politicians. The same reason applies in both cases: in the absence of a mass socialist consciousness in the electorate (or, more precisely, given an anti-Soviet consciousness), practical politicians will not make themselves vulnerable by proclaiming themselves socialist, and insurgents flying the socialist banner will not defeat them. The most that a socialist campaign will achieve under such circumstances is to give aid and comfort to the conservative opponents. Thus the crucial issue at this point is, How can we change the circumstances that limit our options so severely?

In saying this, I do not for a moment urge a nonelectoral approach to the building of socialist consciousness—to community organization, or mass education, as counterposed to political campaign involvement. The first way in which the intolerable circumstances can be changed is for socialists to participate alongside liberals in their common struggle for immediate reform. That is easy enough, particularly since so many liberal demands are, as I have already noted, quite socialist in content. In the course of that joint effort, what socialists must stress is the necessity that an idea of socialism should animate and radicalize all those socialist ideas.

This, clearly, is going to be done in the liberal wing of the Democratic party, which, for better or for worse, is the home of the mass Left in America. At present, all that can be done is to create a very modest socialist presence within the Democrats: open, candid, self-avowed, nothing like boring from within. And, rather obviously, the difficulty here will be to define socialism as a legitimate tendency within the mainstream of American politics.

That does not mean proposing that the Democratic party become socialist, which it is not in the least ready to do, but insisting that socialists have a role in helping to make it consistently liberal, an idea whose time has more than come.

In the process, the socialist Left will have to break completely with some of its most cherished sectarianisms. More often than not, American socialism saw liberalism as its immediate enemy, as the program for crumbs that kept people from demanding the whole loaf. In breaking with this tradition, I think the argument for American socialism must be made in specifically American terms, i.e., with the understanding that any possibility for mass socialist consciousness must emerge out of the present liberal consciousness. Socialism must, therefore, be put as a logical next step for liberalism, indeed as the only way to assure the actual achievement of liberal values. That is not only good rhetorical strategy; it also accurately describes the only way socialism can possibly become a serious political movement in America.

And there are reasons for hope. George Meany, Pat Gorman of the Meat Cutters, the Minnesota AFL-CIO, and other influential labor figures and organizations have been talking openly of the possibility of nationalizing the energy industry. The liberal organizations have moved a long way programmatically in the direction of socialist ideas. The women's movement is developing a consciousness of its need to confront basic economic issues, a fact symbolized by the impressive beginning of the Coalition of Labor Union Women and by NOW's boycott and other activities on the job front. And although students are not joining any organizations these days, there is a considerable residue of Left ideas from the 1960s.

The question is, will there emerge a socialist Left capable of seizing these opportunities? In helping to organize the Democratic Socialist Organizing Committee around the strategy described in this article, I have tried to build a positive answer to my own question. For we cannot repeat the experience of the 1930s. American socialism emerged from the catastrophic collapse of the capitalist system weaker than ever before, and not the least because of its sectarianism. American communism made real gains, in considerable measure because the Popular Front tactic decreed in Moscow forced it to adopt the kind of approach to liberalism that I have described here. But then in 1945 the Communists were ordered to smash all the progress they had made, and they both obeyed and succeeded.

Is it now possible for a new American socialism to arise, a movement that can speak the genuine accents of this country and find a place within its mass Left? It is urgent and necessary. And, yes, it is even possible.

# PART 7

# 19
# The Corporate Mouse

In the fall of 1982, the NBC "Today" show flew me to Orlando, Florida, to participate in a telecast that originated from the EPCOT center at Disney World. On the morning of the show, they had set up an entire broadcasting center on the shores of one of EPCOT's lakes; there was a blimp overhead for the panoramic shots; and I was told at the last moment that I had been upgraded from four to four and a half minutes. The producers were afraid that their program would simply be one long ad for the new Disney enterprise and they were anxious to have a few voices of protest. Since I was, to the delight of my children, a Disney World expert, I was an obvious choice.

I had been concerned about the social implications of great art, almost from the very first, but it was those listening trips around the United States that began to sensitize me to the consequences of popular culture. When I first went to Disney World—as a father and tourist, not as a social thinker—I liked the place very much as an amusement park. So did my kids. I thought that the history and the politics acted out on its stages and in its exhibits—which were sentimentally liberal, even though Walt Disney was a conservative—were so much hokum.

But then I became aware of the futuristic technology that undergirded the banal model of a nineteenth-century American town. My original reaction was very positive. Socialists have been asked for generations, "Who is going to collect the garbage in the good society?" That was supposed to confront us with an unanswerable objection: that there would still be dirty work and alienation in the best of all possible worlds. But after the experience with Disney World I gleefully told audiences that the mouseketeers in Florida had found the solution to that socialist problem.

So it was that when I proposed writing on Disney World to Lewis Lapham at *Harper's*, I intended to do a positive piece. In part, the hospitality of the Disney World publicity staff was less than overwhelming, in part I began to think more seriously about . . . an amusement park. And gradually, Disney World turned into a symbol—a compelling symbol, I think—of the all pervasiveness of corporate logic in American society as it becomes a technique for organizing hokey old-fashioned ice cream parlors as well as for the creation of multinational corporations. I took sides against Mickey Mouse's keepers.

Indeed, the thinking in this article points directly toward the next chapters: the problem of socialists making a transition toward the new in a society that is still dominated by the old. For if even "theme parks" are big business—and in 1984, the Disney organization was the subject of a very serious takeover attempt in which the raiders put up millions to get control of the enterprise, and forced management to buy up its own stock in defense, a tactic promptly dubbed "Greenmail"—where is the Archimedean point, the noncapitalist space for socialist leverage, in Western society? That thought, suggested by the offspring of Mickey Mouse in Orlando, Florida, is relevant to the problems of François Mitterrand and the French socialists, as chapter 22 will show.

Rereading my analysis in 1984, I also felt a sense of schadenfreude. I had attacked the ideology of "capital shortage" so assiduously propagated by Chase Manhattan and William Simon in the 1970s. I did not know how right I was. For, it now turns out, at the very moment that they were lamenting the lack of capital for all of the very wonderful investments they wanted to make in the United States, they were so awash in recycled OPEC money that they were going on the irresponsible lending binge in the Third World that led to the crisis of the world financial system in the early eighties.

In short, I think I learned some significant lessons from the corporate mouse.

# 20
# To the Disney Station

*Harper's, 1979*

## Corporate Socialism in the Magic Kingdom

On October 1, 1978, the president of the United States and the secretary-general of the United Nations met to discuss war and peace in the Middle East; later in the afternoon they went to an amusement park for what the *Miami Herald* described as "an economic summit for private enterprise."

Jimmy Carter stood before Cinderella's Castle, the turreted fantasy-come-true that overlooks the 2,700-acre "Magic Kingdom" built by Walt Disney and his heirs in central Florida. He told the 2,500 businessmen who had come there for the 26th Congress of the International Chamber of Commerce (the first such gathering not held in a capital city) of his deep capitalist faith. Then, whimsically referring to one of the nearby theme parks, the president remarked, "I looked forward to seeing Fantasyland because it is the source of inspiration for my economic advisers."

The artificiality of the event no doubt was familiar to the president's audience. Hoopla. Photo Opportunities. Free-Enterprise Ritual. Obligatory Presidential Wit. Even an Amy

Story. The president was turning fifty-four in Florida, and he had phoned his daughter to tell her that they would be celebrating the birthday of one of "the world's greatest and most admired leaders." "Yes, I know, Daddy," she had said. "This is Mickey Mouse's fiftieth birthday."

On reading the accounts of this spectacle I couldn't help thinking that the president had found the appropriate forum in which to present his vision of the American future. Disney World is a corporate utopia, a pretentious and socially conscious fun house that, for all of its evident superficiality, embodies the current dream of American business. Moreover, Carter explicitly identified himself with that dream in his speech, to the extent that it seemed to me plausible that when he described Fantasyland as "the source of inspiration for my economic advisers" he was only half joking. That is why I propose to take Disney's capitalist fairy tale seriously. It is possible that Amy is not the only citizen in the White House who believes in Mickey Mouse.

At first glance, Disney World seems to have nothing to do with politics. It is a sophisticated and frivolous carnival that has been seen and enjoyed by more than eighty million people since 1971. The rides and attractions delight adults—who make up two-thirds of the crowd—as well as children. Who by now is not familiar with at least the photographs of a fraudulently neat Main Street, with an ice cream parlor, a silent movie, and horse-drawn cars followed by sanitation workers plodding ever onward toward Cinderella's Castle and then to Adventureland, Frontierland, Fantasyland, and Tomorrowland?

The less obvious aspects of Disney World are not so easy to see, yet they have been discovered by a fair number of thoughtful observers who have come to admire the futuristic technology, the air-conditioned, electric-powered Monorail that silently circles the place, and the trash disposal system that sucks refuse through underground tubes at sixty miles an hour to a central disposal point. This is the Disney World that captivated Peter Blake, the architecture critic, and James Rouse, the creator of a new city in Maryland. As a German commentator, Dankwart Grube, last year put this socially conscious interpretation of Disney World, "German builders, architects, and, above all, city planners should be forced, in chains if need be, to find out from the Mickey Mouse people how one can create an 'environment' in which laughter flourishes and well-being is produced."

Mr. Carter and the International Chamber also had a chance to see this second Disney World. As the president finished his speech a tropical rain began to fall on the buglers in medieval costume who were playing "Hail to the Chief." Carter retreated into Cinderella's Castle, and, the *Economist* of London reported, "2,500 tycoons were saved from pneumonia by the incredible instant efficiency of the young people who do the work in Disney's fantasyland."

The *Economist* is usually reserved, even dyspeptic, in such matters, and it did note that the presidential address was a speech of "monumental wetness." Even so, the magazine was deeply impressed by the automation and crime prevention, and concluded, "If Mickey Mouse were everywhere elected mayor, the efficiency of local government round the world would rise by several hundred per cent." This Disney World of the city planners does indeed exist and it even has a humane potential, as we will see. But it is a much more ambiguous vision than most of its devotees realize. Perhaps this is because the technological Disney World is encapsulated within the invisible structure of a corporate utopia. The "Magic Kingdom" is designed by "Imagineers"—as Disney Speak calls them—who construct escapist diversions on computers programmed according to a sophisticated calculus of profit. They aim at nothing less than the total control of a physical and human environment of forty-three square miles, which is twice the area of Manhattan. Toward that end, they have banished politics, competition, and excessive individualism from their monopolist's Shangri-la, thus fulfilling the daydream of the American boardroom. In their more ecstatic moments they persuade themselves that their fun-filled Brave New World is, and will be, an Experimental Prototype Community of Tomorrow (EPCOT in Disney Speak).

This, of course, is a fairy tale, and yet, if that gingerbread

Main Street does not really lead into the twenty-first century, as its designers believe, it does embody one of the most powerful desires of the late seventies: that it is possible to reach apolitical, anti-intellectual, corporate, and technocratic solutions to the problems of society. Faced with a simultaneous inflation and recession that none of the established theories can deal with, reading the reports of tax revolts from California and elsewhere, the president of the United States is turning into a born-again free entrepreneur.* It was perfectly appropriate that he should give witness to this faith in front of Cinderella's Castle, which is one of its cathedrals.

## Cleanliness and Control

Let us begin with the life of the saint. Walt Disney's formative years were spent, predictably enough, on a farm near a small Missouri town with a real-life Main Street. He moved to California and, after a number of vicissitudes—including a fight with Eastern bankers who took his first cartoon character away from him—established himself as a leading Hollywood artist. Success came—but so did a union movement that shattered the paternal calm of the Disney Studios. In 1941, Disney faced a picket line with signs asking, "Are We Mice or Men?" Bitter and disillusioned, he became more conservative. During the forties, he was involved in the Motion Picture Alliance for the Preservation of American Ideals, a center for blacklisters and the rest of the Hollywood Right. Later on, in 1964, when Disney received the Medal of Freedom from Lyndon Johnson, he wore a Goldwater button in his lapel.

In 1948 Disney began to dream of a new kind of amusement

*Carter is not, as George Meany says, more conservative than any other modern president except Calvin Coolidge. He is, for example, obviously more liberal than Gerald Ford. But that leaves room for regression. Carter's notion that a balanced budget and a fixed federal percentage of Gross National Product can be set years in advance and adhered to no matter what happens in the economy is pre-Keynesian fundamentalism.

park. Facing financial difficulties, he borrowed against his life insurance and in 1955 opened Disneyland, in Anaheim, California. It was an instant success. But there were problems. The core of the Disneyland site was formerly an orange grove, a mere 160-acre lot. That meant that Disney could not dominate his own surroundings. "The one thing I learned from Disneyland," he was to comment later on, "was to control the environment. Without that we get blamed for the things that someone else does. When they come here [to Disney World] they're coming because of an integrity we've established over the years, and they drive for hundreds of miles and the little hotels on the fringe would jump their rates three times."

Control. That is the key to Disney World and the future it envisions. When Disney was working on his plans for the project, he talked, characteristically, of the need to proceed without any interference from the politicians. Embittered by his experience with Disneyland, the founder decided to insulate his new world in Florida from any outside influences. He managed to buy more than 27,000 acres, of which only 3,000 are currently developed. So competitors and parasites (which is to say, other free entrepreneurs) are kept miles away. That, however, is only the beginning of the control in Disney World. There are no peanuts in the Magic Kingdom, no chewing gum, and no cotton candy. These things are messy, and Disney didn't want them fouling up his fantasy. There are no saloons, either, even though that venerable institution played its part on some of the Main Streets of America (liquor is, however, available in the hotels on the property, and the general stores sell beer and wine). One result is that there is practically no drunken brawling and very little crime.

It was more than a little ironic that President Carter chose this setting for a denunciation of protectionism. "Hardly a week goes by," he said, "but what I have some businessman come to see me and ask for some form of protectionism while deploring the protectionism of others." This was proclaimed in a Magic Kingdom expertly and explicitly designed on the principles of a state monopoly. Walt Disney and his associates, exactly like those anti-protectionist protectionists whom Carter assailed, were, and are, deeply committed to free enterprise everywhere but in their own market. Their dominion extends beyond the economy and controls human beings as well as commodities.

The whole place is run by relentlessly smiling young people, who are, it seems to me, disproportionately blond and blue-eyed. They are uniformed in Disney designs made by Disney workers and coached as actors on a stage. Long hair and mustaches, predictably, are not allowed. So far, one could rightly say, there is nothing particularly ominous about these conditions. If Walt Disney and his heirs thought it good business to keep out chewing gum, to restrict drinking and drunks, and to hire stereotypes, what's wrong with that? Indeed, the Magic Kingdom has to be neater, cleaner, and less raucous than any amusement park for thousands of people that one could imagine.

Things become more complex as soon as one takes a few steps behind this idyllic façade. Just inside the gate of the Magic Kingdom there is a city hall. Downstairs is an information center, upstairs the publicity office. For the politicians have been banished from this kingdom, just as Disney hoped. Sovereignty resides in the Reedy Creek Improvement District. Under Florida law, an "improvement district" has no police or judicial power, but it can legislate with regard to water, building codes, and fire protection. When the planners were dealing with this problem, Disney chose the improvement district rather than a municipal charter, in part because a city would have to deal with civil rights.

So Disney World is under the police and judicial authority of the counties (Orange and Osceola) in which it is located, but in all other matters the Reedy Creek Improvement District remains sovereign. It is democratically run by the forty or fifty people who live within Disney World—all of whom are employees of the company that, in their political persona, they are supposed to regulate. The Disney people admit that this arrangement is not designed to promote adversary relationships, but they insist that Reedy Creek is truly independent of the corporation. They also note that there has never been a serious quarrel between them.

All of this comes fairly close to Disney's dream of EPCOT: "It will be a planned, controlled community, a showcase for American industry and research, schools, cultural and educational opportunities. In EPCOT there will be no slum areas because we won't let them develop. There will be no landowners and therefore no voting control. People will rent houses instead of buying them, and at modest rentals. There will be no retirees. Everyone must be employed. One of our requirements is that the people who live in EPCOT must help keep it alive."

In that statement—which is still Holy Writ in Disney World—the totalitarian character of this utopia begins to show itself. If you can invest $700 million in a domain roughly the size of Liechtenstein, and if you allow only a handful of employee-citizens to live in that corporate kingdom, then you can ban slums, retirees, and most of the rest of social reality. But what relevance, prototypical or otherwise, such an exercise has to any possible world of tomorrow is unclear. Moreover, even this attempt at utopia has not achieved the total control of which the founder dreamed.

In July, when I was last there, pickets from the Hotel and Restaurant Employees Union shuffled back and forth in front of the Royal Plaza Hotel, an inn that leases from, but is not run by, Disney World. This was the first strike within the Magic Kingdom, but, if the *Economist* is right, it may well not be the last. The "pay is low and jobs often part time," the *Economist* noted in July. "Many workers have long journeys because, although villas and tree houses have been built as well as hotels, Disney has built no low-cost housing for its employees."And the stand of the black women picketing, the *Economist* noted shrewdly, "took some courage in a place where the employer pays the police."

The hired help are not the only ones made to endure the indignities appropriate to commodities. So do the paying customers, and their plight casts some doubt upon the vaunted efficiency of the place. The Magic Kingdom has been fulsomely praised for the Monorail; its "people mover system" has been awarded a grant by the Department of Transportation. True enough, inside the park, where transportation efficiency is necessary for quick, paying circulation, things move relatively fast. But when it is a question of access to Disney World from one of the independently run hotels on the property (which are not, like the Disney-owned operations, hooked into the Monorail), there is another story. Crowded buses, sometimes with their air conditioning out of order in the middle of the humid summer, carry people from the periphery to the Magic Kingdom. Once past this inconvenience, things become easier—and also profitable for the system. At one point last July, it took me an hour to get from my hotel, on the Disney property, to the gates of the park, and the experience was reminiscent of the decaying central-city present, not of the urban future.

That same point applies to children, who, in theory at least, might be thought central to an enterprise built upon their devotion for more than half a century. That children are routinely shoved out of vantage points for the various parades by adult bullies can hardly be blamed on the Disney people. It is, after all, just the reality of American society that, for all of its stated veneration of kids, it pushes them around given half the chance. But the officials I talked to didn't seem to take a great interest in the problem or to respond to suggestions that they might take some steps to guarantee that the kids have access to what is supposed to be a kid's show. That access cannot be fed into a computer and quantified as contributing to profits; it does not, therefore, exist as a concern.

So Disney World is not a company town; it is a company state. Free of the pressures of democracy, it treats employees, customers, and children as so many pawns on the corporate game board. But isn't that just one more—vivid, perhaps bizarre—manifestation of some classic capitalist contradictions? Don't all competitors want to succeed so well as to drive out the competition, the Department of Justice to the contrary notwithstanding? And in the late sixties, American business spent $45 billion a year on advertising and other sales promotion (which was slightly less than the nation's outlays for health or education). Wouldn't every corporation like to dictate to the sovereign consumer in the name of free enterprise? Disney's only innovation, it might be argued, is that he bought enough land to make his the only voice in a tiny kingdom.

These objections, however, miss the implications of the corporate utopia in Florida. It is not just that Disney World has turned those priorities into a seemingly coherent philosophy. More to the point, that philosophy states (and anticipated) the fashionable corporate ideology of the late seventies. To be sure, that philosophy is as absurd as the idea of locating Shangri-la in a real corner of Florida rather than in the imaginary Himalayas. But these utopian themes are playing a significant part in American politics.* So I treat the pretensions of EPCOT with a provisional seriousness.

## Banning Controversy and Ideology

Let me return to the beginnings. Walt Disney was not simply a small-town boy turned successful businessman who became conservative and virulently anti-Communist when unions disrupted his paternal studio. That obviously relates to the corporate side of Disney World. But the founder was also the son of a socialist, and that, it seems to me, has something to do with his futurism and that of his disciples.

One may be quite speculative. Elias Disney was a turn-of-the-century American radical. When he and his family were living near that small Missouri town, for instance, he tried to organize the local farmers into an American Society of Equity that would focus their hatreds of the middlemen and the railroads. He voted for Debs and he read the *Appeal to Reason*, the famous radical paper published in Kansas and reaching a mass audience of the Left. And even in the thirties, not long before his death, he told his son that he was not sorry that all of the candidates for whom

*Thus the Kemp-Roth bill is a curious mixture of left-wing Keynesianism and right-wing dreams from Adam Smith. It would cut individual income taxes by one-third over a three-year period, reduce corporate levies, and count on the great surge of initiative that these incentives would incite to generate enough production to counter the inflationary impact of all that buying power. This is a utopian reliance on Adam Smithian motives in a post-Keynesian society.

he had voted had lost. "We have won," he told Walt. "We've won a lot. I've found out that things don't always come out in the way you have advocated. But you keep fighting and they come about in some way or another. Today, everything I fought for in those early days has been absorbed into the platform of both major parties. Now I feel pretty good about that."

Those sentiments are in the Norman Thomas tradition and they are hardly sinister. But there is another aspect of American socialist history that is much more ambiguous: it sometimes expresses a warmhearted, futuristic authoritarianism. That sentiment, which was completely alien to Thomas, can be seen in Edward Bellamy's *Looking Backward*, a book that was much more influential in defining socialism for many Americans of Elias Disney's generation than *Das Kapital*. It presents a neat, rational, crisis-free society with distributional justice—and without any visible democratic noise, conflict, or argument.

Was Walt Disney influenced by that misunderstanding of socialism that prepared the way in some instances for an acceptance of Stalinism? The evidence I have seen permits only a deductive guess. But the possibility is fascinating, since Disney's EPCOT is a curious mixture of planner's futurism and free-enterprise faith, i.e., it seems to yoke two conflicting aspects of Disney's heritage. In and of itself, that hypothesis would be worth the trouble of a devoted Disney biographer. Its larger importance derives from the fact that it foreshadows a major trend in the American corporate ideology of today and tomorrow. First, look at the Disney World statement of it; then place it in that broader, American context.

"During 1977," the annual report of Walt Disney Productions announces, "our Imagineers at WED [Walter Elias Disney] Enterprises have concentrated their primary creative thrust on EPCOT, the Experimental Prototype Community of Tomorrow. Working from concepts to renderings to study models, they have achieved in Master Plan 5 the conceptual breakthrough we have sought." When I first heard Disney Speak talk of Master Plans and conceptual breakthroughs, I was reminded of Ely Culbertson, the bridge champion who had a brief career as an international peace planner. World War II, he wrote later on, interrupted his work on a new slam convention.

But when I went to the "presentation" on EPCOT, I did not know whether to laugh or cry. The preview of the Disney future was held in an air-conditioned auditorium across the street from "City Hall," i.e., the publicity office. There was a huge mock-up of the entire park, with the EPCOT addition, and a smaller model of EPCOT itself. At the proper moment someone pushed a button and the exhibit sank with electronic grace as a screen came down to present the posthumous voice and person of the founder. All of this reminded me of a Strangelovian war room, only it had to do with expanding an amusement park rather than with World War III. It was as if George Orwell had written *Alice in Wonderland*.

EPCOT, we were told, will have two major sections. There will be Future World—science-fiction writer Ray Bradbury is working on a script for it—and the World Showcase. The whole thing will be financed by corporations and governments and will cost in the neighborhood of $500 million (which will bring the investment in the Florida plant to more than $1 billion). The companies and the governments will get the chance to present their message in return for paying the bills. But, and this is a critical element of the whole undertaking, politics and ideological conflict will be kept out. This will be so despite the fact that "Communicore," "the global marketplace of new ideas, will be the communications center of EPCOT. Here, *industry and public* will participate in a 'hands on' exchange of new and exciting ideas, systems, products, and technologies" (italics mine). But as the enterprise is now projected, "industry" will speak, the "public" will listen, and the controversial will be filtered out.

Indeed, the "ideas" in the Communicore, as now planned, will be mainly technological gimmickry. There will be an "electronic travel port where visitors can 'dial-in' their travel interests and other itinerary requirements and watch an 'instant preview' of their upcoming vacation." A "Casino of Information" will use a game-playing format to update the penny arcade and make it relevant to the "information age." And so on. Exactly how this will promote "the advancement of international understanding and the solution of the problems of people everywhere through the communication of ideas" is left marvelously unclear. Back in 1933, Disney boasted that Mickey Mouse was the one thing on which the Chinese and the Japanese agreed, and the naïve hope in that thought—which ignores the fact that those admirers of the mouse then tried to annihilate one another—is alive and well in Florida right now.

In this nonideological environment—which, as we will see, is a profoundly ideological concept—Exxon has already signed on to present the problems and solutions of the energy future. General Motors will lend its benevolent expertise to the challenge of twenty-first-century transportation. And there will be an exhibit on the seas. Guests will board the clipper ship *Spirit of Mankind*, and, after a simulated journey through the deep, will arise at "Sea Base Alpha," where they will "experience an authentic ocean environment with marine life, an undersea restaurant, and a showcase of oceanographic exhibits and displays."

Will there be a word of the debate that has been going on for more than ten years on the law of the sea? Will there be a discussion of the relative merits of the American corporate proposal for the private mining of the wealth of the oceans and the counterposed notion that the deeps are "the common heritage of mankind"? The answer is clearly no. Indeed, the American Adventure, the attraction that will link Future World and the World Showcase, is going to give an uncontroversial—which is to say, necessarily bowdlerized—version of this country's past. This is all the more amazing when one realizes that the chronicle will be dominated by "animatronic" figures (full-scale talking, moving models invented by Disney and currently on display in Disney World's Hall of the Presidents) of Ben Franklin, Mark Twain, and Will Rogers. How those witty, contentious, sometimes bitter and acerbic Americans will do that job is difficult to imagine.

The World Showcase is supposed to be a sort of permanent international exposition where the various nations can communicate with the millions who come to Disney World. But here, again, there is a ban on ideology. Of course, most of the countries that have thus far shown an interest in the scheme—Iran, Canada,

West Germany, Japan, Mexico, some Arab states, Costa Rica, and Morocco—are safely on the corporate side of the world divide. But just to be sure, the exhibitors will have to confine themselves to presenting their culture. The Arabs and Israelis have been told that they cannot speak of their rivalries, and the young people who come from various lands to work on the project will be expected to live together in a World Village.

This anti-ideology is, of course, an ideology. It is the key to Disney World and, more importantly, to much of the American political mentality of recent years. The bias appears throughout the spectrum of political debate, in the dreams of urban planners sponsored by the Ford Foundation as well as in the moral blueprints designed by the sociologists in the universities. Corporate technology, we are told in stunning television commercials and newspaper ads designed to look like serious comment, can solve our social problems—if only the bumbling politicians and regulators will leave the businessmen alone. There is an objective, one-best-way to do things, and it is the private property of the experts at General Motors and Exxon. Conventional academic wisdom says much the same thing in learned journals and the popular press.

There is a surface plausibility to these claims, which is why they convince so many people. That is vividly in evidence at Disney World. The entire park is built over a system of tunnels—Utilidors, in Disney Speak. All of the air-conditioning apparatus, the utility lines, and the like are down there, easily accessible for repairs and never requiring that the streets be torn up. Garbage, as we have seen, is collected through that sixty-mile-an-hour evacuation system. On the back lot, the Reedy Creek Utility Company has constructed a building in which solar collectors are on the roof and the energy collected provides all of the air conditioning and all of the heat for the offices.

Disney even used futuristic technology to build his park. The Contemporary Hotel is the most famous hostelry in Disney World, not the least because the Monorail runs through its gigantic lobby. The Contemporary's huge A-frame was constructed as a shell, and then prefabricated rooms—which, not so incidentally, also fit into the pseudo-Oceanic Polynesian Hotel—were inserted by cranes. An even more interesting innovation is found in the Magic Kingdom's power system. Two huge jet turbines do the generating, and their waste heat stokes boilers that yield hot water, which is then fed into four cooling machines and used for air conditioning in the hotels. The water left over from the whole process is purified and piped out to the tree farm where Disney World produces eucalyptus trees. Small wonder that various urban planners have gone starry-eyed in the presence of so many prodigies.

Given this recycling technology, it is also not surprising that "Spaceship Earth" is "the major theme show and introduction to the concept and meaning of EPCOT." But, on second thought, what is an environmental concept like "Spaceship Earth" doing in a corporate-dominated exhibit at a time when business daily tells us that environmental and safety regulations are undermining our productivity and thereby threatening the entire system? The answer is relatively simple. Disney World is going to "communicate ideas" and ban controversy and ideology at the same time. The communicators will be big businesses, and they will present themselves, not as profit maximizers, but as problem solvers. Only their "objective" solutions will conceal a highly controversial, very partisan corporate self-interest.

Some simple examples from Disney World illustrate this point quite well. Let the customers endure delay and frustration as they come on an inefficient transportation system to the gates of the Magic Kingdom—and then move them with award-winning efficiency once they are in the park and turnover rings the cash register. Let the children persuade their parents to take them to the home of Mickey Mouse—and do nothing to help the kids see the parade when their elders blot it out of sight. The environment as a market for big-business technology is marvelous; the same environment as a cost for big-business technologists is to be derided and plundered. It was Exxon and associated companies that, with the help of enormous direct and indirect subsidies from the government, made the nation dependent on Middle Eastern oil and refused to develop the very technologies that it will now present in Disney World. One might as well have the homesteader's exhibit organized by the cattle rustlers.

These deceits are made all the more plausible by what might be called the moon-shot illusion. If we can go to the moon, people in the thrall of a technological euphoria sometimes ask, why can't we build decent cities, teach Johnny to read, end poverty in the Third World, or what have you? That cliché overlooks a simple fact: that there are no people on the moon, and getting there is merely an engineering problem. Indeed, Disney World is a sort of man-made moon, an extraterrestrial, unpopulated place. Yet the management constantly refers to a park without people—except for that corporal's guard of hired citizens—as a prototypical "community" of tomorrow. But it is precisely the absence of any community that allows the corporate commissars to experiment at will on their Florida moon.

## The Magic Kingdom as Potemkin Village

And yet, this reactionary ideology can be given a liberal surface. The fraudulent nineteenth-century charm of Main Street is the front for a fraudulent twenty-first-century version of the future. Therefore, Disney World can claim to be forward looking, progressive, even utopian. The hero of its Hall of Presidents show is an animatronic Abraham Lincoln (surrounded by animatrons of all the other presidents, including Jimmy Carter). And in the Small World attraction—originally designed for UNICEF at the New York World's Fair in 1964—one rides in boats along a waterway bordered by animatronic dolls of all colors and races singing of the unity of humankind. In EPCOT itself there will be the World Showcase and the World Village. Why this liberal gloss in a corporate, technocratic enterprise?

Because the multinational corporation is, in one of its most important modes, internationalist and even pacifist. To the organizers of the World Showcase, the Arab-Israeli dispute is an inconvenience, and therefore the Arabs and the Israelis in EPCOT will not be allowed to mention the unfortunate fact of its very existence. Anything that disrupts the global factory is considered intolerable since it disturbs business-as-usual. To be sure, radical democratic change, as in Allende's Chile, calls forth countermeasures seeking the law and order of a graveyard. That, however, only illuminates the basic point that disruption is to be avoided at all costs. So the Imagineers exclude the political differences between countries from their "world," much as they ban the politics of technology in favor of corporate objectivity. What remains is cultural charm and business expertise.

A Marxist analysis of Disney's comics—*How to Read Donald Duck*, by Ariel Dorfman and Armand Mattelart—was published during the Allende regime, and it captured this point. In Disney's cartoons, the globe is a saccharine Small World in which the nonwhite natives are innocent, ignorant, charmingly primitive, sexless, and all male. But this fond and paternalistic attitude toward the childlike peoples of the Third World, this refusal to hear their political demands, is a liberal and "humanistic" way of holding them down.

So Disney World's internationalism and futurism, like everything else in this seemingly charming fantasy, are predicated on real-world corporate purpose. Moreover, it casts some light on both the so-called liberal and so-called conservative ideology of the late seventies.

Ideology, it must be remembered, is not given, for once and for all. On the contrary, it is as faddist and modish as jet-set fashions, which should give one pause when it claims to be able to shape the far future. In the sixties, when Kennedy-Johnson liberalism was on the ascendant, the companies followed in the steps of their liberal critics in government. There was much talk of the social responsibility of business, of a partnership between the private and public sector, even of a "social-industrial complex" (which I described in this magazine in 1967). *Fortune* magazine was a cheering section for this movement, documenting how dogooding could be profitable. Perhaps the high point of this development was the support given Lyndon Johnson in 1964 by the American haute bourgeoisie under the leadership of Henry Ford.

In the seventies, as popular dissatisfaction with government mounted, the boardroom and the university changed their tunes. Government's function was now to leave business alone—or, more precisely, to subsidize corporate investment by holding down social spending, restraining wages, and encouraging profits as a means of generating jobs. A series of Chase Manhattan ads argued that if the yield on unearned income were only increased then business would solve our problems. William Simon, as secretary of the treasury, used some misleading statistics to show that there would be a capital shortfall in the trillions if new benefits were not conferred upon the wealthy. So it was that Jimmy Carter, who had campaigned against the privileges accorded capital gains in the tax code, came to advocate only a modest increase in their basic unfairness.

In his Disney World speech, Carter explicitly embraced this newest version of the American philosophy. He talked of the battle against inflation in terms that could have resounded in a Gerald Ford campaign speech in 1976. The government, he said, was "cutting unnecessary spending, reducing federal pay increases, removing unnecessary regulations, cutting the federal deficit, and letting the free market set prices wherever it can." That is also the program of the American corporate elite and the ideology of Walt Disney's amusement park. There are, they are saying, nongovernmental—nonpolitical—technological solutions to the nation's ills. The private sector will plan and build the future according to its specifications, and that will maximize the common good. So a top General Motors executive says of his company's projected exhibit in EPCOT: "It will be one of the best investments we make. It will be a good opportunity to point out how technological progress has contributed to the world and the free enterprise system."

One problem with this free-enterprise idyll is marvelously illuminated by Disney World itself: it has little to do with free enterprise. The Magic Kingdom merely requires that the state of Florida confer political sovereignty upon a private, profit-making corporation. There is no Adam Smithian invisible hand, but the visible hand of the company deciding everything, including how long the employees can grow their sideburns. There is an ideology of market choice, only all competitors are banned. There is, in short, a controlled, monopolistic, state-supported capitalist reality of the late twentieth century that pretends to be a capitalist utopia of the eighteenth century. But that, after all, is not simply a description of Walt Disney's little experimental prototype community in central Florida; it is an accurate depiction of the entire American system today.

If that is the case, the system is in deep trouble. On returning from Disney World, one might paraphrase Lincoln Steffens: "I have seen the future and it does not work." For the embarrassing truth about Disney World is that, for all the philosopher-kingmanship of Disney and his disciples, the place is still an animated cartoon. *Business Week* grasped an aspect of this fact last summer when it reported of EPCOT: "Many of the 'new' plans are leftover ideas of Walt Disney himself, giving rise to speculation that a conservative and inbred management is pursuing them more out of respect for the founder than because of any belief in its own planning process. Disney lacks not only a corporate planning department but a long-term strategic plan as well." The planners of the community of tomorrow have no plan of their own for today.

*Business Week* speculates on another, and even more remarkable, reason for Disney World's commitment to EPCOT futurism. The company has the problem of being too liquid: "The corporate treasury is loaded with more than $200 million in cash, while the company's long-term debt stands at a mere $8.4 million." This is the result, *Business Week* comments, of a corporate "lethargy" that saw no new major projects over a seven-year period. So one motive for going ahead on EPCOT and other innovations is to spend money and thereby to avoid being a target for a takeover. The Imagineers, it would seem, have not been imaginative, and they are deciding the fate of the twenty-first century because they have nothing better to do.

These reports suggest an analogy. Disney World is not Huxley's Brave New World or Orwell's world of 1984, since both of those anti-utopias are as believable as they are ominous. Rather, the model for the Magic Kingdom is the Potemkin Village. Potemkin, it will be remembered, was the Russian official who took Catherine the Great on a tour of the marvelous villages he had built. In fact, there was only a single, bogus village, which was assembled for each royal visit, then dismantled and sent down the line to pose as progress again and again. The Disney people have created a similarly fraudulent exhibit, even if it is stationary. They have demonstrated that some technologies will work on a man-made moon without any people, and have hoked up that irrelevance as if it were a prophecy.

And yet, if Disney World is not the wave of the future it is a portent of the present. Jimmy Carter, like Walt Disney, is a business executive from a small town who believes in science and is an antipolitics politician. And he is in the process of adapting the worldview that is fantasized in Florida. It asks government to socialize the costs of business, and to turn the planning of the future over to the executives, even to the point of granting political sovereignty to private corporations. This system of administered and controlled markets is then legitimated in the name of free enterprise. Only the capitalist Imagineers don't really believe in their own dreams any more than the Disney World people do. Right now they, too, are awash with capital, and uncertain and afraid about investing it; they, too, talk of innovation, but they have come up with few serious new ideas. All these things are writ small in the Magic Kingdom and large in the American economy.

# PART 8

# 21
# Socialism in Crisis

I took sides for socialism, in an armchair intellectual way, in 1948 at the end of a year at Yale Law School. I became serious about that radical commitment in 1951, when I went to the Catholic Worker, and in 1952 when I joined the Socialist Party.

In keeping with a great tradition, I adopted more than a few leftist simplifications about society in those first years of militancy. Marxism—the serious Marxism of Marx, not the vulgarized, or totalitarianized, caricature that is so much better known—is a complex, rich world of its own. In a first and youthful immersion in it one can even think that you have discovered the key to all of existence. So it was that I wrote about trade unionism, civil rights struggles, ballet, and poetry. After all, each was a part of that intricate and interrelated whole that Marx had mapped.

And yet I was saved from some of the most crass errors because I was a poet. I knew, out of my own personal experience, that poems could not be reduced to a reflection of some underlying economic reality. They had a life of their own, a certain autonomy; and if they refracted the society in which they were written, they did so like a prism that disintegrates the overwhelming fact of the sunlight into so many different colors. And since I knew that the "superstructure" was not simply a projection of the "base," I also insisted that socialism itself was a matter of new ways of living and not just a question of new forms of social ownership.

As I grew older, I realized that the side I had taken was more complicated than I had first thought. But then, in the late fifties and the sixties, many of the practicing socialist politicians of Europe thought they had finally discovered the royal road to socialism itself: a socialist government in charge of a growing mixed economy appropriating part of the surplus for decency to those at the bottom and the middle. In the seventies, that proposition became problematic as the great postwar boom turned into a decade or more of stagflation, of erratic growth and high inflation.

It was at this time that I came more and more into contact with the leaders of world socialism. At the 1976 Congress of the Socialist International (SI), Willy Brandt became its president and committed the organization to a much more activist role and, in particular, to reaching out toward the Third World. It was my good fortune to represent the Democratic Socialist Organizing Committee, and then Democratic Socialists of America, at the meetings of the SI from 1976 on. In the process, I got to know—sometimes well, sometimes superficially—Brandt, François Mitterrand, Olof Palme, Felipe Gonzalez Marquez, Guillermo Ungo, Carlos Andreas Perez, Shimon Peres, and many other socialist leaders.

After a while I began to play something of an ironic role in the SI. As a native-born English speaker and a professional writer, my command of the organization's official language was greater than that of almost all of my comrades. As a leader of a small organization that was never in danger of taking up the burdens of national leadership that weighed so heavily upon the other party leaders, I had the time to think and speculate more than they. In 1983, I was elected secretary of the program commission of the XVIth Congress of the International and it adopted, with very few changes, my Manifesto of Albufeira (we met at the Portuguese resort town of that name).

More recently, I have written the first draft of a new declaration of basic socialist principles for the International. It will, I am sure, be subject to considerable discussion and revision, but the fact remains that I will be involved in that process too. The point is, the three essays on the socialist crisis that follow in this section are not simply the work of an academic intellectual but also the product of a personal and activist involvement with the leaders of the sixty-five socialist parties that make up the SI.

Chapter 22, which is abridged, approaches the socialist crisis by trying to imagine how the contradictory process of democratic socialization within a society that is still capitalist can take place. Chapter 23, "The Misfortune of 'Great Memories,'" is apparently a scholarly gloss on the history of the Paris Commune but, like almost all accounts of the past, it is written from a present perspective, warning against any notion of a simple, or heroic, transition to socialism. The third chapter confronts one of the greatest socialist disappointments of recent times, the experience of the Mitterrand government in France between 1981 and 1984.

Yet that disappointment has not in the least shaken my socialist commitment. A century and a half ago, at the beginning of the modern socialist movement, Marx said that capitalism was a system of private socialization, that it organized a cooperative, interdependent world which put the collective wisdom of humankind, science, in the service of production, but under the auspices and control of elites concerned with their own gain and unconcerned about the needs of the whole society. That was profoundly true and it was, moreover, an extraordinary intellectual achievement to have understood that Adam Smith's laisser faire capitalism turned itself into a monopoly corporate capitalism.

Since Marx wrote, the trends toward unsocial socialization have become infinitely more pronounced. In Communist countries they are directed by a bureaucratic, dictatorial elite; in the West, they are under the guidance of a partnership between governments and corporate leaders. Nowhere in the world are they subject to the will of that vast majority whose labor and ingenuity are the source of the socialization process. To democratically control a socialization of the very planet which has thus far taken place behind the backs of the people: that is the task of democratic socialism.

In the late twentieth century, with an unprecedented technological revolution, a vast shift in the international division of labor and the multinationalization of corporate capital, unsocial socialization has become even more intense—and even more problematic as the ruined cities and towns of the American heartland or the hungry children of Africa show. So the basic socialist goal is even more relevant than it was more than a century ago.

But the socialists are bewildered. As bewildered as they were in the 1920s, as bewildered as they will be in the midst of some future transition. For the means and tactics of effecting that basic socialist goal have to change in every generation in response to new, unanticipated developments and that has not been, and will not be, done smoothly.

My socialism, then, is not a faith, in that it is based upon the rational, analytic assessment of an economic and social necessity which I see before my very eyes—the necessity of creating an utterly new form of society if human freedom is to survive the results of human creativity. And at the same time, my socialism is a faith, for I will end my life without ever knowing if the wager I have made, that the necessity will become possible, is true or not. Whatever the outcome, it is a privilege to be part of the struggle.

# 22
# What Socialists Would Do in America—If They Could

*Dissent, 1978*

Let's pose a far-reaching question, without pretending to answer it fully. What would happen in America if we were able to make socialism come to pass? How would we move beyond the welfare state? What measures would be taken on the far side of liberal reform, yet well short of utopia?

These questions are not academic. In Europe today there are democratic socialist mass parties that are putting them on the political agenda. In America there is, of course, no major socialist movement, yet. But this society is more and more running up against the inherent limits of the welfare state. We can no longer live with the happy assumptions of sixties liberalism—that an endless noninflationary growth would not only allow us to finance social justice but to profit from it as well. So, for instance, a Democratic president is told by key economic advisers that workers will have to bear the consequences of breathing cotton dust because industry "cannot afford" the cost of protecting their lungs.

In the United States, at present, the dominant reaction to such structural problems is to sound retreat. This may well strike cruelly at the poor, the minorities, women, and all other vulnerable people. But ultimately the forced march to the rear will not work. For there are limits to the ability of the nation to impose the social costs of late-capitalist production upon those least able to defend themselves.

So I baldly assert that old-fashioned reaction is not, in the long run, a feasible way of dealing with our problems. There will either be a new-fashioned reaction—sophisticated, modern, planned—or there will be a socialist alternative. It is with this thought in mind that I undertake an attempt to define a socialist policy for the (still unforeseeable) middle distance. First, I will try to outline some of the general problems raised by such an imaginative definition of the future. Then, there will be a brief sketch of that possible socialist future. And finally, I will try to relate these speculations to the immediate present, since I am convinced that projecting what should be must help us, here and now, in devising what can be.

## Some General Problems

Capitalism is dying. It will not, however, disappear on a given day, or in a given month or even year. Its demise will take place as a historic process that could lead to democratic socialism—or to a new kind of collectivist and authoritarian society. And one of the key problems of locating socialism in this process is that it must emerge in a society that is not capitalist or socialist but something in between, with elements of both.

Let me now hastily sketch in a few details to support the sweeping statements I have just made.

The way capitalism ends defines the terrain on which socialism becomes possible.* Present-day capitalism is more and more collectivist, that is, it increasingly makes its economic decisions politically. This happens because the inherent tendencies of

*In what follows, I have summarized the arguments detailed and documented in *The Twilight of Capitalism*. Readers who seek proof for my various assertions will, I hope, find it there.

the system subvert the always imperfect "free markets" of an earlier age and because, in any case, those markets could not organize a system of such interdependent complexity. Thus far, this process of collectivization within capitalism has been dominated by corporate priorities, even when the collectivizers have been liberals, trade unionists, or socialists.

This last trend is not the result of a conspiracy on the right or of betrayals on the left. It is a consequence of the fact that, as Claus Offe put it, the capitalist state is not itself a capitalist. The economic and political health of the government thus becomes dependent on investment decisions made in private boardrooms. Those decisions are critical determinants of the Gross National Product, the level of employment, and indeed of the government's own revenues. The rulers of the welfare state therefore must adapt themselves to corporate priorities—"win business confidence."

Those corporate priorities center on the maximizing of profits. This, obviously, is no longer done in an entrepreneurial or "robber baron" way. The nonowning manager has a much more sophisticated calculus and, corporate collectivist that he is, takes political and even social factors into account. Yet, even in this new guise, capitalism remains dangerously and fundamentally antisocial. Capacity is expanded in good times as if there were no tomorrow—or more precisely as if the ability of the society to consume were not limited by the very income structure that capitalist production enforces. In consequence, there are periodic crises. At the same time, the growing social costs of the system are imposed upon those least able to pay—a fact cruelly visible in the devastated cities of the Northeast and industrial Middle West. Markets are rigged with increasing expertise, which is one source of inflation in the midst of recession. Inequality persists because, under capitalism, private wealth, personal and corporate, is the main source of new investment funds.

The welfare state reinforces these trends. Since the health of the entire economy is seen to depend on the will of those who control investment, "trickle down" becomes the ideology of late capitalism. Thus the political representatives of the rich are now demanding—in the name of the common good—that further tax privileges should be conferred on the wealthy, while government spending for everyone else is curtailed.

This corporate collectivism is not, however, a stable system—as anyone who has lived in the seventies can testify. The private, and antisocial, priorities that inform public action are becoming more and more destructive. The anticapitalist measures used to shore up capitalism create a crisis of legitimacy. And eventually, the contradictions of "private socialization" will require basic structural changes. Those could move in the direction of a new class society, a bureaucratic sort of collectivism, or toward a new communitarianism, a democratic socialism.

This summary analysis points to a key assumption of all that follows and helps to define a central problem for socialists seeking to transcend the welfare state. *Socialism will have to define itself in the course of a contradictory transitional period in which elements of both traditional capitalism and corporate collectivism will coexist with, and threaten, socialist innovations.*

It is foolish to imagine a day, a month, or a year when society suddenly "leaps" from capitalism to socialism; the very complexity of modern society precludes that. Where, in some brief period of time, will one suddenly find a socialist cadre capable of taking over from the capitalist managers? How can new psychologies, and new ethics, be created quickly? Moreover, one must have a due respect for socialist ignorance. We know the evils of the old order in great detail, but we do not have all the plans for the new order in our hip pocket. Even if we did, that would be of small help, since a socialist society must be built democratically and cannot be proclaimed from on high.

After all, socialists do not simply propose a new economy. We realize that there must be a transformation of culture, of individual and collective values, if the new structures are to matter. As Antonio Gramsci rightly insisted, socialism is the work of an epoch and it has to do with an entire society, not just with property forms or tax laws.

But that fact creates enormous problems. How, for instance,

does one avoid the cooptation of partial measures of socialization in an economy in which corporate collectivism retains considerable power? In a recent book, Serge Christophe Kolm analyzed what this meant in the Chile of Unidad Popular. One of the first measures of the Allende government was to increase enormously the wages of the poor while holding down prices. This meant, however, a reduction in the profits of the private sector—profits that had been the traditional source of new investment funds. At first, the problem was not too serious since the wage policy set off a consumer boom. But eventually, there occurred a slowdown and the corporations had to borrow, thereby setting into motion the inflationary spiral. The Nixon administration, the CIA, the copper companies, the world financial community (including the World Bank), all did what they could to make matters worse.

Still, the relevant point here is that Chile demonstrates the inherent difficulties in introducing socialist measures in an economy still manifesting strong capitalist tendencies. So, alas, does the Tennessee Valley Authority. From its inception under the New Deal until the early fifties, the TVA managed to control floods and generate power in a way that enormously stimulated the region's economy. But from the early fifties on, this public property behaved more and more in a classic private way. It moved from hydropower to coal and in the process was a major initiator of the destructive strip-mining of Appalachia. Indeed, it is possible to make a sad generalization: *most existing nationalized enterprises in the world behave about as badly as private enterprises*. When one adds that those nationalized companies constitute, more often than not, the collectivization of private losses and inefficiencies, one gets a sense of the enormous difficulties of a transition toward socialism within the contradictory world of late capitalism. In that setting, the danger of cooptation does not arise, primarily because of the personal corruption of leaders or bureaucrats; it is a structural tendency of the society.

So in imagining socialism as it would emerge just the other side of the welfare state, the imagination must be realistic. How does one begin to create a new society in a world in which there will be capitalist striving for gain, socialist egalitarianism, and "communist" free goods in the libertarian sense of the word as used by Marx in his "Critique of the Gotha Program." Under such difficult conditions, how is it possible to transfer the control of basic investment decisions from private boardrooms to the democratic process?

In facing up to these issues within the framework of a brief essay, much that is enormously important will be placed in parentheses. I will deal with a single developed society and ignore the international implications of socialism that are, in other contexts, decisive. I will posit the existence of a political movement capable of taking the lead in implementing the proposals I make, and I will focus on economic and social structures and present my illustrations as evocative symbols of a possible future, and not at all as a fully worked-out program.

## Speculations and Possibilities

First, socialism proposes a national planning process in which all the people would have an *effective* right to participate.

Through a political process, the society would consider its basic options. Put in American terms, the administration would outline the needs of the next period and the resources available to meet them. Since the latter would not be infinite, there would have to be proposed "trade-offs." A crash program for the improvement of health might limit the growth of education; the decision to take the benefits of increased productivity in the form of more leisure time would mean that the same productivity could not be spent on more consumer goods. This last point is particularly important because one would hope that, as socialist consciousness rose, so would the tendency toward the decommercialization of life—toward communal, noncommodity forms of consumption, like neighborhood centers or public theaters.

Under such conditions there obviously would be debates over priorities. These would be resolved by a democratic process in which parties would compete with one another over conflicting programs. That, however, would not mean a mere extension of present-day "pluralist" theory, which ignores the way formal democratic rights, precious as they are, can be subverted by economic and social inequalities. In the period of transition, there would not simply be a corporate sector striving to impose its values upon the polity; the government itself would obviously be (and already is) a center of power. For democracy to work in such a context, it would have to be much more profound and real than it is today. Let us imagine two quite unutopian aspects of such a deepening of democracy.

First, if the administration or even the administration and the major opposition have an effective monopoly on the machinery and personnel of the planning process, then the formal right to challenge the plan becomes almost empty of content. In French "indicative planning," for instance, the workers are legally guaranteed representation at every level of the system. But they, unlike business and government, do not have the expert staff, the computers, the "knowledge technology" so important in a modern society. Therefore, they normally don't bother to participate in the exercise.

If, then, planning is to be a critical instrument of the assertion of popular control over the investment process, there must be effective provision for democratic participation. Any significant group of people—much larger than a *Kaffeeklatsch*, much smaller than a majority—should be given the means to challenge the official plan(s). This could be done in at least two ways. Such a group could be given the funds to hire its own experts and computers; or it could be given the right to have the official bureaucracy work out the details of its counterplan(s). Within such a framework, when the administration and the Congress went to the various regions and asked for popular inputs, there would not be the *pro forma* hearings that so often prevail today. The critics would be technically as well prepared as the establishment.

Second, the political process itself should be democratized. Here, some of the West European countries now are far ahead of the United States. All television time available to candidates for federal office should be allocated according to a democratic formula. And each significant group should either get subsidies for its own press, or else—as is sometimes the case in this country with intraunion oppositions in campaign periods—have legally guaranteed access to the print media.

Let us assume, then, that truly democratic procedures could be established within the planning process, given a little imagination and a mass socialist political movement. What of the content of the plan(s)? How would it (or they) be rationally debated and worked out? How would it (or they) be implemented democratically without an enormous proliferation of bureaucracy?

It would be of utmost importance that everyone in the planning debates know the real costs of all the proposals. It was thus not an accident that, on the few occasions when he explicitly referred to the socialist future, Marx spoke of the need for careful bookkeeping. Like Max Weber, he regarded bookkeeping as one of the great accomplishments of the capitalist era, and then added that it would be even more necessary under socialism precisely because production would be planned. And it is, of course, one of the central themes in a contemporary indictment of late capitalism that this system falsifies prices by imposing its social costs on helpless people and/or the government.

But does this mean that socialism will operate according to the criterion of profit? And if so, what of the claim that it entails production for use *instead* of profit?

Profit, I would argue on the basis of historical evidence, is the specific form that the surplus from production takes in, and only in, capitalism. Such a surplus exists in all but the most primitive of subsistence societies; it will certainly have to exist under socialism. Under capitalism, the surplus is appropriated by the owners and managers of the means of production, and it is both a title to wealth and to the right to make basic investment decisions about the future of the economy. In precapitalist systems, the surplus was appropriated by political and ideological, not economic, means, i.e., on the basis of "God's will" as backed by the human sword.

Under socialism, there will be a social dividend to provide for those who do not (usually because they cannot) work, for depreciation and for expansion (on the last count, it should be remembered that I am speaking of the socialist transition when there will be many urgent needs for new investment, both at home and abroad). But that social dividend will not be a "profit." It will be appropriated by the society and allocated after democratic decision-making; it will not go to individuals in the form of wealth or elite power, as is now the case. Furthermore, although a socialist society will have to create a surplus and will want to measure the return on investments as precisely as possible, the resulting "interest rate" will be an accounting device and not a flow of income to private owners. The socialist accounting will compute social cost and social benefit in a way that capitalism, for systemic reasons, does not and cannot do. For instance, mainstream economists today defend the ruin of the Northeastern and Middle Western cities as an inevitable—tolerable if unfortunate—consequence of making a more "efficient" use of resources. But efficiency, it must be understood, is not a mathematical absolute obeyed by technocrats; it is always defined in relation to the interests of different groups and individuals. Under capitalism this is done behind a veil of mystifying rationalization and in the interests of a minority. Under socialism, the term will be democratically defined in public debate in relation to the needs of the majority.

Let us assume, then, that the democratic planning process has determined the basic priorities of the society. How will they be implemented?

There are two existing models, neither of them applicable to democratic socialism. In the Soviet Union and other Communist countries, there is centralized command planning with the bureaucracy setting thousands of prices and production targets. The system is politically totalitarian and economically inefficient—two facts that are closely related to one another. I therefore reject this model: it does not satisfy basic socialist goals. The other model, that of indicative planning, is also not the way to democratic socialism, but it is worth examining more closely for a moment since it highlights one of the critical differences between liberalism (in the American sense of that term) and socialism.

Here is how Stephen S. Cohen described French indicative planning in a 1977 paper for the Joint Economic Committee. There is, he says, an economic "concert" achieved without the participation of the unions, consumers, or small businessmen.

> The economic concert is based on a simple political ideology and defines a simple political role for planning. The state needs a high performance economy. This has come to mean a fundamental commitment by the state to the expansion and modernization of the big business sector. Big business needs the active cooperation of the state. It needs the state to maintain a high level of effective demand and to socialize many of its costs. It also needs the aid of the state in managing its own affairs. The overarching organization provided by the state helps industry to regulate competitive forces. In brief, big business finds that it needs a cooperative economy and it needs the state to organize that cooperation. Most modern capitalist nations are doing some variant of the state–big business partnership model, but nowhere with such clarity and enthusiasm as in France.

The French planners assume that private corporate priorities are the pivot upon which all decisions turn and that it is, therefore, the role of the plan to facilitate, and sometimes humanize, the work of big business in the name of the common good. This, it will be noted, is the tacit assumption of much of American liberalism. However, it should be emphasized that in technocratic, *dirigiste* France, what is implicit in America has achieved the status of an ideology. I insist upon this point for a political reason: the American liberals (including labor liberals) who unconsciously accept the corporate premise are often also hostile to corporations and in the future could become socialist. This is not true of a principled French technocrat; or, rather, the conversion required in the second case is much more profound. One of the hopeful aspects of American liberalism is its contradictory character.

In any case, we have come to a fundamental divide, one that marks off socialism from all variants of capitalist reform. The latter believed that liberal goals can be limited to a late-capitalist economic and social structure, while socialists define that structure as the core of the problem. What, then, is the socialist alternative? How will socialists actually implement the lovely choices made in the democratic planning process?

Not by command of the Soviet, or any other, model. However, in rejecting indicative planning within a late-capitalist society that is economically and politically dominated by corporate power, one is not ruling out indicative planning in an utterly different milieu. For in imagining a socialist transition from capitalism toward the good society, I hypothesize two different kinds of motivation.

The first motive is individual gain. The goal of socialism, clearly, is to transcend greed as far as is possible, and to act upon the basis of "to each according to his/her need, from each according to his/her ability." This lies in the distance, although approximations of it should begin on the first day of socialist transition. But as socialism emerges from capitalism, there would be differentials in wages within an enterprise and even differentials between enterprises within the same industry. At the same time, there would be a progressive, egalitarian tax program to reduce radically the outrageous spread between executive and worker pay in capitalism today. Managers receiving hundreds of thousands a year—and setting their compensations for themselves—are not being paid wages, but if I may speak in an old yet useful language, they are appropriating surplus value in the guise of wages.

The wage structure, then, would be infinitely more progressive than it is within capitalism and would follow the biblical injunction by exalting the lowly and making plain the high ones. Yet there would be differentials related to skill and output, and these would be tolerated, precisely as an incentive for individuals and enterprises to produce more efficiently. Moreover, the differentials between enterprises, even though carefully limited, would be the basis of a certain competition between them. It would obviously be preferable if moral incentives alone guaranteed efficient cooperation with the planned priorities. But in this transitional stage, there is simply no realistic reason to suppose that this would be the case.

The second major motivation would be moral. It would not suffice, in and of itself; but it is absolutely essential as the growing edge of socialist possibility. The point, however, is not self-evident. In the United States moral incentives have played a role during wartime, but only then. Moreover, the American labor movement has been particularly hostile to "work enrichment" schemes, regarding them as artfully designed programs to get more work out of fewer people. More often than not, this judgment has been accurate. Why, then, assume that American workers as they are will be moved to change their attitudes in a socialist transition?

It must be obvious—not simply the fact, but a fact plain for one and all to see—that the savings of productivity will primarily go to the workers who make them or to the society as a whole. If they go to the workers, then old-fashioned capitalist psychology would explain why this incentive would work. But what does it mean to say that the gains would go to the "society"? Why would that motivate the average worker? The answer to this question is best given in the form of a generalization about the socialist wage in a transition period.

Wage, then, will be composed of three different elements (I borrow some insights from Serge Christophe Kolm). It would be capitalist in the sense that there would be differentials based on performance; it would be socialist in that an egalitarian tax policy would severely limit the differentials and work toward a redistribution of income and wealth; it would be "communist" (in the libertarian sense) in that an increasing part of people's incomes would take the form of "free" goods, i.e., collectively paid goods and services, such as health, education, transportation. So a part of the wage would be received collectively, as a social dividend from heightened productivity.

Farfetched? Not at all. Right now, the socialist parties of Sweden and Holland are moving in the direction of such collective payment, proposing that corporations pay a portion of their tax in stock placed in a worker-controlled mutual fund. And one of the reasons for this development is, precisely, to give workers a communal stake in productivity. This is not, it should be noted, a traditional stock-sharing device where the individual workers get shares in lieu of certain wage increases. In Sweden, this is the conservative alternative. It is a proposal for the *social* sharing of productivity gains.

One last point on wage structure. The capitalist component would be settled by collective bargaining. That issue, and the more general question of working conditions, would provide one of the bases for the continuing existence of a trade-union movement. The socialist and "communist" components would be determined by a political process in which unions, parties, and other voluntary institutions would be involved. Here again, I am positing the necessity of conflict among organizations that would interpret the common good in terms of the particular good of different strata of the citizenry.

So individuals would be motivated to cooperate in the work of the plan on the basis of capitalist, socialist, and "communist" incentives. What about enterprises? Given the previous analysis, I assume that there will be three main types of economic organization: socially owned; privately owned large enterprises; and cooperatives. There will also be a stratum of privately owned small businesses, but these will function primarily in the area of consumer markets and are not likely to play a decisive role in fulfilling the society's democratic priorities for production.

In all three of the major sectors there will be elected worker representation at every level. This is not merely desirable as a way of dealing with alienation. It is a practical necessity if the sense of communal solidarity—the socialist motive—is to grow. And that, in turn, increases productivity. It is also essential to the antibureaucratic aspect of the socialist program, institutionalizing as many local, face-to-face controls on authority as is possible.

So far, this may sound like the socialist version of apple pie. It is much more problematic—and important—than that. Contemporary capitalist technology, Harry Braverman persuasively argues in *Labor and Monopoly Capital*, did not evolve in a value-free, technical way. It had, and has, social and even ideological functions. Specifically, it is not an accident that this technology worked at every point to expropriate the skills of the workers, to dispossess them of all decision-making, and to try to turn out automatons. Therefore, as a technology incarnating capitalist values is extremely difficult to run on a socialist basis, one of the goals of the transition will be to build different kinds of factories—and offices.

I make the last point about offices for an important purpose. Most socialist language and imagining is focused in terms of plants. But what about the "postindustrial society"? Without going into all the complexities of that question, it should be noted that a major part of the "tertiary sector" is made up of service workers in large, anonymous, factorylike settings, e.g., typing pools, supermarkets, the middling and lower levels of the information industry. Moreover, the skilled and educated reaches of this sector—engineering, universities—often in themselves require collegiality. So I am not projecting workers' control as an exclusively blue-collar proposal.

But then neither can workers' control operate as an absolute. In the socialist transition, as many functions as possible will be located on the most immediate level, where the majority of the people work. But individual enterprises or industries cannot be given the right to veto the democratic plans of the entire nation. It is possible, as the Yugoslav experience shows (and the authoritarian character of that country's political structure is not relevant to this point), for worker-controlled enterprises to develop a collective egotism. The Yugoslavs, for instance, have found it difficult to persuade the more affluent collectives to invest their surplus in high-risk underdeveloped areas. So workers' control is not a panacea, and it will require democratic political checks on the part of the society as a whole. It even demands the redesign of technology and economic organization, in the postindustrial as well as in the industrial sectors.

Workers' control will function in all the enterprises of the society—but those enterprises will have different structures.

First, there is the social property sector. I say social, not nationalized, property for a reason. Any fool or charlatan or dictator can nationalize a plant. In and of itself, nationalization is neither good nor bad. Or rather, to the degree that nationalization suggests centralized state ownership, it is bad. It is not necessary to argue the almost self-evident point that such ownership is politically hostile to democracy and economically inefficient. "Social property" stresses both the direct participation of the actual producers *and* democratic control by society rather than administrative control by bureaucrats.

It is painfully obvious that it is simpler to stitch together such harmonious formulas than to realize them in practice. As John Kenneth Galbraith emphasized in *The New Industrial State*, elected bodies either lack the competence to oversee the managers of public property or, if they acquire that competence, they create a second bureaucracy to regulate the first. Galbraith was thinking of existing nationalizations, which do not involve workers' control, but still his point is a substantial one. As I mentioned earlier, in the very first stages of the transition it will be difficult to impose participatory socialist values upon an antiparticipatory capitalist technology. Therefore, I do not see socialization as an act, a law, or a charter, but as a *process* in which democratic forces will have to struggle during an entire historic period to give real content to their legal rights.

In this same spirit, social property will obviously not be operated as departments of the state run by civil servants. They should be constituted on the model of the Tennessee Valley Authority, as authorities with relative independence but ultimate responsibility to the elected representatives of the people. Another check upon their power will be economic. There will be a multiplicity of such authorities within each industry. The size of American enterprises, as Robert Lekachman has pointed out, is not determined by the technical requirements of "economies of scale" but is the result of the drive of major corporations to control markets, politics, and consumer taste. Within a framework of democratic planning there would not be an antitrust utopia of Adam

Smithian competition among tiny economic units in a perfect market, but there could be a rational policy on corporate size and a consequent decentralization of economic power.

With certain carefully defined exceptions, social enterprises would be required to pay their own way and return a surplus for depreciation, new investment, and the social dividend. Obviously, there would be cases when, in full consciousness of the cost, society would want to continue subsidizing production for "noneconomic" reasons (in the callous, capitalist sense). That, it should be noted, is the case in most nationalized industries today, and although it might also be true under socialism, it would hardly be the dominant model. The point would be to locate social property in surplus-yielding activities. For example, the present private energy industry is completely unwilling to develop alternative sources of energy without huge government subsidies. If it gets that money from Washington it will surely develop a socially inappropriate technology. This, therefore, would be a prime area for society to invest in socially oriented research and development, which it would implement through socially owned enterprises.

Social property would also be a key element in a full-employment policy that would emphasize the growth of all regions rather than a competitive struggle between regions as in the current "beggar thy neighbor" situation in the United States. Instead of providing private corporations with multimillion- (and billion-) dollar bribes to go into the South Bronx or Appalachia—which are always collected and often dishonored—locating new and vital social industries in such areas would do that job much more directly and efficiently.

The second tier of economic activity would be a profoundly modified private sector.

You cannot, I have stressed, *socialize* an economy overnight. It is possible to nationalize the "commanding heights" at a stroke, but that would have the negative consequences I have already described. So we must anticipate a corporate sector in the socialist transition. But if that is a necessary fact of life it is also a problematic one. A major private company, Oskar Lange argued in one of his classic discussions, is not likely to behave responsibly if it operates within a socialist political environment and feels that it is working, so to speak, on death row. Part of that problem might be met because of developments that postdate Lange's fears: the emergence of a Galbraithian "technostructure" that, except at the very summit, will hire out to anybody as long as the pay is relatively good. But precisely that summit is the controlling factor in today's economic world.

This is why workers' control and public participation in the corporate structure are so important. The private title to corporate wealth and a limited profit have to be recognized; but many of the existing functions of corporate power can be socialized. For example, the worker and public representatives on the board of directors should routinely reveal all company secrets to the public. Secret debate and decision-making with regard to plant location, pricing, new products, hiring and firing policy, etc., are today considered to be "managerial prerogatives." In the private sector during a socialist transition such matters would be made as transparent as possible and would be subjected to social controls within the planning process.

Still, a transitional socialism would have to tolerate private profits from this sector. One of the reasons why people would invest in such undertaking would be in order to make money. (I speak here of investment in new physical assets—real investment—not of the shuffling and dealing of stock certificates in the great gambling house on Wall Street, a parasitic, near functionless waste of resources that could simply be abolished.) The deleterious social consequences of the continuing existence of profit would, however, be moderated by a highly progressive tax policy and, above all, an inheritance law that would effectively end the possibility of transferring large concentrations of wealth from generation unto generation. By now, the Ford family has been more than compensated for cantankerous old Henry's genius.

Finally, there would be a major cooperative sector, an idea much stressed in nineteenth-century socialism.

In the United States, cooperatives account for less than 1 percent of GNP; in Finland, their share is 10 percent; in Israel, 30 percent. There is, then, enormous room in this country for expansion of the cooperative principle. During the socialist transition we might make great use of one of the Rooseveltian reforms: the Rural Electrification Administration. Under that system, the government has supplied cheap (subsidized) credit to cooperators and thereby accomplished a decentralized, locally controlled electrification of the countryside. (The private sector opposed the program in part on the grounds that farmers did not need electricity!) That strategy could be a major level of socialist policy in the future. It would allow for a proliferation of locally controlled, face-to-face undertakings, including community corporations. In this sector, the capitalist motivation would be most attenuated, the socialist most emphasized as the "associated producers" would actually run most of their own working lives.

The goods and services of these three tiers of production would be distributed in two ways. First, there would be free goods and services collectively paid for by various levels of government. How would one control waste and overuse in this area? A New York *Daily News* dispatch on the thirteenth anniversary of National Health in Great Britain suggested that the problem itself might be somewhat exaggerated. Not only is British medicine superior in some important indices to its American counterpart, it is also less costly as a percentage of GNP and has a lower rate of patient utilization. Even so, there obviously should be some checks on the provision of free goods and services. An idea that is already partly at work in the United States might be generalized well beyond its present use. Health maintenance organizations now provide lump-sum payments for the care of an entire group. If the providers can maintain set standards but reduce costs, they are able to get some of the savings from their own productivity. This principle might be tried out in some areas, e.g., in transportation.

Second, a transitional socialist society would make full use of the virtues of the market mechanism in the areas where consumers would choose, and pay for, their goods and services. To be sure, there is no point in investing markets with the mystical powers claimed for them by their capitalist advocates—advocates who love to ignore the essential. Thus, after Charles Schultze devotes a lyrical hymn to the power of the "unanimous consent arrangement" within markets, he adds, "if the income distribution is grossly unfair, the concept of voluntary decision and unanimous consent is a charade. . . ." Since this is the prelude to a book that praises markets in the extreme, Schultze never so much as bothers to ask whether the data show that his argument is a charade.

Socialists, however, can do more than probe the question that Schultze sidesteps; they can create a new answer to it. That is, if an egalitarian tax policy has enormously reduced the discrepancies in income *and* if public control of the private corporation has severely limited, or even abolished, monopoly pricing—*and* if the engineering of consumer taste is replaced by straightforward information—*then* markets can really function as they are supposed to. They can operate within the broad limit of the democratic plan, and alongside the free sector, in order to communicate the desires of the people and to maximize their choice. The existence of such a market would not determine the basic priorities of the economy, but it would provide more real consumer freedom than capitalist society has ever offered.

Fine, someone might reply. Sitting in a study, socialist writers can conjure up all kinds of glowing dreams. But who will pay for all of these utopian proposals?

The largest single source of corporate investment funds in the United States today is found in retained profits. Within the limits already discussed—relative autonomy of the enterprise, but under the ultimate control of a democratic society—that could well be true under socialism. For, as Marx foresaw before anyone else, capitalism has more and more "socialized" itself within its private framework. Horatio Alger and the individual stockholder long ago ceased to be that important to the investment process. Moreover, as the Meidner Plan of the Swedish trade unionists and similar proposals by the Dutch socialists indicate, a democratic sharing in an essentially social surplus could provide the basis for higher rates of capital formation than are now possible under capitalism.

Furthermore, a useful if somewhat capricious book by a corporate apologist, Peter Drucker's *Unseen Revolution*, helps to focus on a socialist solution to the question of who pays. Private-sector pension funds, Drucker said in 1976, own 25 percent of the equity capital today, and the pension funds of the self-employed, public employees, and teachers account for another 10 percent of the total. By 1985, Drucker calculates, the pensioners will "own" between 50 percent and 60 percent of equity capital, and 40 percent of debt capital. I put "own" in quotation marks for a reason. Most of those funds are employer-controlled and are invested, as required by law, in an utterly capitalist fashion. The workers cannot sell their pension interest during their working life, borrow on it, etc. It is available only upon retirement; and, since some of those claims are not fully funded, there are even questions about payoffs.

However, the point here is not the inadequacies of the existing pension system; it is to take Drucker's rhetorical fantasy—that "pension-fund socialism" now exists in the United States—and try to turn it into fact. Roughly two-thirds of domestic welfare expenditures now, in 1978, are for people over sixty-five, and there are in addition the private pension claims Drucker cites. Socialists, I suspect, would want to create a single and uniform system, since current practices give government support to enormous inequities. But the point here is that societies committed to the decent care of the aging—as all the welfare states, to one degree or another, are—will indeed have to set aside or provide for huge sums of money.

In Sweden some of those funds are already used for investment in housing. Here the AFL-CIO has a program to attract union funds, where possible, into similar undertakings. Why not generalize again? An intelligent and socially motivated investment of pension funds would provide an enormous pool of capital for all three sectors of the economy in a socialist transition.

And then, some individuals might want to save more of their

income than others. Within the constraints of a socialist commitment to wealth and income redistribution, that could be accomplished by the revival of an old American institution: the Post Office savings system. And there is still another source of savings: the people would pay for the nonfree goods in the society and the cost would include, as it now does, funds for depreciation and new investment—but not, as now, under the control and to the benefit of wealthy individuals and their hired managers.

Finally, there is another important source of savings in the elimination of some of the outrageous waste inherent in American capitalism. Business in 1977 spent about $38 billion on advertising. A little of that money provides the public with useful information about products people truly want and need; a major portion of it is employed in a corporate disinformation program to gull the supposedly sovereign consumer. Strict standards for private advertising and public support for a variety of (competing) consumer services could free much of those outlays, and a fully employed economy could find useful work for the people now living off them.

I mentioned earlier the parasitic character of a great deal of the activity on Wall Street and in the financial industry as a whole. A portion of the American legal profession thrives on the pervasive venality of the society. A radically progressive income and inheritance tax law, to take but one example, could free the graduates of many of the elite schools from essentially wasteful and antisocial lives. There are other activities—those of antiunion consultants, managerial psychologists, etc.—that are a cost of capitalist production but not of production itself. Here again, socialism, even in the confused period of transition, could offer a more efficient system (always on the premise of a social, not a corporate, definition of efficiency).

It would thus be possible in a socialist transition to plan democratically, to effectuate that plan realistically, and to finance the entire process. In making this point, I have not tried to be complete and detailed in my analysis, only to evoke the direction—and the problems—of socialist solutions. Moreover, I have been "economistic" on purpose and not indulged in the poetry of socialism. This is not to suggest that the culture and personal dimensions of socialism are unimportant. On the contrary, the economic programs are only means to the noneconomic end of human liberation. But the cynics impugn those ends by saying that we socialists cannot realistically present a program of means. And that is what I have tried to do here, in briefest outline.

## A Vision of That Socialist Future

I am writing this essay during the summer of discontent of 1978. Proposition 13 has just passed in California and polls in that state show that the voters want welfare to be cut, first and foremost. There are many other signs of a growing social meanness. The hope and good feelings of the first half of the 1960s seem to lie a century or so behind us. Is this description of measures that go far beyond the welfare state then a simple exercise in social fantasy? I think not.

The problems of American society today are structural and they require deep-going changes. Those, as I noted, could be undertaken by sophisticated and modern reactionaries—or by democratic socialists incorporating the best of liberalism in a movement that goes beyond the welfare state. If it is thus necessary to project the middle-distant future in an open-ended way, with both rightist and leftist possibilities, it is certain that incantation, conservatism-as-usual, or political temper tantrums against our complexities will not work. The ideas I have described here are, I believe, more realistic than most of the popular panaceas of the late seventies.

Another reason I am hopeful is that all utopian anticipations of the future are also descriptions of, and prescriptions for, the present. This effort at imagining socialism is rooted in—and, more important, relevant to—the America of the late seventies. In the briefest and sketchiest fashion, let me simply list some urgent and possible contemporary approximations of the more distant hopes whose realization and beginnings I have just imagined.

Here and now the democratic Left should:

- Challenge corporate control of the investment process by insisting that public policy concern itself with what is produced, and how it is decided, instead of confining itself to Keynesian "aggregates" and leaving all the details to the private sector. This would include public controls over private investment decisions, such as specifying the conditions under which corporations can leave a locality or oligopolies can raise prices, as well as such public undertakings as a democratically owned and controlled gas and oil company.
- Demand national economic planning for full employment, with the implementation of the Humphrey-Hawkins bill as a first, but only a first, step.
- Suggest public cost-conscious and accurate definitions of economic alternatives in which corporations are charged for their use and destruction of social resources.
- Propose sweeping tax reform aimed at a redistribution of income and wealth and, in particular, at the unearned income of rentiers and the untaxed wealth of successive generations of the rich.
- Suggest a rethinking of the entire American pension system, public and private, with emphasis on using such funds, theoretically "owned" by the people, for social purposes as determined democratically by the people.
- Urge employee and public representation on the boards of directors of all major corporations and a radical increase in democratic decision-making by primary workers in factories and offices.
- Propose federal support for a vast expansion of producer and consumer cooperatives, including funds for community corporations.

Some of these proposals are more difficult to imagine in the near future than others, yet none of them requires a commitment to socialism and most have been approved in principle by major institutions of the mass of the democratic Left. But why burden such empirically justifiable ideas by relating them to an ideology called "socialism"? There are two reasons why I do that. First, time is running out on the very American creed of utopian pragmatism, i.e., the religious conviction that all problems can be solved in the middle of the road by a process of bumbling along. The ills that afflict our society—which, to repeat the most obvious and appalling of current examples, are laying waste entire cities as effectively as a rocket attack—are systemic. They are the product of a late capitalism that collectivizes on the basis of anti-social, corporate priorities. Either the democratic Left will find a systemic response to that challenge, which is fairly called socialism, or the undemocratic Right will.

Second, America—Western capitalism, the world—desperately needs, not simply a legislative shopping list, but a vision. Not a religion, not a secular salvation; but a new sense of purpose. And so, in the details sketched out hopefully here there is not only a rational response to immediate issues but also the intimation of some tentative steps in the direction of a new civilization.

# 23
# The Misfortune of "Great Memories": Historical Remarks on the Paris Commune

*Dissent, 1971*

> *The misfortune of the French, even of the workers, is that they have* great memories. *It is necessary that events once and for all put an end to the reactionary cult of the past.**
>
> —Marx, to César de Paepe,
> September 14, 1870

Marx's bitter comment to de Paepe just before the Paris Commune was typical of his mood in those days. The French section of the International Workingmen's Association had, in the midst of the war between France and Prussia, turned back to the rhetoric of 1793 and called for a revolutionary war against the invader. In a letter to Marx on September 7, 1870, Engels gave a pithy summary of their common, and outraged, view of the French socialists. "These people," wrote Engels,

*Karl Marx and Friedrich Engels, *Werke* (Berlin: Dietz Verlag, 1957-1978), vol. 33, p. 147.

> who tolerated Badinguet [Napoleon III] for 20 years, who only six months ago could not keep him from getting 6 million votes as against a million and a half opposed, or from provoking Germany without reason or warning, these people, now that the German victory has given them a republic—and what a republic!—insist that the Germans must promptly leave the soil of France or else: *guerre à outrance*! It is the old presumption of superiority, the attitude that the land is sanctified by 1793 and that no later French swinishness can desanctify it, the superiority of the holy phrase, Republic.*

I recall these remarks of Marx and Engels on the reactionary cult of the French revolutionary past for a purpose. We have reached the one hundredth anniversary of the Commune, and throughout the world the Left has celebrated it with appropriate piety. In part, this speaks to a genuine identification with the brave Communards massacred by the bourgeois terror. In part, it derives from the fact that Lenin made his interpretation of the Commune a crucial precedent for his seizure of power in October 1917, so that every state and party that venerates his memory must also acquiesce to his version of what happened in Paris in 1871.

The Commune has become, in short, a *great memory* in precisely the sense that Marx used the phrase: a mythic moment in the past that confuses our understanding of the present. Moreover, Marx and Engels knew—and said—that it was a myth. During and immediately after the event they defended it out of honorable motives of solidarity with the victims of a terror imposed in the name of law and order—and they also had factional reasons for playing down its extremely un-Marxist character. But both before and after the Commune they expressed their real—and historically much more defensible—attitude: that the courageous Parisians had sacrificed themselves in a badly led, tactically botched movement, which set back the socialist cause in their country for at least a decade.

*Ibid., p. 56.

In the months prior to the Commune, Marx was first of all concerned about the low level of leadership in the French movement. "If a revolution breaks out in Paris," he wrote to Engels, "one must ask oneself, do they have the means and the leaders for serious resistance against the Prussians? One cannot hide from the fact that the 20 years of Bonapartist force had been enormously demoralizing. One is hardly entitled to rely on revolutionary heroism."* And Engels wrote to Jenny Marx: "The worst thing is—in case of an actual revolutionary movement in Paris, who will stand at its head?"†

Shortly after these letters, in early September 1870, Marx wrote the Second Address of the General Council of the IWMA on the Franco-Prussian war. He said:

> The French working class finds itself in an extremely difficult situation. Any attempt to overthrow the new regime while the enemy is at the very door of Paris would unquestionably be a folly. The French workers must perform their duty as citizens, but they must not let themselves be dominated by the national memories of 1792, as the French peasants allowed themselves to be deluded by the national memories of the First Empire. They must not repeat the past but build the future. *Let them calmly and patiently utilize the means that republican liberties grant to them in order to carry out the basic organization of their own class.* That will create a new, herculean force for the rebirth of France and for our common task—the emancipation of the proletariat.‡ [Italics mine—M.H.]

This theme of utilizing the new civil liberties in order to carry out basic organizational work runs through their correspondence of the period. In praising Auguste Serraillier, the International's envoy in Paris, Engels remarked that "his ideas about the situa-

*Ibid., p. 32.
†Ibid., p. 117.
‡Ibid., vol. 17, p. 278.

tion are clear and correct: use the freedoms guaranteed by the Republic for the organization of the party in France, act when the opportunity offers itself after effective organization, and restrain the International in France until peace is achieved."*

They were thus concerned with curbing their French comrades because they had little confidence in them. "The French branch," Marx wrote to Engels in September 1870, "is committing all kinds of stupidities in the name of the International. 'They' want to overthrow the provisional government, establish a Paris Commune, name Pyat [a French radical particularly disliked by Marx and Engels] as French ambassador in London, etc."† And Marx was personally outraged when the French Internationalists telegraphed him instructions on how he should carry on the agitation in Germany.‡

In the spring, however, the Commune became a fact. Marx's attitude changed, and changed radically for a number of reasons.

To begin with, a struggle was under way, and Marx had no doubt as to his side of the barricades. In a letter to Ludwig Kugelmann he wrote enthusiastically, "What resiliency, what historic initiative, what capacity for sacrifice in these Parisians!" And then, in the very next line, he reversed the position he had taken in the Second Address, using almost the same words to come to an opposite conclusion: "After six months of hunger and ruination, caused at least as much by internal betrayal as by the foreign enemy, they rose up under Prussian bayonets as if there never had been a war between France and Germany and the enemy was not at the very gates of Paris!" This, he ended, "is the most glorious act of our party since the Paris June insurrection."§ The problem is, as will be seen, and as Marx was later to admit, that the act was not carried out by Marx's party at all or, in the majority, by socialists of any kind.

* Ibid., vol. 33, p. 57.
† Ibid., p. 54.
‡ Ibid., p. 60.
§ Ibid., p. 205.

In a second letter to Kugelmann, Marx attempted to give a more developed rationale for his new position:

> World history would be quite accommodating if the struggle would only break out under unerringly favorable conditions. It would be quite mystical if "accidents" played no role. . . . The decisive unfavorable "accident" in this case is not in any way to be found in the general circumstances of French society but rather in the presence of the Prussians in France and their position right before Paris. The Parisians know this quite well. This, however, the bourgeois canaille of Versailles understands just as well. Precisely for that reason they presented the Parisians with the alternatives of either taking up the fight or else surrendering without a struggle. The demoralization of the working class in the latter case would have been a far greater misfortune than the succumbing of any number of "leaders." The struggle of the working class with the capitalist class has entered upon a new phase. Whatever the immediate outcome, a new point of departure of world historical importance has been achieved.*

In short, even when he rallied to the Commune, Marx regarded it as an experience imposed in considerable measure upon the workers by their enemies, and he did not predict victory ("whatever the immediate outcome" would imply a pessimistic assessment of the future).

Hal Draper, in his introduction to a new collection of Marx's and Engels's writings on the Commune, points out that Marx's illness in April 1871 had a psychosomatic component because he knew that the collapse of the Commune was only a matter of time.† Indeed, in May 1871 Marx's wife wrote a revealing letter to Kugelmann that corroborates this psychological assessment of Marx's illness and also shows that, even as he was writing his

*Ibid., p. 209.

†Karl Marx and Friedrich Engels, *Writing on the Paris Commune*, Hal Draper, ed. (New York: Monthly Review Press, 1971), p. 13.

ardent defense of their revolution, he privately retained all of his earlier criticisms of the Parisians.

Mrs. Marx wrote to Kugelmann:

> You can't have an idea of how much my husband, the girls, and all of us have suffered because of the French events. . . . The lack of military leadership, the entirely natural distrust of everything "military," the insistent interference of the journalists and of knights of the phrase like Félix Pyat, the quarrels, irresolution, and contradictory actions which necessarily result—all these evils, inevitable in a movement so audacious and so youthful, would certainly have been overcome by the core of the sound, self-sacrificing and self-confident workers. But now I think that all hope is lost, now that Bismarck, getting paid by German gold, is handing over not only all prisoners but all fortifications to the French canaille . . . , every one of whom represents some infamous crime. Another June massacre lies before us. . . .*

In other words, the fears Marx and Engels had expressed prior to the Commune about the weakness of the leadership in Paris had been confirmed. Yet in *The Civil War in France*, Marx celebrated the Parisians as the discoverers of "the political form . . . under which to work out the economic emancipation of labor."† In part, this was because he was clearly determined to defend the Commune against its detractors and therefore to put the most optimistic interpretation on everything that took place during its brief existence. In *The Civil War*, for instance, Marx writes, "The financial measures of the Commune, remarkable for their sagacity and moderation, could only be such as were compatible with the state of a besieged town."‡ Yet, as will be seen in a moment, he really thought that the financial measures of the

*Ibid., pp. 222–23.
†Ibid., p. 76.
‡Ibid., p. 81.

Commune—above all, the failure to move against the Bank of France—constituted a crucial tactical error.

Marx was also defending himself against critics on his Left. It was with some justice that Bakunin wrote,

> The impression made by the communist insurrection [the Commune] was so powerful that even *the Marxists*, all of whose ideas had been tossed overboard by the insurrection, saw themselves forced to take off their hats in its presence: they did even more. *In contradiction to all logic and to their own feelings they made the program and aim of the Commune their own.* It was a comic, but forced, travesty. They had to do it or else they would be repulsed and left behind by everyone, so powerful were the passions this event had excited in the whole world.*

Karl Korsch would later develop this point from a Marxist perspective. *The Civil War in France*, he said, was written at a given historic moment in a spirit of "blood and fire." In order to defend the essence of the Paris Commune, Marx had to play down his criticisms of its political form. His purpose, Korsch writes, "*was not only to annex Marxism to the Commune but thereby also to annex the Commune to Marxism.*"† His problem, Korsch writes, was to take a federalist, anticentralist reality and give it a centralist interpretation. This was particularly difficult since there were only twenty-five workers among the seventy revolutionaries elected in the Commune on March 26, 1871, and, in any case, Proudhonists, Blanquists, and Jacobins were far more numerous than Marxists.‡

In order to do this, Marx had to adopt a strange device in describing this precursor of the socialist regime, a supposed

*Bakunin, quoted in *Schriften zur Sozialisierung* (Frankfurt am Main: Europäische Verlagsanstalt, 1969), pp. 102–03.

†Ibid., p. 104.

‡Karl Kautsky, *Terrorisme et Communisme* (Paris: Povolozky, n.d. [orig. German ed., 1919]), p. 84.

archetype of the most conscious society human history would ever know. "The great social measure of the Commune," he wrote in *The Civil War*, "was its own working existence. Its special measures could only betoken the *tendency* of a government of the people by the people." [Italics mine—M.H.]. * In other words, it was not so much what the Commune did but the fact that it existed at all that was crucial in Marx's most enthusiastic interpretation. In a letter to Eduard Bernstein in 1884, Engels was quite specific on this count: "That in *The Civil War* the *unconscious* tendencies of the Commune were credited to it on a more or less conscious plane was under the circumstances correct and even necessary."†

Finally, Marx and Engels were considerably more candid about the Commune once the attacks upon their position, from both Left and Right, had receded into the distance.

In a letter to Ferdinand Domela Nieuwenhuis in 1881, Marx made a stunning reassessment of his interpretation—or, more precisely, he surfaced all the criticisms and misgivings he had suppressed in *The Civil War*. Nieuwenhuis, a Dutch socialist, had asked Marx what measures a victorious socialist movement would take, a question that was to be discussed at an international meeting in Zurich in October 1881. Marx replied that what could be done would depend upon the circumstances. Then he added that a socialist regime could come to power only when the circumstances were so developed that the regime could take all the crucial measures to intimidate the bourgeoisie so that the first desideratum—time for sustained action—could be won.

> Perhaps you will refer me to the Commune: but, abstracting from the fact that this was a mere rising of a city under exceptional circumstances, the majority of the Commune was in no way socialistic, and also could not have been. With a little common sense it could have reached a compromise with Versailles useful to all the people—which was all that could have

*Marx and Engels, *Paris Commune*, p. 81.
†Marx and Engels, *Werke*, vol. 36, p. 79.

> been gained. The appropriation of the Bank of France would by itself have put an end with terror to the boasting of Versailles.*

Marx's reference to "terror" here is ironic. The Commune executed the archbishop of Paris and sixty-four hostages; Marx felt that Versailles would have been much more terrorized if the insurrection had seized their treasure.

Here the Commune is no longer the discovery of "the form of proletarian rule"; it is now the "mere rising of a city under exceptional circumstances." Moreover, Marx's comments are not isolated and casual. His criticism of the decisive failure of the Commune—that it did not seize the Bank of Paris—was repeated by Engels in 1891 in his introduction to a new German edition of *The Civil War in France*. "That was a serious political error," Engels wrote. "The Bank in the hands of the Commune—that would have been worth more than ten thousand hostages."†

At the very end of his life, in the 1895 introduction to *The Class Struggles in France*, Engels was even more explicit. He argued that the events of 1870–71 proved that

> In Paris no revolution is possible except a proletarian revolution. After the victory, power fell undisputed into the hands of the working class. And once again it was shown how impossible even then, 20 years after the time described in this work, the rule of the working class was. On the one hand, France left Paris in a lurch, looked on while it was bloodied by the bullets of MacMahon; on the other hand, the Commune consumed itself in fruitless argument between the two parties that split it, the Blanquists (the majority) and the Proudhonists (the minority), neither of which knew what to do.‡

*Ibid., vol. 35, p. 160.
†Ibid., vol. 22, p. 196.
‡Ibid., pp. 516–17.

Given this history of Marx's and Engels's attitudes toward the Commune, it is time to disabuse ourselves of some "glorious memories." The Commune was courageous and revolutionary, and is hallowed by its sacrifice of blood. (Given my Irish background, I am particularly sensitive to the idea of heroic defeat; Ireland had nothing else for centuries.) But it was not the model of the socialist revolution to come, as Marx and Engels themselves understood and said, once they were no longer under political pressures, from Left as well as Right, to defend the courage of the Parisians.

Hal Draper begins the introduction to his collection of writings on the Commune with the conventional leftist statement: "One hundred years ago, on March 18, 1871, a working-class-led revolution took power and established a new type of state for the first time in the history of the world—temporarily, in one city."* This thesis is not, I believe, supported by a careful reading of the very documents that Draper himself has quite usefully assembled. The Commune was not primarily led by workers and, in Marx's opinion, it was badly led in any case. It did not establish a "new type of state," even if Marx projected a vision of one on the basis of the "tendencies" of what took place there. It did not even appropriate the Bank of Paris and was not "socialistic" or even very conscious of itself, for neither its majority nor minority, as Engels pointed out, knew "what to do."

There is good reason to be clear about this glorious, and inaccurate, memory. The myth of the Commune has been used, from Lenin on, to propagate the notion that there is some simple way to smash the bourgeois state apparatus and to proceed to create new and lasting revolutionary forms. That was not true in Paris in 1871—and it was not true in Petrograd in 1917 or Peking in 1949. There is no "day" of the revolution on which history makes its leap from past to future. Since Marx once helped make the myth that there was, one should pay some attention to his more considered opinions when he helped to unmake it. The bravery of the Parisians in 1871 will be no less magnificent if one is truthful about it.

*Marx and Engels, *Paris Commune*, p. 7.

# 24
# Is There Socialism after France? 1984

Is there socialism after France?

May 1981. François Mitterrand is elected president in an upset election. The euphoric crowds demonstrating at the Place de la Bastille in the traditional spring rain chant, "Mitterrand, du soleil!"—"Give us some sunshine, Mitterrand!"

June 1981. The Socialist Party wins an absolute majority in the National Assembly with a five-year term of office. Since Mitterrand has taken over the extremely strong presidency created by Charles de Gaulle, the Left has more power than ever in its history, much more than in the legendary days of the Popular Front of Léon Blum in the 1930s.

April 1983. I am a visiting professor at the university—at Paris VIII in St. Denis, one of the most radical of the institutions created as a result of the cultural explosion of 1968—and watch with a kind of fascinated horror as the riot police with their tear-gas launchers run down the Boulevard Saint-Germain almost nightly in pursuit of rightist student demonstrators. There is talk of a "1968 in reverse."

July 6, 1984. The *Wall Street Journal* editorial is titled,

"Hooray for Mitterrand." His refusal to bail out Creusot-Loire, the nation's largest industrial equipment maker, "shows that market forces can redeem even Socialists." "On the whole," the *Journal* pontificates, "we suspect the Mitterrand government has learned some valuable economic lessons." A final, friendly word from Wall Street: "If Mr. Mitterrand wants more hoorays from free marketeers, he can start by selling back the nationalized banks."

It is rather obvious that this chronology records a failure, but I suspect that only socialists understand how profound and bitter it is. I remember, for instance, the enormous stir the new French Socialist Party made when it attended the Congress of the Socialist International in Geneva in 1976. The old Socialist Party of Guy Mollet—which had played the game of musical cabinet seats under the Fourth Republic, backed the repression of the Algerian national movement, and even supported Charles de Gaulle when he returned to power in 1958—had disintegrated. In its place there was a vibrant movement led by François Mitterrand, the very traditional Fourth Republic politician who had, to the surprise of many, dug in his heels against de Gaulle in 1958 and managed to create a born-again socialist movement over the next decade and a half.

To be sure, some of the members of Mitterrand's Socialist Party had once followed Mollet. But many more had come into politics in the sixties in the struggle against the Algerian war that Mollet supported. And others were graduates of the street battles of 1968. The party's symbol, which was quickly adopted by socialists around the world, graphically dramatized this strange amalgam: a fist, the traditional icon of Left power, now held a rose that represented, not simply rising GNP, but the possibility of a different way of living.

Indeed, the new French party refused to call itself social democratic. It was, most of its leaders said, socialist, seeking a radically transformed society and not just a better, more humane, capitalism, which was all that the Social Democrats had achieved. There were imaginative plans for decentralization, for a "self-managed socialism" controlled by the workers at the base rather than by some bureaucrat in Paris. The Mitterrand coalition even contained a "second Left," opposed to Jacobin centralization and the technocrats, committed to a politics of genuine popular participation.

Socialist hopes soared—which is why the subsequent events were to be more wrenching for them than for anyone else, and not merely in France. But what, then, did happen between 1981 and 1984? Why could Roger Ricklefs write in the *Wall Street Journal* last September that "French socialism is an idea whose time has gone"? Worse, is that patronizing "Hooray" from the *Journal*'s editorialists the epitaph for a socialist ideal that is in trouble all over the world?

In dealing with these very serious questions, it is necessary to get some American superficialities—the kind that one finds in the *Wall Street Journal*'s praise for Mitterrand—out of the way. It is often assumed that the last three years have decisively proved the superiority of capitalism, personified by Ronald Reagan, over socialism, in the guise of François Mitterrand. The somewhat more complex truth can be put paradoxically: the United States is the only country in which Mitterrand's program might have worked.

There were, we will see, two very capitalist constraints that weighed heavily upon the French Socialists: the world market would simply not allow them to keep running higher balance-of-payments and governmental deficits. But America under Ronald Reagan was immune from such old-fashioned economic discipline. So this country stumbled into a demand-side recovery while pursuing failed supply-side policies and generated both trade and governmental deficits that made Mitterrand look Milton Friedmanesque by comparison. In comparing the two nations, then, it is well to remember that the French Socialists had to play by capitalist rules that the American "free enterprisers" could—for a while, at least—ignore. (Adam Smith, we will see, is the ghost at Ronald Reagan's feast, but that is another, and quite unfinished, story.)

So it is necessary to be aware of the very French factors in Mitterrand's predicament. And one can best understand the Socialist failures in that unique country by looking at their successes. The two, alas, are linked.

The Keynesian stimulus policies that Mitterrand hoped would set off a demand-side recovery were all designed to benefit the poorest in the society the most and were financed, in part at least, by taxes on the wealthy. "SMIC" is the acronym for the French minimum-wage law and the "Smicards" are the lowest-paid workers who receive it. Everything was done to increase their income more than anyone else's, and the policy worked.

Between March 1, 1981 (two months before Mitterrand was elected president), and July 1, 1982, the wages of the Smicards were increased by 29 percent! And in 1982, when the first reversal of Socialist policy occurred and wages were frozen, an exception was made for them. This was in a context in which the real value of all wages rose by 3.5 percent in the first year of Socialist rule and the buying power of social benefits climbed by 6.2 percent. Family allowances were increased, Social Security agreed to pay for abortions, special programs for training women workers were launched, there were new outlays for the aging and the handicapped.

At the same time, the Socialists carried out the greatest political decentralization in France since the first Napoleon concentrated political power in Paris, a move that benefited the opposition—which was always announcing the appearance of the "Gulag" under the Socialists—more than the government. And the concept of decentralized socialism was acted upon in the "Auroux laws," which gave the workers the right to speak on economic policy at the workplace. The Right hailed this very democratic initiative as yet another sign of the second coming of Joseph Stalin.

Jobs were created in the public sector, and there was a concerted effort to shorten the working life in order to spread employment around: a fifth week of vacation for all, a right to retire at sixty years of age, even earlier retirement for some in troubled industries, the 39-hour week as a first step toward the 35-hour week. After the first year, when this Keynesian stimulus had not succeeded well enough (it did increase GNP in France at a faster rate than in the United States), and the government began to accept an increase in the unemployment rate, there were attempts to soften the impact of the trend.

For some there were "reconversion leaves," two years with pay during which a worker could prepare himself/herself for a new job. And when Peugeot proposed to cut 6,000 workers, the government insisted that only 4,000 could be let go and that the reduction be accomplished through early retirement and the voluntary repatriation of immigrants.

The Socialists thought that this socially oriented stimulus would lead to the economic growth that would make it possible to pay for their decency. At the same time, they embarked upon an industrial policy to restructure the economy, nationalizing significant sectors in the process. To most Americans this was the most distinctively "socialist" aspect of the Mitterrand strategy. In fact, it was nothing of the sort.

In September 1981, the new president held his first major press conference. What was striking was that the reasons he gave for the increase in state ownership were eminently capitalist. The private sector, Mitterrand said, had not been investing in new production. Therefore it was necessary to take over some of the capitalist enterprises because they refused to carry out the normal process of capital accumulation. Nationalization was not, at this point, a way of striking at the social power of the bourgeoisie but a means of correcting their very unbourgeois patterns of conduct in recent years.

In understanding this paradox, one begins to turn from the early Socialist successes to the failures they helped create. Charles de Gaulle had carried through the process of modernization that had begun in the years right after the Liberation—but he had done so in the most conservative social and political way. A society that was being urbanized at breakneck speed was run on the basis of traditional peasant and petit-bourgeois values. That prepared the way for the political-cultural upheaval of May 1968, when a student rising culminated in a gigantic strike wave and almost toppled de Gaulle from power.

De Gaulle was, of course, a *dirigiste* in that great French tradition that goes back at least to Louis XIV. So he sought to create a strong, independent economy as the basis for the renaissance of French *grandeur*. He was, for instance, furious that his country—and its military—had to depend upon American computers, and he used all of the power of the state to fight IBM. But his successors, particularly Giscard, took a different tack. Rather than trying to master the global economy, they sought to adapt to it. As a result, a significant portion of the manufacturing sector, including capital goods, was partly deindustrialized.

That prepared for a Catch-22 for the Socialists in 1981. They could not finance their social initiatives without growth; but growth required capital goods, 50 percent of which were imported, and that led to pressures on the balance of payments; and the constraint of that growing external debt—which was also fed by the generous social policies that provided the middle and bottom strata with the money to buy imported consumer goods—convinced the government that it had to cut back on the economic stimulus and social policies. So growth was the road to stagnation. Moreover, if one reacted to the rise in consumer spending by devaluing the franc (which, all other things being equal, was indeed necessary), that would even further increase the cost of the imported capital goods.

A good many of the Socialists' problems were, then, quite French and, worse, an inheritance from the conservatives who went before. Indeed, there is good reason to believe that, because of deindustrialization and an overvalued franc, Mitterrand generated more jobs in West Germany than in his own country. At the same time the French Socialists were under yet another attack, one mounted from within a historic bastion of the Left. When the latter was in opposition, it dominated the culture, giving rise to the famous cliché, A Frenchman's heart is on the Left and his wallet is on the Right; but at the moment of Socialist triumph, its philosophy lost a good part of its hold over the French mind and heart. Why, the wits asked in 1983 and 1984, is Paris so "morose"? Because there is no François Mitterrand in the opposition to tell, with blinding clarity, why the government is failing.

This "treason of the intellectuals" is a complex phenomenon, but surely one of the reasons for it has to do with Stalinism. In the postwar years, Stalinism was seen as genuine Marxism and, for many of its friends and enemies, as the only authentic socialism too. In part that was because the social democratic movement seemed consumed by bourgeois opportunism while the Stalinists, barricaded in their proletarian ghetto, had the luxury and weakness of being utterly irrelevant to everyday political life. They built a genuine mass movement of the working class that was as isolated as a tiny sect. That allowed them to seem noble and pure, uncontaminated by capitalist corruption.

In the seventies, a number of activists who had been under the Stalinist (or Maoist) spell suddenly discovered Solzhenitsyn and the horrors of the Gulag. But if the previous illusions had been dedicated to real socialism and Marxism, then their disillusionment pointed them in the direction of free enterprise. For example, Yves Montand, a lifelong leftist, became so critical of the Socialists in early 1984 for continuing their governmental coalition with the Communists that he refused to support a united front against a racist candidate.

As a result of these trends, a cover story in an October issue of *Le Nouvel Observateur* was entitled "The Free-Enterprise Madness" ("La Folie du Libéralisme"). Even Guy Sorman, a leading French exponent of Reaganomics, wrote that things were getting out of hand as irresponsible managers used the newly fashionable ideology to justify an old-fashioned social meanness. And Jacques Julliard commented—in an article entitled, in English, "Good-bye Mao, Hello Ronnie"—that many intellectuals had simply shifted their allegiance from one simplistic monomania to another. "Mao," Julliard concluded, "is being reborn in the visage of Adam Smith." So precisely at a moment when the Socialists were confronted with an economic reality they had not dreamed of in their program, they were deprived of at least a part of their intellectual and moral legitimacy.

Most of the causes of Socialist failure I have just recounted are, like the faddishness of Parisian political intellectual life, very French. But there is another aspect to this process that is Western and capitalist. Americans, who will not forever be exempt from the discipline of a world market that they extol in theory and ignore in practice, might take note.

The Socialist Project, drafted by the leader of the party's left wing in 1980 and put into practice in 1981, differed radically from Ronald Reagan's supply-side economics, of course. Washington saw the road to the future in cutting back on social programs and providing huge tax cuts to the wealthy, who were supposed to use them to finance an investment-led recovery. Paris looked to the stimulus of a socially oriented, redistributive Keynesianism and favored the working poor rather than, as was the case with Reagan, depriving them of food and medical care. But on one point, Paris and Washington did agree: the goal was a self-generating, self-reinforcing boom, a "virtuous circle" in which growth creates growth . . . endlessly.

Some of the shrewdest French intellectuals have a name for this vision: they call it "Fordism." This is an ironic homage to the American industrialist who did not simply create the assembly line but also paid his workers the unprecedentedly high wage of five dollars a day in 1914. That combination of mass production and relatively high wages, these theorists persuasively argue, was the secret of the glory years after World War II. The governments of advanced capitalism effectually nationalized the auto entrepreneur's private innovation.

So it was that a combination of private-sector pay and government social expenditures created consumers capable of buying the growing output of an increasingly productive economy. That yielded high profits, which allowed further wage hikes, more social outlays, and additional investments to generate yet more productivity. Had the French Socialists been able to set such a virtuous circle into motion, their strategy of economic stimulus through social justice, coupled with an industrial policy to restructure the economy the conservatives had crippled, might have worked. But Fordism, this theory concludes, is no longer possible.

To cite but a few of the possible reasons for this shift: mass production can be—and is being—sent to the low-wage periphery; the welfare state turns out to be too socialist to let capitalism work and too capitalist to permit socialism; multinational corporations subvert all national economic strategies; the technological revolution creates a bifurcated occupational structure with an affluent elite, a "sliding" middle, and new strata of the impoverished; and so on. The Socialist failures, then, are not merely a result of French exceptionalism, or even of the Mitterrand government colliding with the most severe recession since the Great Depression. More profoundly, they also have to do with a new stage of capitalism, one that will, in the not too distant future, bedevil policy makers in Washington as viciously as it has already attacked the Socialists in Paris.

But then, am I arguing that François Mitterrand and his comrades are simply the victims of an historic fate that is part French and part capitalist? If that were the case, socialism might acquire a certain tragic dignity as it turned into an utter irrelevance. This is hardly my point.

Even as the Socialists were making their momentous policy choices in their euphoric first year in power there were those on the Left who, in basic sympathy with the regime, understood that some basic errors were being made. Michel Beaud is an economist who is a partisan of the "second"—decentralist, anti-Jacobin—Left. Alain Lipietz is a dynamic young (democratic) Marxist who, though critical of Beaud on other counts, agrees with him in terms of the theory of what went wrong. When critics with very different views converge, it is often the case that truth is being spoken.

The traditional French Left, and particularly its Communist wing, Lipietz notes, has always believed in "soaking the rich." In essence they thought that the capitalists were hoarding an enormous hidden treasure that, if only shared around, would stimulate economic growth as well as satisfying the demands of distributive justice. There may be something to that argument, Lipietz continues, in times of an expanding economy where there is enough of a growth dividend to give to the rich for investment and to the poor to raise the level of their life. But in the crisis of the 1980s, characterized precisely by a low yield for capital and a consequent reluctance and/or inability to invest, soaking the rich—or even increasing payroll taxes to finance some minimal decency for the unemployed—subverts the expansion of production.

In a similar vein Beaud holds that capital accumulation—which is necessary in the state enterprises as well as in the private sector—requires a growing, nonconsumed surplus to finance future production. Moreover, the Socialists had thought that the workers would, under a government of the Left, want to work harder and more productively. In fact, for quite understandable reasons, they had long looked forward to working less, and assumed that they would be able to do so when their friends, rather than their enemies, were in power.

I would add a related point: that the crisis of the eighties is much more profound than that of the thirties. On the face of it, that proposition is absurd. During the early years of the Great Depression, GNP declined by 50 percent; in the recession of 1982 it went down by a mere 1.9 percent. In the thirties, the unemployment rate hit 25 percent; in 1982 it was less than half of that at its peak. How, then, can one say that our current plight is more profound than during the greatest collapse that capitalism has ever known?

When the thirties ended and Dr. Win-the-War put America back to work, the economy was structured more or less as it had been when the bottom dropped out in 1929. The mines and mills were as they had been. When the crisis of the eighties ends, the very economic landscape will have been transformed. What we are going through now is a period of fundamental restructuring that resembles the last decades of the nineteenth century, when the nation made the transition from entrepreneurial to corporate capitalism, from Adam Smith to oligopoly. So too in France. It was impossible for the Socialists to run the system better than the conservatives because the system itself was changing. Candidate Mitterrand's program was permeated by the economic assumptions of the early seventies (when the new Socialist Party was created) which were contradicted by the economic realities that President Mitterrand faced in the eighties.

But what, then, should the Socialists have done? What will they do if, as I assert, socialism did not die on a rainy night in May 1981?

The Swedish socialists had the benefit of hindsight upon the French experience when they returned to office in 1982. On his first day as prime minister, Olof Palme devalued the currency by

16 percent, i.e., he consciously reduced the standard of living of the people who had just elected him (Felipe Gonzalez Marquez in Spain acted in much the same way). Last winter, Palme gave the Jerry Wurf Memorial Lecture at Harvard and told an audience of trade unionists and students that he not only favored holding down consumption but wanted to increase profits as well as a means of financing investment and an export-led boom.

It should be added that when Palme talked of the very modest social innovations possible under such conditions of austerity, he described advances that the trade unionists in the audience would have greeted as the millennium in this country. But that does not change the fact that the Socialist, Palme, was playing by the capitalist rules much more than the "free enterpriser" Ronald Reagan. He had heeded the criticism of economists like Beaud and Lipietz, but what does that have to do with something called socialism? Indeed don't the French and Swedish experiences simply prove that Lenin was right, that any democratic and gradualist attempt to transform a capitalist economy will simply turn the socialists into the Left cover for a perpetuation of the status quo?

Many of Lenin's negatives, my friend Irving Howe ruefully observes, were indeed true. The logic of the capitalist system is fundamentally hostile to socialist values, particularly at a time of radical restructuring such as the present. The attempt to create a new society takes place on the terrain of, under the rules of, the old order. That creates intolerable contradictions whether one tries to move rapidly, as Mitterrand did, or accepts the constraints imposed upon one by the antisocialists, as Palme did.

Lenin got these negatives right in most cases. The problem is that his solutions were, and are, either utopian or a step in the direction of totalitarianism. Stalin cut the Gordian knot and succeeded in creating a society that was indeed anticapitalist and also completely repressive and economically inefficient. Mitterrand, Palme, and the democratic socialists generally, reject such an approach on basic principled grounds, and rightly so. They choose to accept the tortured and difficult challenge of democratic change, with all its contradictions.

But that does not mean, as the *Wall Street Journal* editorialists and other simplifiers suggest, that the French Socialists have simply been metamorphosed into closet capitalists. They have had to pay a terrible price for the errors of the first year; they endure, as Jean Daniel has said, a kind of a political Calvary. How bitter it must be for them to hear the Gaullist mayor of Paris, Jacques Chirac, discover a "new poverty" in the summer of 1984—a poverty primarily the consequence of the fact that a quarter of those who are twenty-five years old or less are jobless—and to realize that Chirac is, in considerable measure, right on this count and wrong on almost everything else.

It is also true that the present Socialist response to the structural crisis is to make it easier to fire a worker in France, to take back some of the historic gains of the French Left. But it would be terribly wrong to assume that they have thereby accepted the tenets of American capitalism. Laurent Fabius, and his predecessor as prime minister, Pierre Mauroy, have tried to cushion the impact of those changes. Fabius, for instance, is developing a program in which every one of the jobless youth will either go to school, receive skill training, or be placed in a new job.

So it is true that the Socialists have reduced the duration of unemployment coverage from three years to eighteen months—and also true that this retreat still provides benefits three times as long as those in the United States. Indeed, one of the reasons why there is such a crisis in France is that the government is not willing to simply abandon the new poor, which is what Reagan has done. Strangely enough, the ultra-Left joins with the *Wall Street Journal* in ignoring such distinctions. Mitterrand, the Marxist, writes James Petras, practices "Reaganomics with a socialist gloss." But then Petras, among other fantasies, argues that France under the Socialists should have based its economic program "on an internally oriented development," a tactic that, given the openness of the economy to international pressures, would have been a sure way to economic disaster.

Still, a rejection of the Reaganite and ultra-Left theme that Mitterrand has simply gone back to capitalist economics should not obscure the depth of the French Socialist crisis. Their basic program has failed and they are paying an extremely high price for having implemented it; they do not have anything that remotely resembles a new and coherent alternative to their discredited strategy; they hope desperately that their retreat from euphoria to austerity will generate enough economic gains to keep the 1986 legislative elections from turning into a rout. And I should add that in foreign policy, a subject I will not deal with in this article, Mitterrand's praiseworthy initiatives toward the Third World coexist with a defense policy that I find profoundly disturbing.

Given all of these devastating admissions, I might be excused for extending sympathy to friends in deep trouble; but how can I rationally be hopeful about their future?

To begin with, the anti-Socialist opposition in France—led by Jacques Chirac, Valéry Giscard d'Estaing, and Raymond Barre—offers no workable alternative to Mitterrand. Indeed all of them accept some of his reforms, like five weeks of annual vacation for all workers. And all of them are pushing some kind of Reaganite politics for France—business incentives, tax cuts, deregulation. Chirac, having lost votes to the far Right in the European elections, is also coquetting with the racist, law-and-order vote and thus counterposing himself to one of French socialism's greatest accomplishments in recent years, the reform of the criminal justice system under the attorney general, Robert Badinter.

The problem with this counterprogram of the Center and Right is that Reaganomics will not work in France, a fact that has been decisively demonstrated by François Mitterrand. That country simply does not have the margin of economic maneuver that permits a Ronald Reagan to violate the economic principles he says he holds so dear. Indeed, there is a European name for Reaganomics, and it stands for 13 percent unemployment: Thatcherism. Earlier this year, Mrs. Thatcher's own chancellor of the exchequer, Nigel Lawson, was quite blunt about these matters: "The American option, which rests on the unique position of the dollar as the world's reserve currency, isn't open to any other country." The French Center-Right has not yet heard this important news.

There is another problem with the opposition's strategy.

Right now Ronald Reagan stands tall in America, and his economics of joy have helped stimulate the free-enterprise madness in which Chirac, Giscard d'Estaing, and Barre participate. But suppose that the French legislative elections in 1986 and/or the presidential campaign of 1988 take place while Reaganomics is coming apart at the seams. That possibility is not a product of a fevered leftist imagination. Reagan, the sophisticated and conservative London *Economist* remarked after the 1984 elections, will have to act quickly "if the free lunch provided by tax cuts and defense increases is not to be found to have been rather expensive after all." The recovery, the *Economist* continued, was "fuelled by falling commodity prices and a federal deficit financed by unlimited international credit." It is, then, quite vulnerable.

The very week that the *Economist* was throwing this bit of cold water on the Reagan triumph, *Business Week* reported that the foreign trade deficit had become an enormous drag on the economy, more than offsetting the economic stimulus provided by the huge federal deficit. It would be a politically dangerous irony if the French anti-Socialists managed to completely identify themselves with an economic strategy that was failing at election time as spectacularly as it seemed to succeed in 1984. It can happen here—and there.

Secondly, the failures of the Socialist policies in 1981 should not come as a surprise. They were, we have seen, anticipated by Alain Lipietz and Michel Beaud. Indeed, they are inherent in the Socialist position at a time of economic crisis when the Left is called to run a malfunctioning economy that is, however, designed to operate on anti-leftist principles. A Mitterrand inherits the terrible failures of Giscard and Barre and is supposed to make radical new departures at the same time.

That contradiction was not invented by the French in 1981. It haunted the British Socialists when they came to power for the first time after World War I. The Labour prime minister, Ramsay MacDonald, was so bewildered by the ambiguities of socialist power in a capitalist society that he followed economic policies to so orthodox a degree that he was attacked from the Left by the Tory liberal, Harold Macmillan. Labour split in the midst of all this confusion and could not even return to power during the Great Depression, the greatest catastrophe in the history of capitalism. Yet it was this very same, humiliated party that won a landslide in 1945 and institutionalized the welfare state revolution.

In doing so, they built upon the experience of the Swedish Socialists, who had invented Keynesianism before Keynes—but did so in a language that practically no non-Swedes read—and then put it into practice. Is it possible that the European socialists are groping toward such innovations in the eighties and that this might lead Mitterrand and friends to a new program? I think so. The Swedes are pioneering again with Wage Earner Funds, a form of decentralized social ownership, which puts worker and community representatives on the boards of private corporations. Strangely, Olof Palme, the Swedish prime minister, is downplaying the inventiveness of the Funds, not the least because the conservative opposition has attacked them as a step toward Stalinism. But it is conceivable that Palme's actions are better than his words and that, in the eighties as in the thirties, very practical socialist ideas could flow South from Scandinavia once again.

But I do not want to base my hopes for Mitterrand and Company on such a short-run speculation. I am simply convinced that, for all their problems and failures, the French Socialists are the only possible source in that country of a humane response to the greatest world economic transition in a century. Their opponents are intoxicated with the idea of importing a Reaganomics that certainly will not work in France and most likely won't work much longer in the United States. And if the Socialists are still confused after their dramatic failures, they keep searching for a way out that will not impose the costs of change on the most vulnerable citizens. They remain, in short, Socialists, the very antithesis of Ronald Reagan.

That last point has American implications. The household gods of this country regularly punish presidents by decreeing landslides for them. After 1936, Roosevelt lost effective control of his own party; after 1964 Lyndon Johnson was forced to resign from a probable second term; after 1972, there was Watergate.

When the *Wall Street Journal*, its editorial tongue fairly bursting through its cheek, sounds its patronizing hooray for Mitterrand, perhaps it is inviting Reagan to act on that post-landslide hubris that so often unmakes our presidents.

Eventually, this nation is going to have to face some of the problems that sandbagged the French Socialists, above all those limits imposed by the internal and external deficits. While Mitterrand agonizes over every trade-off between justice and efficiency, Reagan does not even seem to recognize that the trade-off exists and celebrates an economy with nine million out of work as his supreme triumph. But if Adam Smith takes his revenge upon his faithless American disciple, as I think he will, things may not look so simple, so condescending to the French, as they now do on the *Journal*'s editorial page and in the Oval Office.

Of course you cannot conjure up the sun on a rainy night in Paris or carry out an orderly advance to the left within a single second-rank economy particularly open to the tumultuous pressures of the world market. But the crisis is far from over and the French Socialists far from finished. Solutions may yet come—will only come in France—from their compassionate improvisations. Two cheers for them!

# Epilogue
# Paradise or Disintegration: James Merrill's Unique Search for New Myths

*Commonweal, 1983*

In the introduction to these essays, I argued that the young poet who took sides and turned into the militant socialist intellectual did not disappear. He was, I said in Hegelianese, *aufgehoben*—incorporated into—that socialist intellectual. In this last essay I prove my point.

During the five months I spent in Europe in 1983, I was haunted by James Merrill's *The Changing Light at Sandover*. It was then that I read, and twice reread, that intricate poem. But even as I reverted to the aesthetic passions of my youth—and to the very careful explication de texte that I had learned from the Chicago Aristotelians—I was deeply involved in my political work. The poet and the militant were each other's doppelgänger.

I began reading *Sandover* at Albufeira, a resort on the Southern (Atlantic) coast of Portugal where the Congress of the Socialist International was held. The last day of that meeting, the moderate Palestinian leader, Issam Sartawi, was murdered in the lobby of the hotel while we were in session in a nearby room. I went from Portugal to Paris, where, in the endless rain of April and May, I taught at the Paris VIII campus of the university, a shabby place peopled by exceptional students who would not have qualified for entry at the more traditional branches of the system.

I continued to be absorbed by the poem when I went to Greece and Israel in June. When I returned to Paris, my wife and children came over and we traveled to England, Greece, and Italy. I kept up my political work—lunch with the international secretary of the Labour Party in London, discussions with the Papandreous in Athens, and so on—even as I immersed myself in *Sandover*. I wrote the review of it as I was leaving Europe, and two days after I returned to the United States I was speaking and demonstrating in Washington, D.C. as part of the twentieth anniversary of Martin Luther King, Jr.'s March on Washington.

This chronology, I suggest, is a living proof that the poet was *aufgehoben* into the militant. So is my essay published in Commonweal which follows. Indeed, as I said at the outset, I think that the political and the aesthetic ideal are related, that, just as Goethe said, a free people—I would say, a socialist world—is a vision of loveliness.

It is possible that James Merrill's *The Changing Light at Sandover* is one of the significant works of the second half of this century.

It would, of course, be foolish to try to be more precise. It is simply too early even to hazard the semblance of a definitive judgment. Time must participate in a decision that can only be made looking backward at a distance; the book, like the shades of the dead whom Merrill summons back to life, must be seen in a rearview mirror. But to say that the future might well regard *The Changing Light* as major is to make a very large present claim for a powerful and unique poem.

Before supporting that claim, however, I should admit to at least three reasons why I might be overly enthusiastic. First, Merrill is culturally (and chronologically) of my generation. His points of reference—Blake, Eliot, Auden, Stevens—are my own, and there is even a passing reference to the Village bar in which I gloriously misspent most of my twenties and early thirties. Second, I read, and reread, *The Changing Light* during a five-month stay in Europe, in a time when I was deprived of the boring reassurance of everyday life and perhaps became hypersensitive as a result. Not so incidentally, I visited two cities—Athens and Venice—that figure in the poem, and even went sightseeing with its images in my mind. And third, I came upon the book shortly after finishing my own analysis of what is one of Merrill's central themes, the effective decline of religious belief in Western society. The poem therefore had—has—a relevance for me that could be personal and exceptional.

Even so, I am convinced that *The Changing Light at Sandover* is an event of importance in our culture and not just in my own life. Why?

The book is "about" a series of revelations from heaven and the dead, communicated to a ouija board whose "Hand" is "DJ" and whose interpreter is "JM" (David Jackson and James Merrill; but both are characters in a fiction and I will call them DJ and JM when they appear in that guise). The setting is the religious social crisis of the contemporary world, which, with its menaces of atomic and population explosions, must face the question of whether reality is ultimately benign or whether it is tending back toward the chaos from which it emerged. These issues are posed in terms of new myths—the old faiths, Merrill thinks, are unbelievable. Will God B (for biology) and Mother Nature triumph over anti-matter and disintegration? Will the spiritual forces accumulated over the generations produce "a great glory or a great puddle?"

More simply put: modern men and women have lost that basic, essentially religious, trust in the ultimate goodness of existence at the very moment at which they themselves have acquired the power to destroy, if not the cosmos, then a good part of our small corner of it. Two previous worlds, we are told, did self-destruct, either through a nuclear blast or by a Malthusian conflict between a race of centaurs and their batlike helpers. Ours is the third and last world.

My summary and prose brutalization of the poem should not be taken to suggest that it is a compound of cobwebs and weltschmerz. On the contrary, *The Changing Light* is intricately architectonic and intellectually serious. Like *Finnegans Wake* it comes full circle: it concludes as JM begins reading to a heavenly audience all that has gone before, and intones its first word as its last word. This preposterous notion, and many others, is so totally and convincingly imagined that, when JM and DJ finally break off contact with three of the dead, there is a poignant sense of present loss. Indeed, if all of its parts failed, which is in no way the case, *The Changing Light* would still be a triumph as an incredibly realized whole.

The poem is divided into three main sections and a brief coda. The first book, *Ephraim*, consists of twenty-six separate poems beginning with the successive letters of the alphabet. It establishes the basic dramatic premise about the ouija board and introduces some of the central themes: the decline of the old myths, presented in a lovely elegy telling how

> *Venice, her least stone*
> *Pure menace at the start, at length became*
> *A window fiery-mild, whose walked-through frame*
> *Everything else, at sunset, hinged upon—;*

a debate between JM and his artist nephew over realism (science, facts, this world) and faith-art (the otherworldly); the fearfulness of power as JM learns that the bomb at Hiroshima destroyed souls as well as bodies; and, with an allusion to Wallace Stevens, the idea of God as that which (who) conserves an unstable universe whose black holes are scientific intuitions of an unthinkable and metaphysical possibility.

*Ephraim* also contains a poetic fragment of a lost novel that is confusing and wisely forgotten, and many more personal references than the rest of *The Changing Light*, references that are sometimes excessive and obscure. The whole project, one suspects, did not become clear to Merrill until he began to work on the next book, *Mirabel*; and thus *Ephraim* is marred by some loose threads. It is in *Mirabel* (twice as long as *Ephraim*, followed by *Scripts for the Pageant,* which is even longer) that the dramatic fascination of a marvelously articulated fictional (symbolic of the real) world becomes quite dominant.

"Mirabel" is a batlike creature, the survivor of one of those self-destructed worlds, who becomes a peacock as he talks to JM and DJ. Indeed he turns a scientific account of the genesis of reality into a poetic myth so that his own transformation from bat to peacock is a refraction of his subject matter. This section is divided into ten sections, numbered from zero through nine, which, not so incidentally, is the number of heavens in Dante's *Paradiso,* one of the many ghosts that haunt this poem. In *Mirabel* the shades of three dead people—W. H. Auden; Maria Demertzi Mitsotaki, an Athenian friend of JM and DJ and the daughter of a former Greek prime minister; and Robert Morse, a neighbor and friend from Stonington, Connecticut—become central. And a basic theme is fully defined: that there must be "POEMS OF SCIENCE." The supernatural characters speak upper case, a convention that, strange to say, is not at all bothersome. At first, JM is appalled at the notion.

> *To squint through those steel-rimmed*
> *Glasses of the congenitally slug-*
> *Pale boy at school, with his precipitates,*
> *His fruit flies and his slide rule?*
>
> *Not for nothing had the Impressionists*
> *Put subject-matter in its place, a mere*
> *Pretext for iridescent atmosphere.*
> *Why couldn't Science, in the long run, serve*
> *As well as one's uncleared lunch-table or*
> Mme X en Culotte de Matador?

*Mirabel* ends with a serene meditation by JM, to which I will return, and the appearance of the Archangel Michael, one of the key figures of the next book, *Scripts for the Pageant. Scripts* is divided, typically, into three subsections, "Yes," "&," "No." In this poem everything is dialectical, from matter (which is white and black, order and chaos), through images (which, like photographs, are positives of a negative and vice versa), to Michael (who is good, but perhaps a sentimental liberal) and his sometime antagonist, the angel Gabriel (who destroys, but perhaps as a necessary work for the sustaining of life).

In *Scripts,* another shade joins the group: George Cotzias, a Greek scientist. Buddha, Akhnaton, Jesus, Homer, Montezuma, Plato, and a false Mohammed also put in significant appearances. (Plato is, for reasons that will not be explained here, major.) This is the book in which the chaos-order antagonism is explored, and it ends as JM and DJ break a mirror—and thereby their relationship with Auden, Maria, and George. The coda (*The Higher Keys*) ties up various loose ends but also focuses upon the rebirth of Robert Morse, who, in his new guise (which includes a clubfoot, one more sign of the unity of this imperfect world and its ethereal interpretation), will be a great composer. As JM prepares to read *The Changing Light* to twenty-six spirits, including Dante, Jane Austen, and Proust "a star trembles in the full carafe/As the desk light comes on, illuminating/The page I open to." The lectern lamp—the ordinary—becomes a star. As bats turn into peacocks and science into poetry, the poet goes back to the beginning and ends with the first word, "Admittedly. . . ."

Before moving to some of the most important particulars within this extraordinary structure, I should acknowledge some problems. Merrill is possessed, he himself understands, of an "unrelenting fluency," a talent to turn everything into "slant, weightless gold." But does one, then, confuse a craftsman's formal genius with deep meanings, knowing with Merrill that "affection's/Poorest object, set in perfect light/By happenstance, grows irreplaceable"? Bob Adelman, a photographer friend and collaborator, once said to me that you should not cover a war with color film since the carnage will come out vividly beautiful.

That is a problem with Merrill; it is also a glory. For instance, in *Scripts* he describes a changing of the light in a supernatural schoolroom: "not/The lights we've seen according to thus far/—Spectral gems, first waters of a star—/But Light like bread, quotidian, severe,/Wiped of the sugar sprinkles of Vermeer; . . ." And there is ubiquitous wit in this poem, sometimes as frivolous as a pun, sometimes more ingenious as when Jane Austen addresses the newly dead Robert Morse "As *Mr. Robert*—a shrewd estimate./He's after all not Heir to the Estate,/Its goods and duties, but a Younger Son/Free to be ornamental and have fun." My greatest difficulty is not, however, aesthetic but political. *The Changing Light* has, as we will see, a very explicit political content: antinuclear, environmental, and sometimes a kind of upper-class, elitist Malthusianism. It is that last attitude, I will suggest, that creates problems.

With these qualifications, let me return to the poem and a very basic question: What is it "about"? One answer is, the changing light at Sandover. The name, Sandover, we are told, is a corruption of the French, Saintefleur, or the Italian Santofior, "An English branch of that distinguished tree/Through whose high leaves light pulses and whose roots/Rove beyond memory." It is, as "WHA" (the shade of Auden) suggests, the community of art and spirit that lies beyond doing your own thing, the "ROSEBRICK MANOR" of language and culture whose family includes Shakespeare and Emily Dickinson. "IT WAS," WHA says, "THE GREATEST PRIVILEGE TO HAVE HAD/A BARE LOW-CEILINGED MAID'S ROOM AT THE TOP." "Sandover" is also the ouija board and, I suspect, the heavenly flower at the end of the *Paradiso*. But, for my present purpose, its most significant meaning is the heritage of culture, and that relates to one of the central myths of *Mirabel* and to one of the basic theories of the age.

It was, Mirabel tells JM and DJ, language, culture, that marked the beginning of the transition "OF THE TWO BASIC APECHILDREN" toward humanity. Émile Durkheim, and Friedrich Nietzsche, both of whom thought grammar a key to God, would agree; so would Wittgenstein and, in our day, Jurgen

Habermas. So signal gave way to sign and then sign became symbol and symbol music and the "REASONED INDIRECTION" of the garden of human culture was on the way. But now, the old symbols lose their power and we move from symbols back toward signs: the clock face, Henri Lefebvre remarks, at least imitated the revolutions of the day; the digital watch is pure information. But if, to go back to Merrill, "IN THE BEGINNING WAS THE WORD" and now the word is no longer what it was, how are we to face our crises as the light changes in our culture?

Without the sustaining myths, Mirabel tells JM, "MAN IS AMOK & CHAOS SLIPS IN (UPON/COLLAPSE, IN INTELLIGENT MEN, OF RELIGIOUS BELIEF)." That is hardly an original thought, and a theologian like Bultmann is more radical than Merrill in his demythologizing. But what Merrill makes of this commonplace—both as poetry and poetic meaning—is anything but a cliché. The past two or three hundred years, JM comments, "have been a superhuman/All-shaping Father dwindle (as in Newman)/To ghostly, disputable Essence or/Some shaggy-browed, morality play bore/(As in the Prologue to Faust)." And then there comes a key intuition (it is, I will suggest later, central to the entire poem):

*Why should God speak? How humdrum what he says*
*Next to His word: out of a black sleeve, lo!*
*Sun, Earth and Stars in eloquent dumb show.*
*Our human words are weakest, I would urge,*
*When He resorts to them.*

But if God is in crisis, so is literature. The old vocabulary becomes stale, "translucent, half-effaced," but science creates a new language: "through Wave, Ring, Bond, through Spectral Lines/And Resonances blows a breath of life,/ Lifting the pleated garment." Since JM, openly acknowledging his debt to Matthew Arnold, thinks the scribe must replace the priest, it is therefore incumbent on the poet to marry science and poetry (and music), matter and man, nature and spirit, to reconcile all the dialectical contraries. It is necessary, WHA argues, to bring "WM CARLOS

WM'S THOUGHT THINGS/& THE COLD VIRGIN VERB OF MALLARMÉ/TOGETHER. . . ." One must, JM puts it, "tell round what brass tacks the old silk frays."

In confronting this challenge, JM presents three new Gods. First there is the God who holds back the chaos: a distant figure, not at all as human and compelling as Mother Nature in her best mood (Nature, for JM as for the Greeks, is a trinity). The second God reminds me of the divinity defined by Hegel in the Phenomenology: an imminent transcendence that develops historically, not simply in nature (which would be a rather simple pantheism) but in the evolution of nature and man. As WHA puts it "GOD B IS NOT/ONLY HISTORY BUT EARTH ITSELF. HE IS THE GREENHOUSE." JM is, I think, even more daring: God B:

> *(Who, lacking human volubility,*
> Has *no word for His own power and grace;*
> *Who, left alone, falls back on flimflam*
> *Tautologies like* I am that I am
> *Or* The World is everything that is the case*);*

That is remarkable: to equate the God of Abraham and the empirical reality of Wittgenstein. But then I suspect Wittgenstein might have agreed even though he insisted that this was a matter upon which one must keep silent.

This second, "Hegelian" God is described more prosaically—more scientifically—by the Archangel Michael at the close of *Mirabel.* The genius of life is, he says, its responsiveness to the sun "AND SO AS YOU FACE THE SETTING SUN YOU FACE YOUR ANCESTOR." Cells accumulated energy through the suncycles and "THIS ACCUMULATED ENERGY BECOMES THROUGH EONS AN ANCIENT AND IMMORTAL INTELLIGENCE . . . AND AT LAST AFTER EXPERIMENT THIS INTELLIGENCE FORMED MAN./THIS IS GOD'S NAME." And yet, for all of the demythologizing, *The Changing Light* is a religious poem. In a commentary on Michael's cosmology, Maria says:

*FOR MICHAEL/SUN*
*READ GENERATIVE FORCE FOR*
*GENERATIVE FORCE*
*READ: RADIATION TO THE BILLIONTH*
*POWER*
*OF EXPLODING ATOMS. FOR EMMANUEL,*
*$H_2O$. FOR SEEDS, THAT COSMIC DUST*
*LADEN WITH PARTICLES OF INERT MATTER.*
*FOR GOD READ: GOD.*

Ultimately, all the scientific myths—and, for that matter, the scientific nonmyths—encounter the mystery of the beginning. Kant was, and is, right (and on this count, Hegel agreed with him): you cannot deduce the infinite from the finite. But JM—and Wittgenstein—are right, too: one can imagine in silence or in poetry, a godly source of that beginning. *The Changing Light* does more than that. It projects a supernatural effort to help humans toward an earthly paradise, in part through biology—the "no accident clause" of DNA, time standing still in the clockword of genes—and in part through an otherworldly research lab, making use of the reborn, reapportioned souls of the great dead.

There was, I thought, more than a little poetic license in all of this. Wasn't the transmigration of souls merely a way of saying that Shakespeare and Buddha still live in us? But then I happened to read the comments of a French scientist, Claude Allegre, in an article in *Le Monde*: "To know that the stars are immense nuclear laboratories whose activities continually change the chemical composition of our galaxy . . . to discover that the physical laws that rule liquid crystals, a plate of spaghetti, a pile of sand are finally the same . . . these are some of the elements that today infuse the most profound human thought."

Science, then, is becoming science fiction and *The Changing Light* with its "R" (for Research) lab where new types are cloned is not so otherworldly. But it is here, in the domain of the science God, that the elitist neo-Malthusianism emerges. Of course, the bomb and nuclear power are a threat to human existence; of course, the sense of the holiness of the environment is perhaps the most genuine and spontaneous religious emotion of these times; and of course there must be a limit to population. But to blame and despise the mass of the "breeders" is another thing. Mirabel makes the essentially aristocratic point: "A MERE TWO MILLION CLONED SOULS LISTEN TO EACH OTHER WHILE/ OUTSIDE THEY HOWL AND PRANCE SO RECENTLY OUT OF THE TREES." At the time when Malthus wrote, attacking decency toward the poor as an incentive to excess population, most enlightened Britons thought my Irish forebears—and James Joyce's, more to the point—a race of savages.

There were even those—Nassau Senior, for instance—who thought that the Irish did not die in sufficient numbers during the Potato Famine to restore the proper economic equilibrium between food supply and the "demand" for life. WHA, in welcoming the coming of the "alphas" (from *Brave New World*) asks, "WHAT OF THE OMEGAS?/3 BILLION OF EM UP IN SMOKE POOR BEGGARS?" And JM interjects: "Wystan, how *can* you?" The reply comes: "COURAGE: GABRIEL/KNOWS WHAT HE'S UP TO & (LIKE TIME) WILL TELL." When humans thus play God they take on too great a responsibility, to put it mildly. In fairness, JM has his doubts—and I presume James Merrill does, too—and the worst statements are made by assorted angels and shades.

I don't want to be priggish. Some of the poem's perceptions of the problems of mass society are insightful enough. Finishing this essay in Venice, tramping as a member of the democratic mass through the aristocratic precincts of the Doge's Palace, I would be a hypocrite to deny that an occasional snobbish thought occurred to me. But then the thought was dismissed as both unworthy and untrue, for the point is to expand the human potential of the billions—just as we have already in fact expanded the potential of the millions, including me.

All of this raises the truly vexed question of the relation between art and politics. How does one deal with Ezra Pound's beautiful evocation of the corruption of art by money in the *Cantos* when one knows that it is quite likely inspired by fascist nonsense about the Jewish bankers? Or with the poignance in Brecht's Stalinist play—an agitprop play at that—on the Chinese Revolution? I do not want to equate Merrill's ambivalent and liberal elitism with fascism or Stalinism, yet the problem it poses is similar to the one raised by Pound and Brecht.

Of course one doesn't judge a work of art by political standards. Marx well understood that Balzac, the reactionary, was a greater novelist than Zola, the socialist. And there can be a sort of "willing suspension of disbelief"—I think. But then Balzac's monarchism does not threaten me, while neo-Malthusianism does. Whatever the high theoretical solution to the problem, I must confess that I was aesthetically put off by the suggestion—and it is not made by JM himself—that a famine in Africa may be part of a benign plan for the future.

I regret this criticism, for the objectionable material arises precisely because Merrill is becoming more socially concerned. The transition from *Ephraim* to *Mirabel* is, in part, a shift from the more personal to the more public and it marks a gain in power—it is one of the reasons why this strange poem may be truly great. If in one aspect of that excellent transition Merrill nods as politician and utopian more than as poet, that is to be noted and regretted; it should not be a reason for turning against *The Changing Light*.

In this spirit, I conclude, then, with one of the finest passages in the poem, a key to Merrill's third God and his basic meaning. I cite but a few lines of this magnificent meditation, first about DNA:

*The world was everything that was the case?*
*Open the case. Lift out the fabulous*
*Necklace, in form a spiral molecule*
*Whose sparklings outmaneuver time, space, us.*

Then JM explains that Hell in German means bright,

*—So that my father's cheerful, 'Go to Hell',*
*Long unheard, and Vaughan's unbeatable*
*'They are all gone into a world of light'*
*Come, even now at times, to the same thing—*

But how will Hell—in that double meaning—render what it owes? That is, JM thinks, a "quaint idiom," perhaps "from the parchment of some old scribe of the apocalypse." So then one must

*. . . render* it *as long rendering to*
*Light of this very light stored by our cells*
*These past five million years, these past five minutes*
*Here by the window, taking in through panes*
*Still bleary from the hurricane a gull's*
*Ascending aureole of decibels,*
*As numberless four-pointed brilliancies*
*Upon the Sound's mild silver grid come, go?*
*The message hardly needs decoding, so*
*Sheer the text, so innocent and fleet*
*These overlapping pandemonia:*
*Birdlife, leafplay, rockface, waterglow*
*Lending us their being, till the given*
*Moment comes to render what we owe.*

In Paris at the Beaubourg earlier in the summer, I saw a series of Kandinsky paintings assembled to show his progression (which I am not sure was a progression, in this case) from representational to nonrepresentational art. The first painting was of woods, and the light makes a marvelous pattern upon the dark ground. That, it struck me, was what all Kandinsky's work was about: the light in the woods was the donnée, all else was implicit in it. So with Merrill. His third God is reality, the world that is the case, but enchanted, sheer, innocent, and fleet with its overlapping pandemonia. A page earlier, the same insight in different language:

> *Things look out at us from a spell*
> *They themselves have woven.*

That is, I think, Merrill's perception of God, and it pervades—it illuminates—every page of one of the most extraordinary poems of our times, a theology for the godless and godly.

# Index